A Memoir

Stand Easy
or
The Rear Rank Remembers

The Author in Deputy Lieutenant's Gear. (© *Brian Graves, Folkestone*)

A Memoir

Stand Easy

or

The Rear Rank Remembers

by

Charles Millman

The Pentland Press Limited
Edinburgh · Cambridge · Durham

First published in 1993 by
The Pentland Press Ltd.
1 Hutton Close
South Church
Bishop Auckland
Durham

ISBN 1 85821 087 9

Typeset by Elite Typesetting Techniques, Southampton.
Printed and bound by Antony Rowe Ltd., Chippenham.

This book is dedicated to all those other Rear Rank 'scruffs' who have served all over the world since the end of World War II.

'He has achieved success who has lived well, laughed often and loved much; who has filled his niche and accomplished his task; who has always looked for the best in others and given the best he had.'

adapted from *The Life and Work of Ralph Comba Jackson*

Contents

List of Maps and Diagrams

List of Illustrations

Foreword

by

General Sir Michael Gow, GCB

This autobiography is by a man who is very much a 'soldier's soldier' and who, as is revealed, served with me when I commanded the 4th British Division in Germany. One of my beliefs is that life must be fun, and this especially applies to *la Vie Militaire*. For the Author this was very much so, and certainly when he recalls those days when he was my Head Administrator; I think of many humorous moments which we shared. He writes of 'Rear Div HQ', and in the early stages of one particular exercise I thought it would be a good idea if I paid a visit, partly to show that I wasn't a 'G' snob but also to be educated in matters logistical by Colonel Millman, as he then was, and his supporters. They were established in a wood, so well camouflaged that I could easily have missed them completely, but eventually I came to the Colonel in his 'brain centre'.

'Charles,' I said, 'I simply must have a drink. I'm absolutely exhausted.' He looked somewhat surprised as the hour was well short of midday. 'Yes,' I explained, 'I've never had to return so many salutes in my life as I have since arriving here.'

'Oh, I *am* pleased, General,' he replied. 'I thought the whole Headquarters was a complete shambles so I ordered every member, regardless of rank, to gather round me, and I demonstrated by numbers how they were to salute with their personal weapons or whatever. Important to start the way you intend to carry on!'

Not only did we become firm friends from that moment, but I became so well educated in administration that he and his staff presented me, when I relinquished my appointment, with a beautiful print, entitled 'Commissariat Difficulties – The Road from Balaclava to Sevastopol in Wet Weather', and with a subsidiary caption: 'To a very logistically minded GOC from the Camp Followers and Quality of Life Team. September 1975'.

This is the life story of a man who has loved being a soldier and who particularly has been very proud indeed of his Regiment, despite the many changes that have taken place in its title and structure. He embodies all the qualities of the good officer, not least his understanding of the British soldier. It is, therefore, hardly surprising that he gained the respect and indeed affection of all ranks – from Generals to Private Soldiers. His has been a life devoted to an organisation in which he believes passionately. It was the Army's loss that he was retired before being promoted to higher rank; there are too few officers around of his ability, humour and total honesty and sincerity.

Preface

It was an afternoon in early December 1988 at Mooltan Barracks, Tidworth. HM Queen Margrethe II of Denmark, as an Allied Colonel-in-Chief of the then Queen's Regiment, had just paid a formal visit to the 1st Battalion. As Colonel of the Regiment I had, a few minutes earlier, seen her to the Queen's Flight helicopter for her return to London (the Regiment has since merged with the Royal Hampshires to form The Princess of Wales's Royal Regiment). On arriving back on the parade ground with the Commanding Officer (CO) I found the Battalion in hollow square formation under the Regimental Sergeant Major (RSM). I was already aware that to end the day the Battalion were proposing to make a small presentation to me to mark the completion of my tour as Colonel at the turn of the year. On my instruction to Mr Farrar to 'Carry On' he stood the Battalion 'At Ease' and then cried 'Stand Easy.' At that point Corporal Ron Brill, the senior pioneer and oldest soldier in the Battalion (he had been serving when I commanded some twenty years previous), who had been deputed to make the presentation, marched forward . . .

As he came towards me I was reminded that on an afternoon in early December 1945 I had reported to the Indian Army Cadet Company at 148 Pre-OCTU on Wrotham Escarpment in Kent. Some forty-three years on, and as I was to finally 'Stand Easy', it came to me that after what had been a virtual lifetime of service, there were perhaps some laughs, thoughts and memories worth recording. For as a graduate of the first Post-War Sandhurst Intake my service had spanned the Cold War era, the period of withdrawal from Empire and its associated 'small wars' and insurgencies and more recently, the Ulster troubles. Whilst never a '1st XI player' I had been on the fringe of 'The Squad' and, on occasion, like the 'well-drilled reserve', had been given my head as a 'sub' on the main playing field. In short, this is the story of a 'Rear Rank' soldier who gave much of his life to the so-called 'peacetime' Army. (It is in the Rear Rank that the Sergeant Major generally seeks to hide the 'scruffs' and the least co-ordinated on parade.)

The war and its immediate aftermath determined a chance service career and entry to the Post-War Sandhurst. Commissioned as one of the new breed of Regular Army Officers, I was soon pitched into the Cold War at the height of the Berlin Blockade. I next sampled the National Service training 'sausage machine' before a first spell of active duty during the Mau Mau rebellion. There followed a home stretch in the then struggling Reserves, attendance on the key Staff College course and my first staff appointment in the Ministry. A varied tour as a company commander in the Strategic Reserve was the next landmark and this was succeeded by active duty in Borneo during Confrontation with the Indonesians in the mid-sixties. The last leg to command took in a first tour in Ulster, the Joint Services Staff College and a brief return to a much changed BAOR scene. Command followed and this covered a semi-operational tour in the Gulf, an internal security call to Bermuda, early entry onto the streets of Londonderry at the start of the Ulster troubles and a Public Duties stint outside Buckingham Palace. I then returned to the Staff College on the Directing Staff and from there was despatched to Khartoum to reorientate the Sudanese Staff College to the Western way of thought. There followed a senior logisticians appointment in the BAOR 'shield' at the peak of a 'Pomp and Circumstance' bonanza and a spell at Aberdeen University as a visiting Defence Fellow. In Jubilee Year I arrived at the Ministry, still in my logistic guise, to become heavily involved in some emergency operations and civil contingencies. I completed my full-time service as the Divisional Brigadier, The Queen's Division and as ADC to HM The Queen. Finally I devoted my early retirement years to the then Colonelcy of The Queen's Regiment and the Army Benevolent Fund. In the concluding chapter I reflect on what I believe might have been, where different policies could have changed things to possible advantage and the now likely way ahead for the next generation of Sandhurst graduates. The whole could also be described as a microcosm of the military and social history of the times.

Throughout this forty-three year period I experienced both the rough and the smooth times – there was a fair share of both. I have no regrets and look back without anger. I wouldn't have done otherwise with my life. Above all I cherished that deep family spirit that still pervades the regimental system, 'Options for Change' or otherwise. A family in which everybody matters, everyone cares, nobody will lack comradeship and where sound Christian values and a healthy approach to life abound in plenty. Long may it stay that way for it remains the envy of armies world-wide. It is up to the next generation to see that it does.

Hythe   January 1993

Chapter 1

The Seed-Corn Years

I was born in Herne Hill, a Southeast London Suburb on 18th February 1928 – the sole offspring of a 'Meat Salesman' and 'Bank Clerk' as my parents were described on my Birth Certificate. The former was employed by Armour & Co, the big American meat wholesalers, and my mother by Coutts & Co, the rather 'posh' bankers. She was one of the first ladies they employed. To add to the meat connection, my Grandfather Millman was the Chief Superintendent of Smithfield Market, a post he held from 1904–1942. He also lived in Herne Hill but was a Devonian by origin. My mother's folk had a house in nearby Dulwich and Grandfather Bridger was a Master Mariner. He was Mayor of Camberwell in 1936. It was overall a comfortable and sheltered middle class background in which to be brought up, one in which prime family social contacts centred about the activities of such as the Dulwich Cricket and Tennis Clubs, and where Saturday evening parents' outings favoured the Trocadero or Cassani's (with Charlie Kunz at the piano) rather than the Savoy or Grosvenor House.

During World War I Grandfather Millman had seen service in the Ypres salient as a Bombardier with the Honourable Artillery Company (HAC). In late 1915 he had, however, been recalled to Smithfield Market where it was considered that his expert services were more urgently needed to maintain meat supplies about a nation suffering acutely from the effects of U-boat action. Father had sailed for France on the 14th August 1914 as a Lance Corporal with the London Rifle Brigade (LRB). He gained the Mons Star, was later commissioned and Mentioned-in-Despatches and as a Captain was finally captured at the last stand of the 2nd Battalion. The Devonshire Regiment at the Bois des Buttes during Ludendorff's last fling offensive in March 1918. The Regiment was awarded the Croix de Guerre

1

Grandma Bridger, Uncle Harry and Mother – Dulwich 1916.

by the French for their brave action in saving the Front from total collapse
in this key sector. My father accordingly spent the last six months of the
war as a POW. on the island of Stralsund in the Baltic. Meanwhile, my
mother was employed throughout 1918 as a Red Cross VAD. on the wards
of the then Royal Herbert Military Hospital at Woolwich. Grandfather
Bridger, a Mercantile Marine Captain, and my Uncle Harry, a Training
Ship (TS) *Worcester* cadet, both served with the Merchant Navy on convoy duty in the Altantic. The latter was lost at sea in 1917. Like many they
had all done their national duty and not without human sacrifice. However, there was here no professional nor career soldier background to
influence my subsequent lifetime choice – the Regular Army. The spirit
was rather more that of the true Territorial Army volunteer, as some of
them had indeed been.

    My career choice I believe, like many before me, began to take seed
about the age of seven when I first started to collect toy soldiers and
especially the German-made variety, Elastolin. They were stocked by the
then local Bon Marché Store in nearby Brixton and were modelled on
World War I combat types. A real Christmas treat was to feast one's eyes
upon the Hamley's selection and just hope that Santa might drop off a

parcel or two from it during his rounds. This nursery floor battlefield activity, combined with regular reference to that splendid Annual *The Wonder Book of Soldiers*, and continual war story 'pestering' of father all assisted in developing the mould. There followed major early martial memories like a first Changing of the Guard ceremony, a Royal Review of the HAC at Armoury House in the City, the splendour of the great parades associated with King George V's Jubilee and King George VI's Coronation and a short trip with father to the Flanders Battlefields in the summer of 1939. We visited Hill 60 and the Menin Gate. The latter memorial bore the names of the many LRB chums who had fallen alongside Father in the early days of the war.

Meanwhile, in Europe the war clouds were gathering again and this first became apparent to even me in the autumn of 1938 – during the Munich crisis as it became known. I was then at Dulwich College Preparatory School (DCPS) and over the period of the crisis the Headmaster (the foresighted John Leakey) took us down to his in-law's farm at Coursehorn near Cranbrook, Kent. We occupied an old Oast House and slept on the floor on straw palliasses. All good camping experience and I don't think the true significance of events would have fully registered with me had not mother then joined the newly raised Auxiliary Territorial Service (ATS). She was among the first fifty volunteers to rally at the Duke of York's Headquarters, Chelsea, and was subsequently appointed to raise and command 7 Company attached to the 35th (1st Surrey Rifles) Anti-Aircraft (AA) Battalion, Royal Engineers (RE) at Flodden Road Drill Hall, Camberwell. She was gazetted in the rank of Junior Commander (Captain). In the following summer, and before Father and I did our mini-battlefield tour, we visited her and the company at their first Annual Camp at Horley, Surrey. A large number of faces were familiar to me since, in addition to many family friends, or their daughters, she had by then recruited the majority of the DCPS mistresses.

So certain was our Headmaster, following Munich, that war was inevitable that he persuaded most of the parents to subscribe towards the construction of a hutted evacuation camp based about the Coursehorn Farm complex. Whilst the accommodation was fairly basic it was certainly adequate, in the short term, and was linked to the provision of shared classroom facilities at nearby Cranbrook School. (The site is, incidentally, now the permanent home of DCPS Coursehorn.) Despite increasing tension, a campaign of Air Raid Precautions (ARP) publicity and the national issue of respirators, we still proceeded on our annual summer holiday to Kingsgate on the Thanet coast. Whilst there mother received her mobilisation papers and we all returned to London with her. Within days she moved to Marlow with her Searchlight Unit. On 1st September, the day Poland was invaded, Grandma Bridger took me to West Dulwich Station, respirator, camp bed and all, to join a special school evacuation train to Cranbrook. Meanwhile Father had departed for Colwyn Bay – co-opted by the Ministry of Food, thus leaving Grandma, who had lived with us since the 'Old Skippers' death, as the sole occupant of the homestead in Herne Hill. However, the full significance of what lay ahead did not come over me until the morning of 3rd September as we stood in an orchard beside our huts and listened to Mr Chamberlain say that we were now at war. I then just wondered when I would see our scattered family again. My fears were soon abated as the 'Phoney War' set in along the Western Front and tensions eased. Christmas 1939 was spent at home with the family. Mother had a leave pass and Father, now based in High Wycombe, was home too. It was the last Christmas we ever spent in Herne Hill.

However, the lull ended with a bang as France fell and Dunkirk was evacuated. Appreciating that Cranbrook was now virtually in the 'front-line', the remarkable Mr Leakey produced another trump card from his hand – the Royal Oak Hotel at Bettws-y-Coed in North Wales. What seemed like overnight we packed our bags, folded up our camp beds and clutching our respirators in our tiny hands took another special train, this time northwards to Snowdonia. We settled fast into our new hotel surrounds but despite the invasion threat were permitted home for the summer holidays. In so doing most of us stepped straight into the first phase of the Luftwaffe Blitz on London. Father and I were actually watching cricket at the Dulwich Club when the first daylight raid was launched on Croydon Airport. We were so taken by surprise that it took us some moments to truly appreciate what was happening. A few weeks later, whilst undergoing a minor operation on my neck in the Royal Northern Hospital, Holloway (a latent infection picked up whilst hop-picking the previous September had suddenly developed into an enormous cyst), I had watched from my window the first major attack on the London Docks. With the first serious casualties of the raids now beginning to bring pressures on hospital beds, mine was clearly needed so I was sent home early to recuperate there under our local doctor. Most nights were spent in the cellar where Grandma, a great lady and very much of the old school, always paraded dressed for the big occasion – fur coat, hat, handbag and umbrella. If anything should happen, and we were forced to evacuate our cellar sanctuary, she had a horror of being seen 'improperly' dressed in the street. A fortnight or so later she was in fact able to prove her point when the house was damaged and we were forced to abandon it. Mother, then with an AA unit in Harrow, came to collect us, the Chow dog and belongings (including my toy soldier collection) and take us to High Wycombe to join father. At such short notice he could only find us 'digs'. A lovely old couple, the Brickwells, took us all in without a murmur. I shall never forget their kindness though they are long since departed this earth. By the time I returned for the Christmas 'hols' father had found us a small cottage near West Wycombe Station where we stayed till the end of the War. I left there to begin my military career.

Life in Bettws-y-Coed was far removed from the war except that one November evening, as we were having our supper, a stray Luftwaffe plane, having lost its way to Liverpool or somewhere, and following the line of the Conway River by moonlight, unloaded its bombs across the nearby railway line. The nearest fell some 250 yards behind the hotel and blew in most of the windows. The time had now come, however, to decide my academic future. Normally I would have gone on to Dulwich College. Their initial evacuation to Tonbridge had been terminated by mutual agreement after only one term. They were now back in London – Blitz and all. My father, was however, an Old Citizen and the City of London School (or 'Blackfriars Grammar' as Sir Kingsley Amis, another Old Citizen, has at sometime described it) seemed to be enjoying a somewhat happier relationship with Marlborough College. So it was to Marlborough that I went for the Michaelmas Term of 1941, to join Form Classical IVa – Latin, Greek, Music and all.

The School was billeted about the town and I was resident above Lloyds Bank in that lovely wide High Street, the sky or roof line of which is one of the finest in the country. The Bank Manager's wife was a very worthy soul and it was said that she 'prayed for the children to cross the road in safety' and all that. She certainly insisted on me drinking some supposedly health-giving herbal tea both night and morn. Most of it went down the loo. There were two daughters. One was in the Land Army and the other the Bank. The latter was an accomplished pianist and used to help me to check practically my Theory of Harmony homework for offending parallel fifths and octaves, for I had no ear for music and certainly couldn't read it. I still have neither ability. They were good days and I adapted quickly to my new surrounds. Having been a virtual boarder since evacuation, I had learned to stand on my own feet the hard way and was now not frightened to press my case in most company. I very much doubt that, had I remained a day boy in Dulwich, I would have been as self-confident at the same age.

In sharing the class room amenities we played games in the morning and took lessons throughout what seemed a rather long afternoon. Always a keen games player, I relished the excellent sports facilities to hand and made both the Cricket and Hockey 1st XI before we returned to London. I also, to my father's great pleasure, became a boxing enthusiast. We never, however, matched Marlborough playing standards, though at Light Welter I represented a joint Boxing Team versus St Paul's School (then sharing with Wellington College). However, probably the most significant development at this time in the way ahead was when I joined the School Junior Training Corps (JTC). Previously known as the Officer Training Corps (OTC) that title, it seemed, had of late become both socially and politically unacceptable. I was issued with my first uniform – 'Battledress' as it was then known. It became very useful in the holidays when visiting Mother in that it enabled me to accompany her about her 'parish' with no questions asked. I enjoyed these frequent visits as I got a first-hand feel of Service life and regular outings to the cinema accompanied by some delightful ATS subaltern or staff car driver detailed as my escort for the evening. It helped to introduce me to the charms of the opposite sex at a time when such liaison was not part of the Public School curriculum. My last visit was to Bournemouth in the Summer of 1944 and not long after D-Day. Mother was then an Acting Chief Commander (Lieutenant Colonel) commanding the Bournemouth Garrison Group ATS. She finished as such before going off to be the Welfare Officer at Selfridges. A strong personality, who was greatly liked and respected by all who worked with and for her, she could on occasion ruffle more senior feathers – a trait I no doubt inherited and which coloured her career as it certainly did mine.

Once I had obtained my Certificate 'A' qualification in the JTC I became eligible to join the local Home Guard (HG) Reconnaissance Platoon as a Runner. The Platoon was manned by masters from both schools and was equipped with four Carden-Lloyd Carriers mounting Spandau machine guns taken from shot down German aircraft. According to my now heavily thumbed pre-war *Wonder Book of Soldiers* Annual, the Carden-Lloyd was the first light-tracked infantry carrier introduced with mechanisation. It had since the mid-1930s been replaced by the Bren Carrier – hence its availability to the HG. Whilst I now felt a small cog in the war effort, I was only too conscious that I had some time to go before I could return as an Old Boy properly khaki clad. For every now and then once familiar seniors, especially the 'Y' Scheme University Entrant variety, seemed to make brief appearances as if '*pour encouragez les autres*' at the behest of their Service masters. The urge to become a real part of it all was also fostered by the regular sight of so many Service folk about the town and particularly at weekends. A Battalion of The King's Royal Rifle Corps (KRRC) was stationed at Chisledon nearby on the Downs (a camp I was to inhabit a few years hence), there were many RAF and WAAF on the Stations at Upavon and Yatesbury together with PMRAFNS Nurses and VADs at the Hospital at Wroughton. There were also many Yanks in camps about the area. Every Saturday night the Town Hall reverberated to the sound of the weekly all ranks 'hop' and the popular tunes of the day, 'Moonlight Becomes You' and the like. One felt, and especially with no brothers and sisters, that one was missing out on something – something I now saw as my ultimate destiny, a Service life and a share of the excellent camaraderie that so seemingly went with it. No doubt I was only seeing the glamorous side of it all, for a number of those I encountered over that period in the High Street subsequently, I am sure, made the supreme sacrifice either in NW Europe or in support of the continued Bomber Command offensive. But at that point in time I was not mature enough to view things in their proper perspective and television had not yet brought the real horrors of war nightly into the parlour. My main concern was to grow up faster and to make the Services before the war ended. I am sure there were many youngsters then who saw it my way too.

The School returned to its historic site on the Embankment at Blackfriars (now occupied by an American Finance House) for the Summer Term of 1944. As a classicist I had gained School Certificate the previous year (I missed Matriculation since I failed dismally in Elementary Mathematics) and, now a Prefect in the History V1 Class, was due to take Higher Certificate at the end of term. The decision to return to London bemused many (and certainly my parents) since, whilst D-Day was imminent, the war was far from over. However, London seemed barely threatened by the Luftwaffe these days and the City Corporation (who run the School) were perhaps beginning to feel the strain on their 'coffers' of the prolonged Marlborough sojourn. It cannot have been a cheap operation. Whatever the case, within weeks of our return Hitler launched first the V-I Flying Bomb attacks on London and later the far more sinister V-2 Rockets. All those not taking the Public Examinations were instructed to remain at home. Those who were were required to continue their studies at the School. I came up daily from West Wycombe to Marlybone Station and thence by Tube to the Temple. Over those few months I recall narrowly getting away with it when a flying bomb cut out and fell in Baker Street as I waited at Marylebone to catch the train home. I also remember being in class one morning, when a V-2 rocket fell near

Smithfield Market in the adjacent City. I took and passed Higher Certificate in the basement of Unilever House next door to the School. My
subjects were English, History, Colonial History and French and I'm sure
the examiners were sympathetic in the circumstances. No Maths nor
Science subjects featured and, as I perhaps did not appreciate at the time,
this was to have significant bearing on how I played my career cards
thereon.

   After the Summer holidays I returned to School for my final year. It was
planned that I should seek a History Bursary at Oxbridge, though my heart
was still set on an early Service career and I saw the 'Y' Scheme University Entry as my then best approach. However, events in Europe virtually
overtook the Scheme and I was advised by my Headmaster (the great Dr
FR Dale, a World War I DSO, and perhaps the finest Head the CLS ever
had) to try for Special Entry into the Royal Marines. This was a Civil
Service Examination still held annually despite the war. There was, however, one big snag. Two of the compulsory papers were Mathematics, and
Physics and Chemistry. I had failed the former in School Certificate and
had done none since and I had never learned any Physics or Chemistry in
my life. Believing that the will was probably there, if not the aptitude, Dr
Dale agreed that I should spend the next term trying to do the near
impossible. Despite all the encouragement and help the School could give
me, we made only marginal progress. It was, therefore, decided that in
January 1945 I should go to a well-known Military Crammer. You cannot
though, as they say, 'make a silk purse out of a sow's ear' and after some
three weeks in that excellent Holland Park establishment I went to see the
Principal and said that I thought I was wasting both his tutors and my time
and, more importantly, my father's hard earned cash – he rather agreed.
Thus that afternoon, before returning home, and on the advice of one of
the tutors (who had had similar problem children before) I went to the
India Office to see a dear old gentleman, a retired Indian Army Brigadier
called Ponting, who ran the Indian Army Cadet Scheme. I filled in my
application on the spot and he advised me that within the next few weeks I
would be summoned to attend a Selection Board at the Great Central
Hotel opposite Marylebone Station. I then went home to face the wrath of
my father. He was not pleased with the news, to say the least. He, however, accepted the *'fait accompli'* – he really had no other option. In any
event, the fine competition for a Royal Marine Special Entry place had,
according to our local doctor, been fraught with one other possible complication – my hammer toes. He felt sure these could present a Medical
Board problem. The point was well taken but some forty-seven years on I

still have the same hammer toes and in the intervening years have marched or yomped many, many a mile over a variety of terrain about the world. For all my service I was essentially an infantryman.

A couple or so weeks later I attended the Selection Board and was offered an Indian Army Cadetship. I accepted and was told I would be required to join the Indian Army Cadet Company Wing at 148 Pre-OCTU, Wrotham with the October Intake. I can recall nothing exceptional about the Board – an IQ Test Paper, an interview, a lecturette and some fitness tests come to mind. It certainly wasn't as stiff as I had expected. Nor was I awfully impressed by a number of the candidates. However, I felt sure the system would sift the 'wheat from the chaff'. How wrong I was, as was evident when I came to report at Wrotham later in the year. But then no doubt some were surprised to see me there too.

That weekend Father decided that it was probably time I disposed of my toy soldier collection. I was now a big boy. We, therefore, took it into a shop in High Wycombe and got £45 for the lot. Heaven knows what it would have been worth today, judging by some prices I read in a recent Christie's Catalogue.

Chapter 2

The King's Shilling

I had next to enlist (or take the King's Shilling in best historical military parlance) and this I did at the Recruiting Office in High Wycombe on 18th June 1945. By this time VE Day had been and gone. I was enlisted into The Queen's Royal Regiment for the day and then promptly transferred to the Class W/T Reserve (whatever that may have been) to await my call-up papers to join the Indian Army Cadet Company. The choice of Regiment was later to become significant but at this time simply related to the fact that all cadets in the Company were so badged. Why that was so has been lost in the passage of time. I would like to think, however, that it perhaps had something to do with the legend that prior to the war the Regiment, long India based, had been known as 'The Guards of India'.

Having now spent several months idling my time away under Grandma's feet in the tiny West Wycombe cottage, Father reckoned that it was high time that I did something more positive to bridge the gap prior to my call-up. Above all he was concerned that I should keep myself fit, whilst Mother had laid down some key 'social criteria' she was certain I needed to master before my reporting date. Whether she had been influenced by too many Mess tales concerning the behaviour of the Raj, and rumoured social habits of the pre-war Indian Army and Colonial Forces I know not. She had, however, convinced herself that I needed to learn to ride, shoot, play bridge and dance soonest. It so happened that Father had some good friends in North Norfolk whom I had met and who, once approached, volunteered to help. Ted Chapman was a big farmer and pre-war wool and seed merchant at North Elmham, near Fakenham. In his day he had ridden to hounds and had been a keen Point-to-Point rider. He was also a good shot. Nancy, his wife, also happened to be an expert Bridge player. The youngest daughter, Bridget, a WAAF Officer stationed nearby at RAF

Swanton Morley, agreed to take on the dancing instruction – Victor Sylvester records and all. To keep myself fit it was decreed that I should, when not under 'social guidance', help out on the farm and especially during the harvest. In fact, I spent a blissful Spring and Summer under the roof of this very kind and happy family. I certainly became a fairly competent shot. I mastered the Bridge and Equitation basics though I have never sat at a Bridge Table since and have always studiously avoided any possibility of being mounted on parade. As regards to the dancing I did progress to the waltz, foxtrot and quick-step but it didn't take long to settle into a more promising nightclub shuffle. Finally, at the end of the harvest I returned home to await that expected call-up. Instead I received a deferment notice till November – and later still a summons to report to Wrotham on 6th December. By this time VJ Day had also been and gone and the new Labour Government, dedicated to a rapid withdrawal from India, were positively considering how the transfer of power might be conducted at an early date. But I still wanted to go on.

I reported to the Indian Army Cadet Company Wing of 148 Pre-OCTU at the far end of the rather bleak Wrotham Escarpment above Snodland on a decidedly chill early December afternoon. The environment presented a distinct culture shock as I stepped first time into my Spider Hut to be greeted by a concrete and matless floor, double bunks, straw filled paliasses, no pillows, steel lockers and a single central coke stove. The nearest ablutions were some twenty-five yards away down a covered walk-way. For whilst we were termed 'Cadets', and wore white strips on our epaulettes and a white disc behind our cap badge, we were in effect, no more than slightly 'up-market' rookies about to undergo twelve weeks Basic Training prior to moving on to the Officer Cadet School (OCS) at Bangalore in Southern India. We were known as 20 Platoon (or Intake) but were, in fact, a Company strong. I found myself in 20B Platoon with several I remembered from the Selection Board. The Officers were all Indian Army and most were awaiting demobilisation. A few, however, including my Platoon Commander Captain Bob Fletcher badged Sikhs, were applying for Regular Commissions in the British Army (I was later to meet up with him again in Berlin – in the same Company and in the same Battalion). In addition to map reading and some fieldcraft training they also instructed us in basic Urdu (after all this time I can just remember '*Kitne baje hai?*' or 'What is the time?'). Otherwise our 'welfare' was in the hands of British Army NCOs mostly awaiting demob too. Sergeant Ballantine, a Royal Scots Fusilier and a Regular, was, however, our Platoon Sergeant and whilst a truly human soul was both very tough and

20B Platoon, Indian Army Cadet Company – Wrotham 1946. (The author is first from left in the Rear Rank).

very difficult to understand. The days all began with PT whatever the chill – and before breakfast. The instruction was hard and lengthy but with our JTC (and HG) background most of us had something of a start to ease us in. The 'grub' was mostly stodge but plentiful. We were paid 25s. 0d. per week and were permitted to pocket 15s. 0d. of that. The remainder was put into 'Credits' (or Savings). There were no weekend passes and anyway by midday each Saturday we were generally too 'knackered' to do much. We did, however, manage the odd Saturday night treat – the all ranks dance at the 'Star' Hotel in Maidstone (now sadly swept away by redevelopment). We used to walk to and from Snodland Station (the uphill haul on the return journey was trying) and the draw was, of course, the Wrens from Chatham. I met a rather sweet little RNVAD, Adele, who weathered my laboured foxtrot on several occasions. Sadly she was posted to Haslar late in January.

We did get seven days Christmas and New Year leave. It was the first time we could show ourselves off truly in public. I am sure nobody really cared in the post-war atmosphere that then prevailed – we just hoped they might. After that it was a continued hard slog until we 'Passed Out' in early March. A few fell by the wayside before we reached this point and we were certainly a mixed bunch. I'm sure that several made their way to OCS Bangalore who would not have made it through the then British Army equivalent at the OCS Eaton Hall. After three weeks embarkation leave we returned to Wrotham to receive two pieces of rather surprising news. The 'bad' news was that we were to move the following week to the then Guards Depot at Caterham in Surrey. The 'good' was that Sandhurst was to reopen in January to take in Regular Army cadets. 'NAAFI canteen' rumour had it that the move was occasioned by a serious bout of meningitis in the neighbouring Pre-OCTU Wing. On reflection I think it more likely that a War Office edict had decreed that there was no longer a requirement for Pre-OCTUs and that their functions could now be assumed by a number of designated Training Battalions. Certainly all those who followed me into the Regiment began at such – and notably with the 28th Training Battalion based at Holywood Barracks, Belfast. I have long been a believer in fate and the Sandhurst decision was certainly a key factor in determining my future, for once I heard the news I went to see Captain Fletcher and said I wanted to apply. In the final event some half dozen or so others did likewise. No real effort was made to make us change our minds. One sensed that the management were already aware of what lay ahead, since within a few days of our arrival at Caterham it was officially announced that 20 Platoon would be the last to proceed to India

– and even then they had to wait some weeks before their eventual departure.

The Guards Depot (situated incidentally next door to a mental institution) was an even more severe culture shock than had been the arrival at Wrotham – and we were technically no longer recruits. There, at least, we had been spared a surfeit of 'bull'. The emphasis had been very much on fitness, practical fieldcraft and weapon training. Perhaps our standard of drill was a deficiency in our military education to date. On arrival at Caterham we were directed to Codrington and York Blocks and were greeted by Guards Instructors and Trained Soldiers (they wore a special badge) who were to become our new 'grassroot' masters. Our Indian Army Officer element remained, however, and I am sure suffered much the same 'pain' as we did. There followed a great deal of 'square-bashing' (no doubt to raise that drill standard deficiency), innumerable inspections of our kit (including the very 'painful' standard Saturday performance which demanded that you spent the previous night lying on a 'spare' blanket on the floor beside your made-up bed with all your 'boxed' kit upon it) and a seemingly endless spate of fatigues, perhaps the most puerile of which was 'digging over', with our dinner forks, the flower beds along the way to the Commanding Officers Residence. HRH Princess Elizabeth was to proceed that way during a visit the following day. The Barrack Rooms were even then from a bygone age and I can still recall the murals which were at great pains to enlighten us as to the difference between a 'Gold' Sergeant (proper Sergeant) and a 'White' one (a Lance Sergeant or over-promoted Corporal). It will all come clear when next you watch the 'Trooping of the Colour' on TV – always assuming you have a coloured set. Recruit Training at the Guards Depot has always been a recognised culture shock, and the instructors have their own particular brand of humour. Shouts such as 'Take his name for idle cycling', 'Am I hurting you, lad? I should be as I'm standing on your hair' and 'Look up, lad – you need his help' were legion. I don't, though, really believe the Caterham experience did any of us any harm. It does not hurt in any profession or trade to begin at the very bottom and, at times, to bear with what you may expect others to have to do later in your service. In short, it is important to know first hand when soldiers are perhaps being over-stretched, what makes them 'tick' and when they are plainly being messed about. You cannot learn this in the isolation of a purely sheltered Officer Cadet environment.

Whilst the edict had been issued that 20 Platoon should be the last to proceed to Bangalore no immediate decision was taken to terminate continued Intakes. This decision was not taken until September, by which time the Company totalled some 300 or more cadets with nowhere visibly to go. Those of us who had elected to try our hand at the Regular Commissions Board (RCB) for entry to Sandhurst were then made Cadet Sergeant Instructors and conducted most of the basic weapon training for the remainder. Much to our delight we were also given NCO bunk-type accommodation. Our new elevated status did not, however, cut much ice at the Main Gate inspection conducted by Sergeant George, the Provost Sergeant, prior to walking out. An enormous Scots Guardsman with a great bull neck and huge hands, he 'ate cadets before breakfast'. One was invariably sent back to correct some dress 'infringement'. At the third attempt one generally made it, however. We were next notified that we were to attend the RCB at Knepp Castle, Sussex, in September. Meanwhile, it was decreed that the future of the remainder should be determined by either the RCB (for those who wished to try to be a Regular) and the War Office Selection Board (WOSB) for they that only sought an emergency commission through OCS Eaton Hall. From midsummer onwards this began to visibly thin our numbers as those who opted for WOSB, the majority, either failed to make it or went off to OCS. I went to the first special RCB for Sandhurst at the beginning of September. One had some idea of what to expect but was much shaken, when early on, one was confronted by the totally unexpected – an education test that included papers in both the dreaded Maths, and Physics and Chemistry. It seemed they were to dog me yet again. Whilst both papers contained a set of 'a', 'b' or 'c' answers for selection you were unlikely to win by pure football pools intuition alone. Any background knowledge of the subject and one answer at least would appear as obvious nonsense – I just didn't have this. There was also another obstacle to overcome – the composition of my syndicate and especially for the outdoor group and individual tasks, for of the eight in my syndicate six came from the same Sapper Training Unit and had together been put through some pre-RCB preparatory briefing. Jimmy Ward, from the Royal Armoured Corps (RAC), and I therefore were understandably a little pressed to get in on the act when it came to the group tasks. We also had to fight hard not to be overawed by the majority when it came to act as a team leader for our individual tasks. I, however, passed and was initially graded 'C' or 'Less Suitable'. Jimmy Ward made it too. Some weeks later, when standards had become somewhat clearer, I was upgraded to 'B' or 'Suitable with further education'. This all rather stuck in Father's gullet since he wondered what all that expensive classical education at the CLS had been about. I rather shared his viewpoint. A few days later I received orders to report to No 3 Army Formation College at Chisledon Camp to undergo ten weeks 'further education'.

Since I had left Marlborough some years back the KRRC had departed Chisledon Camp. It was now occupied by an Army Formation College (there was certainly another one at Dalkeith in Scotland where others went) where all ranks, both male and female, could undergo resettlement training in seemingly everything from typewriting to pig farming. It was perhaps a strange environment in which to pitch, if only temporarily, some thirty Officer Cadets who were supposedly dedicated to a future career in the Regular Army. We arrived on a rather dank Friday afternoon in the second week of October. We were promptly sent home for the weekend. On reassembly on the Monday morning it became pretty clear to us that not much thought had gone into laying down a syllabus for our 'further education', for we were advised that the subjects selected were Maths, English Literature and French – and nothing else. The former was conducted by a very elderly Royal Artillery (RA) Major and concentrated, thankfully for me, on a mix of geometry and trigonometry with a distinct gunner slant. I say thankfully since it had always been algebra that had really foxed me. English Literature took the form of the reading and group discussion of Shakespeare's more famous works and was in the capable and very charming hands of a delectable ATS Captain, Penelope Alexander (she later married a University Professor and settled in New Zealand). The French class was run by another delightful ATS Captain. We were given no homework, had each Wednesday afternoon free and fell-out every Friday lunch-time till the following Monday morning. It really was all very leisurely indeed and was something of a lull before the final pre-commissioning 'storm'. Penelope Alexander had a car and on several Wednesdays I re-explored Marlborough in her most pleasant company and took sustenance once again in the well-known Polly Tea Rooms in the High Street. All of a sudden Christmas was almost upon us and we received our Joining Instructions for Sandhurst in mid-January. Prior to leaving Chisledon we were, however, required to sign on as Regular Soldiers on a three years with the Colours and five years with the Reserve Engagement. Once again I was enlisted into The Queen's Royal Regiment. There was, though, a clear stipulation that once commissioned we would be automatically discharged from this engagement under the terms of King's Regulations. If we were sacked from Sandhurst it was also said that we would be permitted immediately to purchase our discharge – we just wondered. This latter 'quirk' had arisen since, unlike before the war, we were to be referred to as 'Officer Cadets' not 'Gentlemen Cadets'. In short, we were being paid to go to Sandhurst rather than our fathers being required to meet the fees – or 'purchasing our commission' over the period we were at either the then Royal Military College (RMC) Sandhurst or the Royal Military Academy (RMA) Woolwich.

Chapter 3

The Wishstream and the Immediate Beyond

The newly titled Royal Military Academy Sandhurst (RMAS) that opened its gilded portals in January 1947 was formed from the merger of the pre-war Royal Military Academy (the 'Shop') at Woolwich and the Royal Military College at Sandhurst. The former, established in 1741, had trained those destined for commissions in the Royal Artillery (RA), Royal Engineers (RE) and Royal Signals. The latter set up in 1802 in Marlow (and which moved to Sandhurst in 1812) had been responsible for the instruction of those Gentlemen Cadets for commissions in the Cavalry and Infantry. During the war years both establishments had been closed, though the Sandhurst buildings had been used as an Officer Cadet School (OCS). This later moved to Aldershot to form Mons OCS for the training of Short Service and National Service Officers. The Wishstream runs through the Sandhurst grounds.

It was into these hallowed precincts that some 320 or so of us stepped with considerable awe one bitterly cold day that January. We had been the so-called pick of some 2,000 plus who had sought entry. All the big names in the Public Schools Yearbook were represented in some numbers and notably those with a long military tradition such as Eton, Harrow, Winchester, Cheltenham, Wellington and so on. There was only one ex-City of London boy listed (me) and certainly this, the less fashionable end of the Headmasters Conference Schools spectrum, was thinly represented. Many of the cadets came from families with long and distinguished military backgrounds. Some of these were there by family direction rather than personal choice. At least one went to the extreme lengths of shooting off a finger to break with family tradition.

Times have changed and the entry sample with them – not all for the best, I suspect.

We were met by a Permanent Staff stacked with Officers of wartime military distinction, the pick of the Army's Senior WOs and NCOs and a plethora of the very best the Army could then produce in a variety of games and sports. Gallantry decorations abounded and an early Platoon Commander of mine (later Brigadier Maurice MacWilliam CBE, DSO, MC, TD) was just one of several who mustered both a DSO and MC. The first Academy Sergeant Major was the great and highly respected Mr (Daddy) Brand. He will always be remembered by his distinctive pre-war style dress and especially those long puttees and highly polished brown boots – and that fearsome parade bark which could be heard as far away as the Yorktown Gate. His College Sergeant Majors included his eventual successor, the equally great John Lord of wartime POW Camp fame – the Regimental Sergeant Major of New College. A very big man in every respect. Both my Company Sergeant Majors, Sid Felton and Jimmy Rioch, made senior Guards Quartermasters – almost a case of 'dead men's shoes' in those distant days. The PT Staff contained Wally Barnes, the Arsenal International footballer, and Ernie Shackleton, the former ABA Champion. The instructors included the Rugby Internationals, Bun Cowie and TGH Jackson, and the County cricketers JH Deighton, WME White and JE Manners (the RN staff member). Every stop had clearly been pulled out to field an all round star studded Permanent Staff. Our problem was, of course, that initially they only had one Intake, us, to which to give their undivided attention. I say this since, while the War Office aim was to produce some 1,200 and more young Regular Officers by the end of 1948, the build-up of the Academy was to be gradual. Intake I (or the 'Guinea Pigs'), as we became known, formed four Companies at the outset, two in the Old College (in what is termed the Old Building) and two in the New College (the Victorian monstrosity). On the arrival of Intake IA, three months later, the organisation was expanded to produce four Companies in each College. At the end of our first term, or the Junior Term, Intake II were posted in and Victory College was established (mostly in huts behind New College and for some years). Thereafter a half-yearly Intake cycle became the norm. However, we always retained one singular advantage over every other Intake. We never had to compete with any cadets senior to us as well as the Permanent Staff – hoorah!

Whilst clearly great trouble had been taken in both selecting and assembling a very polished and high grade staff, both military and academic, one could not truthfully say quite the same as regards the framing of the

Academy curriculum. Perhaps there had been something of a rush to cobble a syllabus together and maybe, in so doing, we somewhat confused the aim. For at the start the latter was said to have been that Sandhurst should, in effect, be 'a university with a slight military bias'. If this really was the aim then we fell far short of West Point academic standards and anybody who stood on the Square as often as we did, day after day, could not have been in any doubt as to the extent of that 'military bias'. In the succeeding years the argument has not diminished. There have been numerous Studies and Reports. Our course was divided into three terms – Junior, Intermediate and Senior – over a period of eighteen months. Later this was extended to two years. Some will always argue that, in the beginning, we should have followed the four-year West Point example with a degree thrown in at the end – especially when 'keeping up with the Jones's in Higher Education' became a fashionable theme. In more recent times things have tended to go the other way and notably since Mons OCS has been merged with Sandhurst. For the current twenty-eight week Standard Military Course is neither one thing nor the other. Or as General Sir Michael Gow put it to me in stentorian tones in the Old College Ante-Room during pre-lunch drinks after one Passing-Out Parade, 'Charles, I thought Mons had been merged with Sandhurst – not the other way round.' Perhaps as part of the 'Peace Dividend' we shall at last have time to sit down and properly think things through. I very much hope so for the sake of both the Army and Sandhurst.

The curriculum included both Military and Academic studies. At the military level we examined the organisation of the Army in great detail, were introduced to the writing of Appreciations and Orders and did some Tactical Exercises without Troops (TEWTs) on the neighbouring Barrossa Common. A good deal of this instruction was at a level which, as I subsequently discovered, would have held me in good stead during my Staff College Examination preparations some ten years later. We never did any practical leadership or command type training in the field. We, however, did a surfeit of drill, both on foot and bicycles (in those days it was said that the finest drill in the world was to be seen at a Sandhurst Passing-Out Parade), a good deal of rangework, a great amount of PT (much of this developed into an exercise in quick changing prowess and I never did master the backward roll) and plenty of sport. Standards were high and we had, for example, four Internationals in the Rugby XV, including the England Half-Backs (later Brigadier Dennis Shuttleworth and Colonel Mike Hardy), and could take on any of the major London Clubs and beat them. Unlike some years later when I left a newspaper cutting on Mike Hardy's mantleshelf which read, 'RMAS 4 – Guildford & Godalming 104'. I made the Hockey XI initially but, once the build-up began in earnest, spent the second season in the 'stiffs'. In the Boxing and Cricket spheres the competition was such that to represent your Company was an achievement and especially in the Champion (later Sovereign's) Company Competition. Academically we studied a language (I chose Russian), International Affairs, English Literature and my 'old favourites' Science and Maths. To put us into Sets, or Classes, we were given some grading tests in the first week. Not unnaturally I ended up in the bottom sets for both Science and Maths. The latter, fortunately, stuck largely to the Chisledon experience whilst the former was solely linked to Meteorology. I can still spot Nimbo Stratus and remain an expert in measuring rainfall. At no time during those eighteen months did I feel that academic levels rose much above the fifth grade at CLS. In short, I cannot say that I was ever academically stretched.

I had begun in Marne Company in the New College. On the arrival of Intake IA I was 'unloaded' with several other ex-Indian Army Cadet 'dissidents' to the newly formed Ypres Company. Our basic problem had been that during our prolonged sojourn at the Guards Depot we had picked up a Trained Soldier type drill style that set us a bit apart from the 'sprogs' (the Corps trained) and did not please our rather toffee-nosed Company Commander and the fiery Sid Felton. Additionally, as the latter was a Grenadier and our Caterham 'breeding' had been largely Coldstream inspired (the Left and Right of the Line and all that), we were, we felt, never quite in favour. I remained in Ypres Company when the final split came to form Victory College and was appointed Cadet Lance Corporal at the end of the Junior Term. I subsequently became the Cadet Company Senior Sergeant – or Company Sergeant Major, one down from those golden few who became Cadet Senior and Junior Under Officers. Perhaps the first signal to me, and one which I accepted, that faced with the top competition, I might always come out as a 'fringe of Squad' player. It was hard to accept but so was the competition. Incidentally, I know of at least one Senior Under Officer (SUO) who never made it beyond Major. On the other hand, Ted Burgess (later General Sir Edward Burgess, GCB, OBE) finished as Deputy Supreme Allied Commander Europe (D SACEUR).

As we got into the Intermediate Term we were required to begin considering a choice of Regiment. Not really knowing one Regiment from the other and with no Regular Army background, this was none too easy. I was, however, clear that the Cavalry and Guards were non-starters. I had neither the up-bringing nor the money to match either. Initially, and rather

unwisely, I chose The Rifle Brigade since Father had served in one of
their TA Battalions (LRB) during World War I. There were, however,
twenty-eight Starters on their 'Dukes List' (The Duke of Connaught and
all that) for what turned out to be a single vacancy and I 'fell' early on in
the selection stakes. I then switched to The Royal Fusiliers (City of
London Regiment). I had been a City of London schoolboy and both my
grandfathers had been City Liverymen. I thought this might be regarded
as some sort of Regimental connection. I stuck with this choice to the very
end, even though I knew the other candidate would pass out above me in
the 'Order of Merit' (he was in fact twenty-second and myself forty-sixth)
since it had been suggested that there could be two vacancies. Meanwhile,
I had put down The Home Counties Brigade (which included The Queen's
Royal Regiment in which I was still a Regular Soldier) as my Second
Choice and that very dangerous last resort, 'Any Other Infantry Regiment', as my Third.

One amusing sideline to this Regimental Selection procedure (now
fraught by all sorts of devious poaching by Regimental representatives at
the Academy) was that, in those early days, one was also required to
nominate a second choice of Arm. I chose the Royal Armoured Corps
(RAC) – or essentially the Cavalry. I was duly summoned to a briefing by
their senior representative from one of the 'cut-price' (or fractional)
Regiments. Early on in the talk he came out with a remark I have always
remembered – 'On your first night in the Mess long green cigarette
holders – no. Scent in moderation – yes!' I eventually was appointed to
The Queen's Royal Regiment (West Surrey). To this day I have no idea
whose First Choice it must have been, for I can hardly believe the 2nd of
Foot, and the oldest English Line Regiment in the Army, had not had its
own front runner. I was indeed a very satisfied customer. There were,
however, a number who left the Academy highly disenchanted with their
lot. They were those who were made to fill vacancies in some of the Corps
and Services. Most left the Army early on feeling that they had been
somewhat cheated. Having won through in the initial and needle RMAS
selection process they felt, and I believe rightly, that they deserved a
squarer deal. Perhaps, and in retrospect, it would have been wiser to fill
these non Teeth-Arm slots from among those who had just missed the cut
for Sandhurst. However, it is always easier to be wise in hindsight.

Towards the end of the Intermediate Term a detachment of 100 of us
were selected to 'Line the Route' for the wedding of HRH Princess
Elizabeth. We spent the previous night in the then Clapham Deep Shelter
(below Clapham South Tube Station) and paraded early next morning at

Wellington Barracks. Behind our Colours we proudly swung down Bird-cage Walk in pride of place behind the dismounted Band of The Life Guards. Once in Whitehall we took up position opposite the entrance to Horse Guards. It was a proud occasion and, if I learned anything from it, it was that if detailed to line a route you always get there last and yet get the best view. In this detachment were many very good friends who have remained lifetime chums. Perhaps one of the great merits of our time at Sandhurst was that we grew up in the Service with true friends with whom we never lost touch and with whom we frequently came into close contact again on operations, in the same garrison or station, at some establishment like the Staff College, in the Ministry of Defence and so on. We could, therefore, always seek friendly advice or a helping hand when the need arose. It has been a great brotherhood and it all began in Intake I. Beyond that deep sense of lasting friendship I believe those eighteen months helped to develop what are sometimes described as the 'Officer like Qualities' (or 'Oily Qs' as they are better known in the Royal Navy). They cannot be taught as a subject but were fundamental to all else that went on within the Academy and were generally acquired by a combination of continued pressures and example. I am, in particular, referring to confidence in oneself, self-discipline, a code of personal conduct, style, polish and an ability to smile when the chips are down. There may be more but these I consider to be the essentials if you are to gain the genuine respect of those serving above, alongside and below you – and that is the starting point for all successful commanders.

There was a lighter side to life since it was recognised that all work and no play would breed a body of dull cadets. So a 'blind eye' was generally turned to a reasonable degree of high-spirited conduct out of hours. Cranwell and Dartmouth visiting teams were always given a 'run around', Inter College and Company midnight 'raids' were fairly frequent, every now and then the more unpopular cadets (including the odd JUO) were made to walk the plank pyjama clad into the lake and pairs of trousers (one belonging to a later very distinguished West Pointer) invariably topped College flagstaffs after dinner nights. This 'horse play' was not always restricted to the Academy grounds. On one occasion I recall a particularly unpleasant SUO being found by the milkman strapped to his bed in the foyer of the Arcade Cinema (now long since demolished) in the London Road, Camberley. The line was, however, drawn when somebody 'hid' the great Field Marshal's double-badged beret whilst he was lunching in New College after an address to us. During this address he gave us a clear target on which to set our sights – Regimental or Battalion command. He described it as the most satisfying level of command in Service life. I never forgot that advice, made it my clear goal and came, in time, to heartily endorse it.

We finally 'Passed-Out' on 14th July 1948. The parade was taken by HRH King George VI and thereafter was designated the Sovereign's Parade. Some 1,400 cadets took part since, by then, Intake III were also in situ. It was the largest parade ever seen at RMAS. The following day we were discharged from our Regular Army engagements. Once our proud parents had departed we, the just over 300 who had survived the Course, prepared for that evenings Summer Ball during which, at midnight, we would become Second Lieutenants. For most of us in Intake I it had seemed a very long haul indeed. In my case it had taken two years and eight months to finally make it. Despite this I had not lost out since my seniority would date from the day of the passing-out and not my twenty-first birthday. I was also advised to hang on to my Regular Army Discharge Book since, if I ever made Lieutenant Colonel, my service in the ranks would count towards where I entered the pay incremental scale in that rank. (This I did and I still have it to prove that once I was No. 6108969 Pte Millman HC) Against this rather special set of circumstances this was an occasion when a high degree of long-pent-up emotion was inevitably likely to explode. In retrospect it would perhaps, therefore, have been wiser had the authorities placed some restriction on the quantity of 'booze' (and especially champagne) available at the party. Suffice it to say that the evening developed into a virtual 'drunken orgy' and brought no great credit to either the Academy or Intake I. For sometime after mothers were somewhat reluctant to let their 'little darlings' attend these Summer Balls. The behaviour of the 'brutal and licentious' cadets had been grossly magnified about those afternoon Bridge Tables. (Thankfully the subsequent 'Guinea Pig' Ball held at the Savoy in London was a rather more couth affair.) I am told the lake was a mass of 'fairy lights' or lighted candles floating in chamberpots and that the grounds were strewn with 'loving' couples. Next morning the Commandant, the great Sir Hugh Stockwell (later the Corps Commander at Suez), sent out the Academy Staff, far and wide, to buy in every possible Press and other photograph taken of this unfortunate ending to what should have been a great occasion. It was never permitted to happen again. But then, of course, the same set of circumstances never pertained again. Like all my chums I left Sandhurst with a very sore head, very jaded and aware that for the first time in my life (though not the last), I had grossly over imbibed – end of message!

During the next few weeks leave we had to complete our fitting out. Unlike today, when one receives early advice as to the names of both the Regimental Hatter and Tailor, none had been forthcoming. So with Mother at the helm I went to both the hatter and tailor who had fitted her out for the ATS in 1938. We, however, only had one 'disaster' and that was not to be determined till a few weeks on. Following our final visit to the hatter we decided to take tea at Fortnum's. We were joined by a former SUO and his mother. He had just been appointed to a Guards Regiment and they had been busy ordering a bearskin, scarlet and the like. A bit of 'one-upmanship' seemed to creep into the conversation between the mums and for the first time, in many, I began to appreciate that there were 'two' armies – the Household Division and the rest. It was to become even more evident years later on the streets of Londonderry. We knew them affectionately as 'The Other Army'. That is not to say that I do not respect them and I have many good Guards friends – they are just 'different', that's all.

Once leave was over I was ordered to report to the 1st Bn, The Royal West Kent Regiment at Moore Barracks, Shorncliffe, Kent. They were the Holding and Training Battalion for the then Home Counties Brigade Group (the others in the group being The Queen's Royal Regiment, The Buffs, The Royal Fusiliers, The East Surrey Regiment, The Royal Sussex Regiment and The Middlesex Regiment). I was not alone since all those who had passed out with me, and who were joining these Regiments, reported with me. They included Derek Bishop, headed for the Surreys in Greece, and Ken Dodson, a fellow ex-Indian Army Cadet, who would be remaining in Shorncliffe. (In due course we three would all become members of the same Regiment and all command Battalions within it.) Also in the party was Mike Wheaton, who had gained that single vacancy in the Fusiliers – he was later to leave the Army early on. A National Service Officer awaiting posting to the Royal Sussex at this time was David Sheppard (later the Bishop of Liverpool) and shortly to play so many fine innings for England. On our first day we were required to dress up in our best to be interviewed by the Commanding Officer. I paraded in my new Service Dress Cap for the first time, whereupon the Regimental Sergeant Major, a Queensman by origin, said, 'That's a nice cap badge, Sir, but sadly it went out in 1922.' Covered in confusion thereafter, I can barely recall the interview. A few harsh words were exchanged over the phone with my hatters (no names, no pack drill but I believe they are more famous for their bowlers these days), and the correct badge was forthcoming by post within days and certainly before I was required to pay a short familiarisation visit to the Regimental Depot at Stoughton Barracks, Guildford. At that time it was in virtual 'suspended animation' and seemed solely concerned with running the Officers' Club, the Old Comrades Association, the Museum and the Cricket Week. On my return from the Depot I expected to be immediately despatched to Berlin to join the 1st Bn, The Queen's Royal Regiment, now blockaded within the City. As it was I had to wait another two or three weeks before moving on and during this time was attached to one of the Training Companies. This time was not, however, wasted and served as a very useful insight into life in the real post-war Army. For prior to this I had really only experienced the rather sheltered all cadet environment and the standards maintained and expected within it. First impressions at Shorncliffe were, therefore, something of a rude shock since standards fell far short of what I had both seen and experienced in a similar Basic Training Establishment at Caterham. Likewise, as Orderly Officer doing the evening rounds of the several guardrooms one came face to face, for the first time, with the other side of Army life – the roughs, toughs and 'weirdos' either undergoing detention, biding time for Court Martial, awaiting escort to Prison or the 'Glasshouse' or merely trying to earn a medical discharge. On one such duty I encountered my first attempted suicide – a bungled hanging. It was not a pleasant sight but it served as harsh experience. I was happy two days later to set off for Harwich and the crossing to the Hook of Holland. We were on our way to proper soldiering at last. Or so I hoped.

Chapter 4

Berlin and the British Zone

At the end of World War II Germany was partitioned amongst the victorious Allies into occupied zones. The British Zone, essentially a combination of the North German Plain and the Ruhr industrial complex, was separated from the Russian equivalent by the River Elbe. At the Potsdam Conference it had also been agreed that the Allies should establish a four-power Council which would rule occupied Germany from Berlin. This required that each of the four powers maintain a 'presence' there, including a token military garrison. The city was, therefore, divided into four sectors each of which, initially, was under the direct control of the Allied military government. The British, French and American Sectors constituted a Western enclave deep in the heart of the Soviet sphere of influence. All went well until there was a direct conflict between Soviet policy towards the humbled Germany and that of the Western Allies. This reached crisis proportions when, in mid-June 1948, the Russians cut all the agreed and specified surface access routes to the city from West Germany. They hoped to make the Western Allies position in Berlin untenable and to force their withdrawal. They did not, however, attempt to interfere with the air corridors to the city. Short of war, there was nothing the West could do but attempt to beat this virtual blockade by launching a massive airlift operation – the Berlin Airlift as it became known. The blockade officially began on 14th June, when it was announced that the Russians had closed the bridge at Magdeburg 'for repairs'. At this time the 1st Bn, The Queen's Royal Regiment (which I was to join) were mid-way through a routine relief road move 'twixt Dortmund and Berlin. Once this was stopped the remainder of the Battalion, together with their heavier equipment and baggage, had to be flown into the airfield at RAF Gatow.

Berlin
(under Military Government)

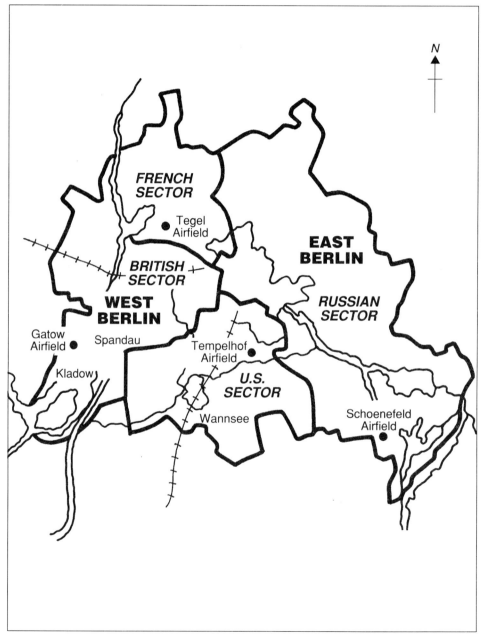

I. The Berlin Military Government Sectors, 1948–1949

It was against this background that I crossed from Harwich to the Hook of Holland on the military ferry one evening in late September. Thence I boarded a military train for Hannover. At this point I was required to spend a night in the transit camp there before being taken to RAF Buckeberg for the onward flight to Berlin. This is where 'disaster' struck in that I became separated from my heavy baggage. I was advised by a somewhat officious Movements Control Officer that, first posting or otherwise, there would only be room for me and my hand luggage aboard the DC3 (better known as the Dakota) that was to airlift us into RAF Gatow. He assured me that my heavy kit would follow within days with other freight. It did eventually make it but not for some six weeks. It was a lesson I learned for life – if humanly possible never let your baggage out of your sight when travelling by air. The flight was uneventful (sometimes aircraft were 'buzzed' by Soviet fighters whilst well within the corridor) and on arrival at Gatow I boarded a unit truck which took me to the Olympic Stadium where the Battalion was temporarily stationed. A few weeks later we were to move to Brooke Barracks in the industrial suburb of Spandau. Whilst the city had been devastated during the final Russian assault, the Stadium had been largely spared. The large swastika emblem that had topped Hitler's podium had been shot away by tank fire otherwise visible damage was minimal. The Officers' Mess was situated in what had been the stadium administration block. I suppose I was greeted with a modicum of interest – the first young Regular 'sprog' from the new Sandhurst. The initial impression cannot have been enhanced when I announced to the Adjutant that I had virtually only the kit I stood up in. However, one of those who immediately befriended me (and I have never forgotten this) was Alec Fearnside-Speed, an Old Marlburian, and we vaguely remembered each other from those earlier days. It also helped to find that Bob Fletcher, from my Wrotham stint, was the Second-in-Command of the company to which I was posted (soon after he married the daughter of the Head of the Canadian Military Mission and, in due course, transferred to the Canadian Army). He also ran the hockey and so I was soon representing the Battalion in the local league. In short, I had a fairly painless, if undistinguished, introduction into the Regiment, far less traumatic than many who followed me and especially once the 'induction ceremony' had got back into its sometimes rather frightening gear.

The teeth-arm element of the garrison then comprised an Armoured Car Squadron ('C' Sqn, 11th Hussars) and three Infantry Battalions – ourselves, 1st Bn, The Royal Norfolk Regiment and The Worcestershire Regiment. We and the Norfolks were based in Spandau and the

Worcesters were out at Kladow adjacent to RAF Gatow and the Russian
Zone. The role of the Battalion was primarily one of guards and duties.
One rifle company was Tiergarten-based, 'shewing the flag' where the
British and Russian Sectors fronted each other near to both Hitler's Bun-
ker and the Brandenburg Gate. Another company met the daily Key Point
(KP) guards and other duties about the Sector. A third was on Internal
Security (IS) standby with one platoon at two hour's notice to move,
whilst the company I joined was responsible for the six-week Continuation Training of the National Service drafts arriving from Shorncliffe. In
addition, once a quarter, we were required to produce the International
Guard at Spandau Prison, a platoon in strength, where Hess, Doenitz and
other major war criminals were detained. On occasion we subalterns were
also tipped out into the chill night to act as observation posts (OPs) to
spot, by bearing and distance, Russian searchlight and anti-aircraft positions attempting to harass Allied aircraft in the near corridor approach to
Gatow airfield. For it was not unknown for the Soviets to attempt to
'blind' pilots with the former, and particularly when on finals, and to put
up warning shots with the latter when an aircraft was in danger of 'stray-
ing' from the approved corridor. To indicate the extent of these
commitments about the Sector it could, as Orderly Officer, take one up to
five hours to do the rounds as one toured the guard posts and sentries at
the British Military Governor's Residence (General Sir Brian Robertson –
later the first Chairman of British Rail), the Villa Lemm home to the
British Troops Berlin (BTB) Commander, the several major ammunition,
POL and stores depots around the city and RAF Gatow. It was during one
of these early duty tours that I began to gather my first real impressions of
life in the beleaguered city. There was little doubt, even some three and a
half years on, that the final Soviet assault had been devastating. Whilst in
the intervening period there had been a determined effort to restore some
degree of normality, a 'Harry Lime' atmosphere remained amongst the
heaps of rubble, where a packet of cigarettes retained a high trading value
and where the population were still largely cellar based. Despite extensive
battlefield clearance rifles, steel helmets, ammunition and unexploded
grenades and shells were still to be found on both the Grunewald Training
Area and the Ruhleben Ranges. The focus of the British Sector then
centred about the Reichskanzler Platz (since renamed) where the NAAFI
Officers' Club was situated, and from where was apparent the impressive
sweep of the Kaiserdamm towards the Charlotteburg Gate and the Russian
Victory Column. The Kurfurstendam, later the mirror of West Berlin
opulence, was largely in ruins. The Sector also contained the scenic

Grunewald, the forested area adjacent to the Havelsee, and from whence the local population sought to scavenge for wood to supplement their meagre fuel supplies during a highly inclement winter. Even the most hardened 'Brit', and youngsters like myself who had been touched by the Blitz, found it difficult not to feel some sympathy, for in changed circumstances that elderly couple sledging a large tree root several miles back to their cellar-type shelter could have been one's own grandparents. It is to the great credit of the Western Allies combined military and civil airlift that they kept the population from both starving and freezing to death during that particularly harsh winter, for few had believed that it would be possible to supply two and a quarter million city-dwellers with food, fuel and raw materials for their industries solely by air. It was and in the Spring of 1949 the Russian reopened the surface communication routes. West Berlin could breathe again, though it remained a 'pressure point' in the deteriorating relations between East and West. Tension was never far from the surface and the newly formed East German Para-Military Police (known as VOPOS) were periodically deployed to promote 'incidents' demanding a 'show of force' from within the IS Company. Those of us who, whilst at school during the war, had sickened of powdered eggs, milk and potatoes had another bellyful during the Blockade. But that is all we really suffered – it could have been so much worse.

The Commanding Officer (CO) at this time was Lieutenant Colonel (later Brigadier) Trevor Hart-Dyke. Another Old Marlburian, he had won a DSO commanding The Hallamshires (TA) in NW Europe. He possessed a distinct charm of manner. He was, however, not one to be crossed. Hence his nickname – 'Tricky' Trevor. Without doubt an able leader, he was a very sound administrator and I learned much in those early days that was to stand me in good stead throughout my service. Whilst my first Platoon Sergeant, now in the Royal Hospital, Chelsea, will tell you that 'I taught him all he ever knew', I believe the credit is actually due to Hart-Dyke. The Battalion he commanded mirrored the immediate post-war Army and was highly variable in quality. The more senior officers and the Warrant Officers and Senior NCOs were all Regulars, whilst most of the junior ranks were National Servicemen. Many of the latter were from the lower Selection Grades (SG) 3 to 5 – or 'chunkies' as we knew them in the Training Company. The Second-in-Command was Major (later Brigadier) Michael Fletcher who, in due course, became our Defence Attaché in Bonn and was another polished and sharp number. My first Company Commander was Major Bill Griffiths (later Lieutenant Colonel and a member of the Directing Staff at the Civil Defence College). He had commanded a TA Battalion of the Regiment with great distinction during the war, gaining both a DSO and MC in the process. Neither were, however, typical of the field officer fraternity, for the majority were charming but somewhat idle with little obvious spark or ability. They were unlikely to make the more senior ranks in the Army – and never did. Seemingly some had chosen to stay on in the peacetime service rather than try their hand or luck in the brave new world outside. Some were decidedly 'punchy' (or in modern OK parlance 'suffering from post-traumatic stress') from their wartime experiences and my second Company Commander was just one such. He had won an MC in Italy but still held himself responsible for some subsequent misfortune that befell him and his Company. He had sadly sought solace in the bottle. The younger officers were a much more promising breed and there were some particularly high grade National Service Officers in our midst. The Sergeants' Mess was headed by a quite remarkable Regimental Sergeant Major (RSM) – Joe Simmons. As a Warrant Officer he held both the MC and MBE – an unusual distinction. He also did seven years in the appointment – equally unusual even in those days. After the war he had gone back to the London buses but had been 'dug out' by Hart-Dyke to bring a firm and guiding hand to a then rather crude and heavy drinking Mess, for unlike today it was, at that time, filled with rather more brawn than brain. Most members were great characters, had good war records and were as loyal as they come. They were just a bit thin where the three R's were concerned. They did, however, love their 'grog' and it was indeed a testing occasion when, as Orderly Officer, you were required on a Saturday evening to close the Mess and collect the takings. Joe Simmons was fortunately always present to 'hold your hand' but not before you had been invited to partake of several 'Advocaat and Soda' – the favourite tipple at that time.

Neither Hart-Dyke nor Simmons were drill 'fanatics' and with our heavy guards and duties commitments we were spared too many formal Battalion parades. Thus each Saturday morning we tended to 'bless our good fortune' as we watched our Norfolk neighbours being put through their paces by their fiery Adjutant – then Captain Tim Creasey. A very big man in every way, and our paths never ceased to cross thereafter as he became both firm friend and mentor. It was only very sad that, after completing his last appointment as Chief of the Defence Staff to the Sultan of Oman, he never lived long enough to enjoy a full retirement.

Just prior to the lifting of the blockade I returned to the UK for eight weeks to attend the Platoon Weapons Course at the then Small Arms

School at Hythe, Kent (a town I was many years later to become very closely associated with). I gained a 'B' (or Above Average) Grading and returned to the Battalion to be appointed Weapon Training Officer (WTO). I also qualified as a marksman on both the rifle and light machine gun (LMG). In those days a subaltern had to be at least a First Class Shot – nothing less was acceptable. At that time we still retained a bolt action rifle and I recall the RSM of the School, a Mr Hale, getting off twenty-eight aimed shots in sixty seconds and all of them in the 'Bull' bar one 'Inner'. It reminded me of Father's war stories concerning the Retreat from Mons and the German belief that, due to the high rate of fire, they were being confronted by a mass of machine guns. This little break in the Berlin tour slightly cut across what had begun to become a promising social scene, for just prior to Christmas I had met a vivacious young American lady at a party held by the 'Cherrypickers' (nicknamed after the colour of their mess overalls) at their Squadron Mess in Scharmgendorf – a rather more salubrious part of the city than Spandau. Martha Rodes (or Miffie as she was better known) was one of the three highly attractive daughters of a US Army 'Bird' (or Full) Colonel stationed in Berlin. The family had a lovely house by the Wannsee in the once highly fashionable part of the city. Meanwhile, at the same party Alec Fearnside-Speed had met up with another American family, the Coopers, who were the US Military Government (OMGUS) and lived nearby in Dahlem. In the week before Christmas we had been taken to the newly revived Opera Company's Bizet's *Carmen* and on Boxing Day had enjoyed a special show at the US Sector Club starring Bob Hope and Jinx Falkenberg (her brother was to win Wimbledon shortly after). Before this welcome widening of our social horizon our vista had been limited, in the strict non-fraternisation atmosphere that then prevailed, to a regular Saturday night visit to the NAAFI Officers' Club. There we dined unaccompanied amidst the marrieds (or 'pads' as they are known affectionately by the 'singletons'). At that time uniform had to be worn on such occasions and so we had to don our 'Blues'. Since we had no private transport we would stand in the bus queue in our dress hats and greatcoats along with the locals and any Soviet Spandau prison guards on 'pass' for the evening (usually very poorly clad junior ranks from one of the Central Asian Republics). Brooke Barracks was just across the road from the prison. It all helped to retain a sense of proportion. We usually made the return journey from the Club in the comfort of a hired Control Commission Germany (CCG) taxi masquerading as 'Mr Thomas, Economics Division' or some such civilian official. The German drivers soon cottoned on and were only too happy to fudge their work tickets for a good tip and a packet of fags. It really did grate to see all these civilians in the Control Commission swanning about in all this transport (and especially the 'fishing fleet', or the mass of rather dowdy secretaries they seemed to employ). On more than one Sunday I borrowed the Company Office bicycle and (recalling that special cycle drill we had undergone at RMAS) rode the twelve miles to lunch at Wannsee. Thankfully I usually got a lift back, cycle and all, in the OMGUS taxi service equivalent – Taxibal – paid for by my hosts. They assumed all subalterns were very poor and they were not far wrong in those days. On my return from Hythe it had been 'all change' in the garrison. 'A' Squadron, Royal Dragoons (once the Tangier Horse, as we were the Tangier Foot, we shared the oldest Battle Honour) had replaced the Hussars, the Royal Welch Fusiliers were now next door and the Gordon Highlanders were out at Kladow. The Royals and the Gordons (including my old chum Bobby Duff from Sandhurst days and later tragically killed by an own sentry in Malaya) were a lively lot and brought new faces (and competition) into the 'younger set' scene. The company of young ladies, such as the Rodes and Cooper sisters, were in much demand and the summer social calendar, which included splendid parties given by all the Heads of Military Mission, also required that we burnt the candle a trifle at either end. We were, however, young, it was all very exciting and enjoyable and one felt that if this was a sample of life in the modern Army, plenty of work and good play, then that long struggle to be commissioned had all been worthwhile. On 'The Glorious First of June' (the Regimental Day) the Hart-Dykes held an excellent champagne party in the grounds of their lovely and spacious house in the Herr Strasse. It came to me that evening that one day I might do the same somewhere. At the King's Birthday Parade on the magnificent Olympischer Platz I carried the King's Colour and commanded the colour party. Shortly after the parade the Rodes very kindly invited Mother to stay with them for a ten-day visit. We had a very happy time with this lovely warm family. All good things have, however, to come to an end sometime and come November I headed with the Advance Party (I was then Assistant Adjutant, Intelligence Officer and Weapon Training Officer) for Iserlohn in the British Zone. We were to do a direct swap with the Royal Fusiliers. The night I left Charlottenburg Station and said goodbye to Miffie Rodes I really felt that my tiny world had suddenly collapsed about me. I recall leaving her with a bottle of 'Ma Griffe' scent and she giving me a record of Edith Piaf singing our favourite – *'La Vie en Rose'*. That tune still touches me to this day and that night I shed a tear or two in the privacy of

The King's Birthday Parade Berlin 1949. (The author is carrying the King's Colour behind the Escort Guard).

my rail sleeper. A month or so later the Rodes departed for Fort Knox near Louisville in Kentucky. Besides being the home of all that bullion, it was also the base of the Armoured School. Father was to be the Executive Officer there in the rank of Brigadier General. I was not to return to Berlin for thirty years and it was a very different city when I did. It still, however, has a very special place in my heart.

Iserlohn, situated on the edge of the Ruhr and bordering the Sauerland, had been largely untouched by the ravages of war. It was the Headquarters of 5th Infantry Brigade – one of the three brigades comprising 2nd Infantry Division. The other Division, 7th Armoured, included a Lorried Infantry Brigade. Full mechanisation had not yet hit the British Army of the Rhine (BAOR) so the big exercise that autumn (Exercise BROAD SIDE in which we took part, was a pretty pedestrian affair in every respect. HQ BAOR was then situated at Bad Oeynhausen, a pleasant Spa town on the Weser. We shared Alexander Barracks with our Brigade HQ and we subalterns, chiefly the 'livers-in' even in those days, had rooms above Block I – Battalion HQ. The Officers' Mess was outside the barrack compound and not far from the rear gate. Prior to the war it had been the Garrison 'Kasino' or Officers' Club. This had been the Germany Army practice whereby officers lived out, whatever their marital status. Typical of these buildings it contained a large and impressive dining hall with minstrel gallery and a few small rooms above no doubt used for bordel type activities later in the evening. To approach it you had to cross a railway footbridge just beyond the back gate. Legend had it that the ghost of a Fusilier Officer, who had thrown himself under a train from the bridge, was prone to make an appearance from time to time. Brave lads that we professed to be, we usually ensured that we were in company as we returned to our quarters in Block I on very dark nights. Following our rather sedentary martial life in Berlin, the emphasis immediately switched to refresher training – first at platoon and company level and thence to battalion training, culminating in a long spring session at the Sennelager All Arms Training Centre (AATC). During this period, now early 1950, the Great Field Marshal himself paid a visit to Iserlohn (this time the famous beret was not 'snitched') and reminded we young Regular officers that our sights should remain set on Battalion command – mine already were after that Herr Strasse party. Just before Easter I took a Quarter Guard to Bad Oeynhausen for the visit of General de Lattre de Tassigny, then Commander-in-Chief (C-in-C) Land Forces Western Europe (France was still a full member of NATO at this time). We were to provide both a Ceremonial Guard and a roving night security picquet. The orders clearly laid down that there was, during the 'silent hours', to be no stamping of feet nor crunching of the gravel paths by heavy hobnailed boots. It was the first and only time I ever mounted and dismounted a picquet in my gymshoes. At Easter I visited Bettie Baldwin (Miffie's eldest sister) at Bad Kreuznach, near Koblenz on the Rhine. Her new husband was the outgoing US Army Liaison Officer (LO) with the 1st French Division. Following a party on my last evening, at which the Pernod had flowed, I was stung by an aside made by his relief as we left the Rathaus where the party had been held, namely – 'You know, Charles, your French never rose above the third grade over the entire evening – not even after all that liquor.' Coming from an American it really hurt – and a Texan at that. Around this time we had a change of CO – Jimmy Sykes-Wright (later Brigadier). Another charmer with a distinguished war record, he did not possess quite the fire of his predecessor. He was nevertheless an able leader of a rather mediocre middle-management team. There was, how-ever, one brief infusion of real talent with the arrival of Major David

Lloyd-Owen (later Major General and GOC Near East Land Forces), the highly decorated wartime commander of the Long Range Desert Group (LRDG). All too soon he was snatched away to be Military Assistant (MA) to General Sir Gerald Templar (later Field Marshal), then Director of Operations in Malaya.

The pattern of life changed markedly when the Korean War began in late June that year. Almost immediately we were required to produce a draft of a Field Officer and 135 Other Ranks to reinforce The Middlesex Regiment. On the parade at which the CO called for volunteers, the whole Battalion took a pace forward. I recall the occasion well and it was a remarkable moment I have never forgotten and am unlikely ever to do. The draft, when it arrived in Korea remained intact and became 'C' Company of the Middlesex. It stayed as such and fought continuously in bitter weather and against great odds for seven long months until relieved. Corporal 'Paddy' King, my faithful Sniper Instructor and WT NCO, was one of those who went. A very likeable Irishman, with all the blarney in the world, I know he survived the campaign. Sadly he and many others, who also made it, never came back to us. Shortly after, whilst on training at Sennelager, we were required to dig and construct a 'model' Korean War style defensive position. During a very hot August we toiled and sweated away with sandbags, corrugated iron sheeting, barbed wire and logs to produce a set of bunkers and support trenches so well protected overhead that they would have done credit to the Japs on Iwojima. It seemed like World War I all over again and, when we conducted a night 'Relief in the Line' Demonstration with the King's Regiment, some of the pages of my now tattered copy of *The Wonder Book of Soldiers* came very much to life. It was not long before the call for further reinforcements, and mostly for platoon commanders, began to become fairly routine. We had by this time some five ex-RMAS Regulars in the Battalion and all were filling designated or specialist platoon appointments. The CO, therefore, chose to meet the initial calls from his National Service (NS) subalterns. After a period this inevitably bred some ill will between the two breeds and this finally came to a head over dinner one night in the Mess. Bryan Cartledge (later Sir Bryan Cartledge, KCMG, our Ambassador in Moscow) had been so detailed that morning. He had taken it very well. However, another NS Officer had not. Over the soup he accused the Regular subalterns of being 'Yellow'. He was promptly requested to withdraw the remark and, when he refused to do so, was invited to 'step outside' by Bob Johnson – the Signals Officer and former Captain of Boxing at Harrow. What seemed like only a few seconds later Bob was back at the table trying to enjoy his now rather lukewarm soup! There was no sign of Mr 'X'. The incident, however, inevitably reached the ears of Joe Simmons (that's what good RSMs are for!) and he told the Adjutant. I was, therefore, summoned the following morning – as Senior Subaltern and Assistant Adjutant – to see the CO. The outcome of this 'dressing down' was that, thereon, all subalterns' names would go into the hat irrespective of breed. A few weeks later there was a further call and this time Mike Reynolds (later Major General MF Reynolds, CB, and Commander of NATO's ACE Mobile Force) drew the short straw. He was on leave at the time and to this day inclines to the belief that he was 'diddled'. I can still assure him that he wasn't. The social scene reverted largely to the early Berlin days pattern – a Saturday night 'run ashore' at the local NAAFI Officers' Club. All dressed to death with nothing to do but wine and dine. We generally walked to and from the Club by the 'back way' – a path through some woods which didn't really do our Mess Wellingtons much good. I did towards the end of my time in Iserlohn make contact with the rather pleasant Women's Voluntary Service (WVS) organiser with the gunner unit in nearby Menden. The problem was, however, once again one of transport, though by then we did have the odd unit Volkswagen 'Beetle' which we could ('*mit*' driver) hire at a pretty exorbitant 'recreational transport' rate. Sports-wise there was plenty of scope and competition. I well recall being flown back off leave from Northolt (then London Airport) for a BAOR Hockey Semi-final match versus The Foresters in Goslar up in the Harz Mountains. Due to a fixture date deadline we were forced to play in several inches of snow with a red cricket ball. Clearly the side who scored the first goal would win – they did. After the Mess 'incident the CO decreed that all the Ensigns (or 2nd Lieutenants) should compete in the Inter-Company Boxing Competition. There were some pretty gutsy performances but it was never repeated. A popular pastime at weekends, under the expert tutelage of Sykes-Wright, were all day shoots. Game of all kinds was then extremely plentiful and the Mess possessed a number of shotguns obtained through CCG distribution of confiscated weapons. The day usually began with an early morning duckshoot and ended around midday with a 'Kesselring' – or a shoot for the pot. Under this tactic guns and beaters encircled a wide area and on a given signal beat inwards. The guns then engaged all that was put up,usually a large number of hares, but by firing out of the circle. Only on one occasion did we have a 'nonsense' when, a US Officer from our affiliated American Regiment, who claimed to be an 'expert hunter', became carried away, shot into the advancing circle and slightly winged

Battalion Christmas Concert Sketch – Iserlohn 1950. (The author is on the left in the sketch 'The Presentation of the Purple Heart with Bar and Cluster'!)

one of the beaters. They were, however, good days and I benefited from my Norfolk instruction. Mother had had it right in this instance. That Christmas Don Donaldson took over the running of the Battalion Concert. Long the preserve of the Regimental Band, the Bandmaster's nose was slightly put out of joint. Don was, however, exceptionally talented in this field and he later went on to produce a Staff College 'best' Panto and to a successful broadcasting career in New Zealand. On this occasion he polished up two or three after-dinner sketches he and I regularly performed in the Mess and notably 'The presentation of the Purple Heart with Bar and Cluster'. These, together with some other acts he garnered from outside the Band, helped to establish a revised pattern for such unit entertainment thereafter. Above all that, the new young officer breed were seen to be happy to laugh at themselves – no bad thing.

An enjoyable session at Vogelsang, a beautiful training area of lakes and wooded hills in the Eiffel near the Belgian Border, opened the 1951 Training season. The place was now run by the Belgian Army. It had been established in 1934 as a Nazi political university and for encouraging the development of the master Aryan race. What had been magnificent sports buildings and grounds had been badly damaged towards the end of the war. It was, however, as its name implies (bird song) a beautiful spot and still reflected the grandiose remains of the Nazi youth image. Not long after our return to Iserlohn I was told that the Regimental Depot was to be reactivated for recruit training purposes and I was to go as the first Adjutant – a Lieutenant's post. The continuation of the Korean War and increasing Cold War tensions in Europe had dictated this course of action. Not long afterwards Bob Johnson was to join me as one of the Training Subalterns. I was not to return to BAOR for many years, by which time I was to be confronted by a level of 'professional mystique' that bemused both me and others.

Chapter 5

From Merrow to Mt Kenya

The Cardwell Reforms of 1881 had afforded Infantry Line Regiments a County connection largely for recruiting purposes. In the case of The Queen's Royal Regiment this had been West Surrey. Rather naturally Guildford, the County Town, was selected as the site for the Depot or 'Home of the Regiment'. However, the barracks was not to be in leafy Merrow but rather in the suburb of Stoughton on the Aldershot side of the Town. As was standard pattern at the time, the central feature of the Depot was the Keep adjacent to an impressive arched main gateway. Since the end of the war the place had virtually been retained on a care and maintenance basis with a minimal staff. The sudden decision to bring life back to the barracks demanded some leeway before training activities could begin in earnest. It was into this vacuum that I was launched in late March 1951, the aim being to set things up for the arrival of the first National Service Intake in early May. In effect there was to be a small HQ with Major Fergus Ling (later Major General, GOC Eastern District and Colonel, The Queen's Regiment (two before me)), another very tried and distinguished wartime soldier, in command and a single Training Company capable of running up to four platoons on a six week entry cycle. The basic recruit training course then lasted ten weeks. Bob Johnson was soon to join as one Training Subaltern. The other came from a Parachute Battalion in Aldershot – Ian Morley-Clarke. An unusual specimen at that time – a married subaltern, for marriage below age twenty-five years was still not encouraged and there was no entitlement to either a quarter or marriage allowance. To get some fresh air out of the office I assisted with much of the rangework and some fieldcraft. We also had a Home Defence role – the security of a small government establishment out near Abinger Hammer that then produced the BBC News 'pips'. On our first night rehearsal

Mau Mau in Kenya

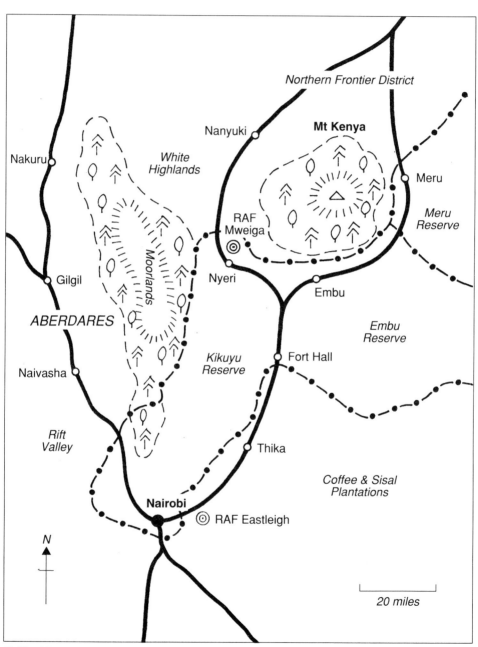

II. *The Mau-Mau Rebellion area of operations, 1953–1955.*

call-out I'm not sure who was more confused by it all – their staff or our part-trained recruits. Beyond the Depot lay the hutted Militia Camp built in 1938 under the Hoare Belisha reforms and which now housed the Depot of The Women's Royal Army Corps (the successors to the wartime ATS and now merged within the new Adjutant General's Corps). It was known as Queen Elizabeth's Camp.

Like all new tasks set against a time limit this was a great and rewarding challenge in every respect. There were inevitably a few teething troubles but I don't believe these were evident to the recruits or the Potential Officers (POs), whom we despatched to the Home Counties Brigade Depot at Canterbury after the first ten days. We had a small training area virtually on our doorstep and had first lien on a perfectly adequate range at Westcott. All in all it was a tidy little set-up and I am sure we produced the goods. Certainly the Mums and Dads who came to the Passing-Out parades seemed delighted with what we had made of 'Jimmy' and 'little Willie'. Having set the cycle in motion we took time out one weekend to compete in the Surrey Rifle Association Meeting at Bisley. It was my first experience of such competition amongst the real 'gravel bellies' in all their elbow-pads, slings, 'Crocodile Dundee' type hats and grossly over-badged shooting jackets. Previously I had only shot in Service Meetings at Ruhleben and Sennelager. I thought it all a bit unreal since I couldn't believe that the enemy would really permit you time to don all that 'clobber' nor quite so many sighting shots. There followed a few weeks later the Regimental Cricket Week, something from the past that the Regimental Committee seemed determined to resume. It began with a two day fixture against HMS *Excellent* (then the RN Gunnery School at Whale Island) to mark 'The Glorious First of June'. The second day's play always suffered from the intervening Dinner Night. On this occasion the opposition wicket keeper was the Captain (later Admiral of the Fleet Sir Varyl Begg, GCB, DSO, DSC). We were next to meet in Borneo at the height of Confrontation on the Sarawak Border. There were also fixtures against the Grasshoppers, Reigate Priory and Charterhouse Masters. I kept wicket throughout and, when it was over, was very happy that I had not decided to try my luck as a County Cricketer. It lasted for a few more years before 'overstretch' began to invade the Service way of life.

By the time that autumn came round any ripples in the training programme had been smoothed out and I asked the CO if I could take my six weeks annual leave entitlement in one lump so that I could visit the Rodes family in Louisville. He very kindly agreed and one early October day I took the train to Southampton to board the SS *Ile de France*. It was the

only part of the journey I did in style (I had a First Class Railway
Warrant) as I had booked Tourist Class (or steerage as it was once
known). I shared a cabin with a Master Builder on a foundation grant to
somewhere in Philadelphia, a London taxi driver who had been saving for
years to visit relations in New York and a sixth-former from St Paul's
School going on a years exchange to St Paul's, Connecticut. It was a
strange mix in a very small cabin. However, we survived the journey
without much strife despite some very rough weather. Light relief in the
evenings was obtained by gate-crashing the dance on the Cabin Class
deck immediately above. The attraction was a group of young ladies from
the famed Wellesley College returning home, having just 'done Europe'
as they put it. On arrival in New York I was met by the Baldwins and they
took me out to West Point where Clarke was now an Instructor. Besides
watching a parade (in all that fancy dress) and a football game, I visited
the Museum in which hung several British Regimental Colours captured
at Saratoga and elsewhere during the War of Independence. After an
evening on Broadway I took a train to Washington where Betty Falck
(another Berlin contact) met me and put me on a plane to Louisville.
During a very enjoyable stay there, deep in the 'Blue Grass' country, we
had only one uncomfortable moment when Miffie, Janet and I were
lunching in Brown's Hotel in downtown Louisville. Suddenly a very
drunken individual staggered across to our table and, with his bleary eyes
fixed firmly on me, said in a very loud voice for all to hear – 'If you're
British you shouldn't be proud of it for we've never forgotten how you ran
at Dunkirk.' He then lurched away out through the entrance to the restaurant. We continued our lunch in peace. At one point in the stay we all
drove up to Indianapolis to attend George Soltan's (a Royal Dragoon)
wedding to Betsy Cooper. On the previous evening we attended a party at
which a number of Philadelphia City Troop Officers (equivalent to our
HAC) were present. They were all National Guardsmen awaiting a draft to
Korea. One of the Ingersoll boys was among them. They got very tight
indeed and, at one point, one of them rose unsteadily to his feet to give the
toast 'The Philadelphia City Troop – the oldest unit in the United States
Army.' Not to be outdone, George promptly rose to his feet and said, 'I
give you a toast, Mr Millman, The Tangier Horse and The Tangier Foot –
the two oldest Regiments in the English Army raised in 1661' and then sat
down to the ensuing silence. On the day I was best man, clad in my
morning dress hired from the local 'Moss Bros', and Miffie was a brides-
maid. It was a very sad moment when I had to retrace my steps to New
York to embark on the SS *Liberté* for Plymouth. Miffie accompanied me. I

was never to see her again. I was not to know this at the time since, whilst I got the 'Dear John' when I was in Kenya, she did not die suddenly until a few years later. It was an uneventful and dull trip home. However, the travel or overseas 'itch' had begun to take hold.

Whilst time spent in a training establishment or unit can be very rewarding in that you can actually see the fruits of your labours, it can, after a time, become something of a 'sausage machine' routine. This was certainly the case during the National Service era. By mid-1952, when we had even repeated the Bisley shoot and the Cricket Week, life had become pretty monotonous. However, there was a lighter side. Ian Morley-Clarke, a Combined Services hockey player, had introduced me to Aldershot Services and I even got an Army trial. We had also established a good fun relationship with the WRAC ladies next door. The then Adjutant, Charmian Mould, remains a valued friend to this day. It helped that Bob had a car and we could thus get around. We were towards the end of our Depot stint to sample the fringes of the then London Season as escorts at Queen Charlotte's Ball and elsewhere. Despite this entertaining and sweeter side to life, I began to hanker for some action and an overseas outlet. I applied for an appointment as a Brigade Intelligence Officer in Korea, only to find that the Brigade Colonel had put it aside. Determined not to be defeated, I noticed another opening a few weeks later. This time they were seeking Ground Liaison Officers (GLOs) for duty in Korea, Malaya and Kenya. My application was successful and I was advised that come mid-June I would be required to attend an eight-week course at the School of Land Air Warfare (long since defunct) at RAF Old Sarum, near Salisbury. Following the earlier death of the King preparations were underway for the Coronation. Charmian and I were already on the Guildford Coronation Committee which had begun to plan a big pageant for Stoke Park. Whilst so engaged Queen Mary, our Colonel-in-Chief, died and we were required at short notice to produce a small detachment to follow the hearse in the funeral procession to Westminster Abbey. It was, however, essentially a Household Division (or 'Other Army') occasion and we were made to rather feel it. The 1st Battalion Colour Party was based on the Depot for the run-up to the Coronation and like the many others, Commonwealth and Colonial Forces included, could be spotted each afternoon somewhere about the local highways rehearsing over the known procession distance. It was all a fascinating sight. The Pageant had to do without Charmian and myself as she left for the Canal Zone and I for Old Sarum. I know however, that my old chum Don Donaldson, my successor, was just the chap to field this one on the day. I passed the

Course at Old Sarum and got the 'plum' posting to Kenya as GSO3 (Air) at HQ East Africa Command in the rank of Acting Captain. In good heart, and having won two tickets to watch the Coronation Parade from a stand in Horse Guards, Bob and I had super view and a high grade champagne buffet to match. It was the perfect end to a happy Depot tour – the time had, however, now come to move on.

I flew in early August by Argonaut aircraft to Nairobi from Blackbushe, near Camberley via Rome and Khartoum (a place I was to know very well years later). Airwork at that time had the charter contract to East Africa. The Mau-Mau rebellion amongst the Kikuyu, and their associated tribes, the Meru and Embu, had begun with surprising suddenness in mid-1952. It had its roots, however, far back in the arrival of the Europeans at the turn of the century. The Kikuyu, the largest, least martial but most intelligent tribe, had ever since nursed a deep grievance at what they supposed the naked theft of their best land by the settlers. Over the years this feeling of injustice had simmered underground. More recently it had been deliberately fanned by such as Jomo Kenyatta in the exploitation of the Kikuyu primitive beliefs in both black magic and witchcraft. From this had stemmed the Mau-Mau Secret Society and the bestial and obscene oaths that became associated with it. Mau-Mau inspired attacks began on European farms in early 1952 and were followed by the murder and mutilation of loyal tribesmen. A State of Emergency had finally been declared on 21st October following the Lari Massacre and the attacks on the Naivasha Police Post and the Gilgil Ordnance Depot. Since when the 39th Infantry Brigade (with Tim Creasey as Brigade Major) had been flown in to reinforce the 70th (East African) Brigade and its supporting 156th Heavy Anti-Aircraft (AA) Battery East African Artillery and East African Armoured Car Squadron (EAAC) (commanded by Henry Houth, a Korean War veteran). A small air element had additionally been established on Peter Marrian's Farm on the edge of the Nyeri Settled Area (or White Highlands) at Mweiga. It was here that I was flown the day after my arrival – tin trunk and all this time. I was to be attached to HQ 70th (EA) Brigade but operate from Mweiga.

RAF Mweiga, as it became known, comprised a tented camp beside a murram airstrip constructed originally by Peter Marrian on whose farmland it was situated. It did also extend to a couple of huts built by the local Public Works Department (PWD) to act as offices and the Operations Room. It was an altitude of some 7,200 feet above sea level and directly between the Aberdares and Mt Kenya. The views first thing in the morning were spectacular before cloud built up to obscure the peaks of both ranges. The air was invigorating – it was a heavenly spot. It was also well placed operationally since flying times to either area of operations were minimal. Operating from the airstrip were 'A' Flight, Kenya Police Reserve (KPR) Airwing and 1340 Flight RAF. The KPR comprised 6 x Piper Tri-Pacer light aircraft. Several had been adapted to carry bombs (6 x 20 lbs fragmentation) and all had fitted an 88 Set ground to air type radio. They were commanded by Punch Bearcroft (Callsign Eagle Red) a one-handed Molo farmer. He was both an intriguing character and a wizard of a pilot. They were mainly ex-RAF wartime pilots who had settled in the Colony post war and answered to such splendid names as Slug Nelson. They provided light aircraft support for reconnaissance, target marking, patrol contact, free-drop patrol resupply and casualty evacuation. They were a superb bunch who never spared themselves, whatever the flying conditions, and more than one sacrificed his life in attempting the near impossible in support of the cause. There was a similar but smaller Flight based at Naivasha supporting operations in the Rift Valley where the Kenya Regiment (my old Sandhurst chum, Roly Guy, was the Adjutant) and Kenya Police General Service Units (GSU) largely held sway. Alongside 'A' Flight was 1340 Flight RAF under the command of Wing Commander 'Judge' Jeffries (Callsign Kitestring One) – another very considerable character. His excellent and high-spirited team had come up from Rhodesia where they had been instructors at an RAF Flying School there. They flew 12 (later 16) x Harvard wartime trainer aircraft. Each plane could carry 16 x 20 lb fragmentation bombs and was armed with one fixed machine gun for straffing purposes. They were used in the close support role and against pre-planned targets – generally suspected hides. The technique, fashioned in the Korean War, whereby a 'mosquito' aircraft marked the target was followed when close support strike sorties were involved. The Harvard was highly manoeuvrable and thus ideally suited for use in this type of operation. Like the KPR the Flight lost one or two of their number, and notably Arthur Pullman, the very image of the wartime RAF pilot type, 'pressing on' (as was his cry) in highly adverse weather conditions over the Aberdares.

The operational area over which the air action took place was a rough triangle in shape, its corners marked by the northern end of the Aberdares, Mt Kenya and Nairobi. The sides of the triangle were approximately 100 miles long and encompassed the Kikuyu Reserve. The whole was bordered by the Aberdare forests to the West and Mt Kenya's forested slopes to the Northeast. Except for the Embu and Meru Reserves in the East, the area was surrounded by the European Settled Areas – and notably the

White Highlands 'twixt Nyeri and Nanyuki (a virtual playground for wild
life and, in particular, the graceful Thompson's gazelle). The slopes of
both mountain ranges were heavily forested to around 8,000 feet, where
they gave way to dense bamboo thicket before opening out into moorland
peaks. It was deep in this very difficult terrain that the Mau-Mau gangs
established their hides and from where they struck out against the settlers
for both food and weapons. From here they also concentrated on their
terrorism of their own people in the Reserve. Having no known outside
support they were always in the market for weapons. Theft was, therefore,
their main source of supply and it is very doubtful that there were ever
more than some 1,000 precision weapons to equip the some 10,000 tribesmen who were believed to have backed the rebellion. Many were armed
with 'home-made' guns which were just as likely to maim the firer as they
were the security forces. Others simply carried the traditional panga or
spears. The Aberdares and Mt Kenya had both been designated as Prohib-
ited Areas and as such freedom of air action obtained in both. In these
early days the targets presented resulted from either positive ground
patrol contacts or visual air sightings of suspected gang hides. A lack of
night flying facilities on the airstrip denied us the chance to get at the
camp fires that were often spotted at last light high up in the Aberdares.
(This limitation was not to be overcome until the Lincoln bombers arrived
and began to operate from RAF Eastleigh in Nairobi.)

   This was the setting into which I stepped as the GLO at RAF Mweiga.
My opposite number, the Air Liaison Officer (ALO), was a very sharp
number called Phil Lagesen (later Air Marshal Sir Philip Lagesen, KCB,
DFC, AFC, and we were next to meet in Rheindahlen some twenty years
later). He was an Afrikaner who had transferred from the South African
Air Force in 1951. Together we were responsible for the operational
briefing of all pilots, KPR or RAF, prior to any sortie. Phil covered the air
aspects and often flew on the strike as well. I handled the ground forces
angle – location of the patrol, their call sign, ground recognition signals
(panels or smoke) and so on. If it was to be an immediate strike, arising
from a snap contact request, I usually accompanied the KPR pilot (Eagle
Red, Blue, Green, etc.) and, once we had established radio contact with
the patrol leader, put down the smoke marker grenade at his direction. The
Harvards (usually a pair) then set about the suspected target area with
their bombs and machine guns. Positive results were not readily determined in such terrain but there is little doubt that the gangs were
continually harassed and kept on the move. Punch Bearcroft and his chaps
were also always looking for an extra pair of hands to assist with free

1340 FLT

Johnny Morris   Mike Watkin-Jones   Tony Train   Mike Holmes   S/LDR JEFFRIES

1340 Flight return from a sortie in the Aberdares – Mweiga 1954.

drops to patrols. Two or three of these five-man packs, at a time, were put down into an agreed forest clearing and would make the patrol self-sufficient for a further forty-eight hours. Like the target marking there was nothing very technical about it – the packs, like the marker grenades, were just heaved out of an open door in the desired direction. Relations with the units we supported, and notably the Devons (they had only lately been in Malaya), was one of mutual respect and whenever possible patrol commanders were invited to join our 'open house' Sunday curry lunch sessions. It was at just such a gathering that I first met the renowned Davo Davidson, the self-styled 'Settler Commando' leader. He was said to have served with Dedan Kimathi (the Mau-Mau 'Napoleon') in the King's African Rifles (KAR). During the lunch session he gave a pistol shooting display that would have put John Wayne to shame. Whilst he and his 'irregulars' had now been sent home with a grateful 'pat on the head' by General Sir George Erskine, the spirit had been willing. That is rather more than one could say for the 'Kenya Cowboys' (as they were termed

by the Security Forces) who daily propped up the Long Bar in the New
Stanley Hotel in Nairobi with their six-shooters firmly strapped to their
backsides. The more 'Tiger' beers they demolished the more critical of
the campaign they became. The social scene did not really extend beyond
these Sunday lunches and the occasional evening at the Outspan Hotel in
Nyeri. The problem with the latter was that one inevitably had to stay
overnight (we were charged 5s. 0d. for the privilege of sleeping on the
floor of the squash courts) as the road between Nyeri and Mweiga was the
main night transit route for gangs and reinforcements moving between the
Aberdares and Mt Kenya. There was also the danger of the ambush of the
lone vehicle. On my regular thrice weekly visits to Brigade HQ, for the
local Operations and Intelligence briefing (better known as 'morning
prayers'), I would often take time out before my return to Mweiga to have
bath or shower at the Outspan, for the bathing facilities in the camp were
primitive in the extreme and one did not want to become one of the great
unwashed. There were already plenty of them about in the forests. The
hotel rather sniffed at these visits and it was perhaps not altogether
surprising when their now derelict Treetops Annexe was slightly damaged
by a 'stray' mortar round during harassing fire along the forest edge (this
was done regularly at last light to deter potential Mau-Mau cattle rus-
tlers); for as hinted above, there was not too much love lost between the
settlers and the security forces at that time. Indeed, they had recently
flayed General Erskine at a public meeting in Nyeri. The rainy season
alternately turned the camp into a murram 'Passhendaele' or a veritable
Safari ant playground as the murram dried, cracked and permitted the
pests to process in dense martial type columns throughout the camp site.
On one occasion I awoke to find them in total occupation of my tent – it
was several hours before I could return. Another morning I opened my
eyes to find nothing more about me than the smouldering embers of my
tent – somebody's discarded fag end had done its worst. So whilst life
in Mweiga had its blissful moments there were distinct 'cons' as well
as 'pros'. I was, however, sorry to leave – it had all been a rewarding
experience, one I am unlikely to readily forget.

Early in April 1954 I moved down to RAF Eastleigh to control the air
effort to be deployed in support of Operation ANVIL or the big clearance
sweep of Mau-Mau sympathisers from Nairobi and its shanty town environs. The Airwing maintained constant air observation over the operation,
ensuring that both the inner and outdoor cordons were kept firmly in
place. The operation began on 24th April and lasted a fortnight. During
that time over 16,000 suspects were detained and many, following screen-

ing, were transported to detention camps such as that at MacKinnon Road. This was the start of what was designed to be the decisive year of the campaign. It was reckoned that by the end of Coronation Year the rebellion had been largely contained. It had not spread and the incident rate was down. To back this major offensive the air element was substantially reinforced, in the first instance by a detachment of Vampire jets from 8 Squadron in Aden. They were specifically brought in to add a hard hitting rocket and cannon punitive punch on the breakdown of the 'peace talks' conducted by Superintendent Ian Henderson (later Chief of The Bahrain State Police when I was there with my Battalion) with 'Generals' China, Tanganyika and others on Mt Kenya. Once this operation had been concluded the detachment returned to RAF Khormaksar. Whilst they were well suited to punitive area type operations, they were not ideal for close support strikes in this sort of terrain and where target marking was the order of the day. The most significant addition to the air effort was a flight of Lincoln bombers with their all weather capabilities. They were provided on a roulement basis by 49,100 and 214 Squadrons from bases in UK. Four aircraft were maintained at Eastleigh at any one time and were rotated, two at a time, on a monthly basis. They carried 1,000 lb bombs and could conduct straffing runs from their front and rear gun turrets. They were supplemented by two Meteors from 13 Squadron from the Canal Zone which conducted extensive photographic reconnaissance largely on their behalf. While some targets produced by the photo interpreters were greeted with 'hollow laughter' or described as 'elephant droppings', the product overall was far better than a blanket map square bombing approach. The primary role of the RAF in this offensive phase, including Operation HAMMER, a major sweep of the Aberdares which numbered the 49th Infantry Brigade a recent reinforcement, was, with the 156th Battery 3.7in. HAA guns in the ground role, to strike at suspected hides and to harass areas which were not under ground forces pressure. A similar policy had proved very successful in Malaya. This sustained air effort was kept up in all weathers and both by day and night. By the end of the campaign the Lincoln Squadrons (who also suffered tragic losses) had flown some 1,100 sorties and the Harvards around 3,500. How many casualties were inflicted will never be known. Likewise the psychological effect remains unproven. Following one heavy raid on the Nyambeni Forest NE of Mt Kenya I do know that patrols found positive evidence of heavy casualties. Sadly there is no doubt that the wild life, and especially the elephant and rhino, suffered badly. In addition, Valletta transports were now made available to bolster air resupply and Austers, fitted with 'sky-shouting' equipment ('Come out, come out wherever you are') to assist with 'Psy-Ops'. It has been said since that the Mau-Mau thought the latter were 'friendly' since they dropped nothing but leaflets. We even had a Sycamore helicopter (on altitude trials) which we used on more than one occasion in the casualty evacuation role. A wide-ranging and varied briefing task gradually developed at Eastleigh and I remained there for the rest of my tour. I still maintained a very close contact with my old Mweiga chums and flew marking sorties with the Airwing when directing Lincoln close support operations.

As had been the case at Mweiga, it was not all work and no play at RAF Eastleigh. Early on I met an attractive but somewhat temperamental air hostess. I introduced her to the Squash Court and she taught me a thing or two. Having only recently received the 'Dear John' from the beloved Miffie I was somewhat susceptible at that moment, so it took a little time for the then popular adage, 'Are you married or do you live in Kenya?' to register. From time to time it was the habit of the Station Commander to borrow one of the Lincoln navigators and to fly the new Communication Flight Pembroke (it had recently replaced a vintage Anson) with a 'Rest & Recuperation' (R&R) party, to Aden via Hargeisa (then in British Somaliland, it always seemed to be deep in locusts). The Aden Protectorate security elements were then exclusively run by the RAF. The 'Duty Free' port, besides being an important coaling station on the sea route to the Far East, was a popular souvenir hunting ground for cruise passengers. There were, of course, two sets of prices in the bazaar – one for the RAF and one for the tourists. There were, however, some very good duty free bargains and especially in the camera line. During one visit 8 Squadron, with whom I had established a good liaison during their time at Eastleigh, took me on a punitive strike in support of an operation being conducted by the Aden Protectorate Levies (APL). It was all rather reminiscent of what I had read about pre-war RAF operations in both Mesopotamia and on the NW Frontier in Waziristan. We simply straffed the terraced livelihood surrounding two 'offending' villages with rocket and cannon fire – to 'teach them a lesson' was the cry. The Gordon Club was the favoured 'nitespot' and our Khormaksar hosts always arranged for some of the Princess Mary's RAF Nursing Service (PMRAFNS) ladies from the local hospital to make up the party. Though discontent in the Colony was then simmering it was not apparent to the casual visitor at that time.

By the autumn of 1954 I had begun, once again, to think about the future and I had some leave due. It also so happened that Father, who had never really got over the full effects of being gassed on the Somme, was suffering from a rather more serious bout of bronchial trouble than was sadly his wont about this time of year. I decided therefore, to hitch a lift home with one of the Lincolns returning to RAF Wittering (now the 'Home of the Harrier') on roulement. I was invited to make a contribution of the princely sum of £5 to Squadron funds for the round trip – a real bargain by any standard, the arrangement being that they would give me forty-eight hours notice of the return flight date. It was a pretty chilly flight both ways in the bomb bay and we stopped overnight at Tripoli where the RAF then maintained staging facilities. I sat in the front turret as we came in over the White Cliffs at Dover – a marvellously welcoming sight as dawn broke even in late Autumn. On arrival at Wittering, still clad in our KD, on what was a chill November day, the Customs 'tore the aircraft apart' looking for Aden-type purchases. For some weeks prior to our arrival another Lincoln, having 'feathered an engine' over the Channel, had made a spurious 'Emergency Landing' at RAF Manston where all the 'loot' had been unloaded on a pre-arranged plan. Once it was safely headed north by road the aircraft resumed its flight to its home base. HM Customs were determined not to be caught again. It was very good indeed to see the family once again after fifteen months and to find Father over the worse. I also used the time to visit the Brigade Colonel at Canterbury to sound out the future. I was then advised that the Regiment wanted me to be the Adjutant of one of the TA Battalions and to begin serious study for that great career hurdle – the Staff College Examination. In due course a Posting Order came through for me to report to The 6th (Bermondsey) Bn, The Queen's Royal Regiment (TA) by late March 1955.

I left Nairobi by Britannia Airways in the first week of March. As if a reminder was needed that the rebellion was not yet over (it was not to end officially until October the following year with the capture of Dedan Kimathi), we included a serious casevac case amongst the passengers. He was a European Troop Sergeant from the EAAC Squadron who had been wounded in the head and was being flown to London for urgent neurosurgery. We took it in turns to try and keep him cool and comfortable during an excruciatingly long refuelling stop at Khartoum. I later learned that he survived the operation. I also heard later that I had been Mentioned-in-Despatches (mid) on the recommendation of my RAF and KPR chums and had earned a Campaign Medal, the African General Service Medal (first issued for 'Jubuland' in the 1880s), on which to wear the coveted oakleaf. Though I always had the cheerful and very smart Lance Corporal Mwangi as my orderly and driver, my Swahili never 'rose above the third grade' (where have we heard that said before). I can, however, still just remember '*pace sana*' (get a move on) and '*kahawa embele*' (coffee for two), two useful cries no doubt contained in some tourist safari phrase book these days. Mwangi, I believe, made it to Sergeant in 7th KAR – I hope he still has the watch I gave him.

Chapter 6

A Home Stretch

There then followed a home stretch which began in late March 1955 when I took over as Adjutant of the 6th (Bermondsey) Bn, The Queen's Royal Regiment (TA). The Battalion had a proud volunteer tradition that went back to the late 1880s and the beginnings of the Territorial Army (TA) as we know it today. In World War I, as the then 22nd Bn, The London Regiment (Queen's), it had fielded three battalions, won two VCs and seen action as far apart as Flanders and Palestine. It had adopted its present title in 1937 and during World War II two battalions, 1st/6th and 2nd/6th, had distinguished themselves in both NW Europe and Italy. When the TA reformed in 1947 the Battalion had been reconstituted with Bn HQ, 'A' Company and Support Company at Bermondsey, 'B' Company in Deptford and 'C' Company 'out on a limb' in Croydon. It was to the Drill Hall at 2 Jamaica Road (now the home of the London Royal Marine Reserves) that I reported that first morning. Clad in my best dark suit and bowler hat, and clutching my rolled umbrella and despatch case, I had taken the Tube from Sloane Square (an early 'Sloane' – but more of that later) to the Monument. Thence I had bussed it via London Bridge and Tooley Street (past Hay's Wharf and Tower Bridge) to the Lilliput Arms pub across the road from the Drill Hall. We were then virtually in the heart of the old docklands and amongst those great folk who lived and worked there. A prior reconnaissance (or a quiet word from my predecessor) would no doubt have saved me some embarrassment on the bus, for I was, needless to say, somewhat 'overdressed' for the neighbourhood. Next day I merely donned a sports jacket and flannels and still felt a bit 'posh'. Or as Phyllis Gobby, the local policewoman, later put it, and who had been on the bus at the time, 'You drew some ribald comment from the lower deck I can assure you.' (A very capable copper she later went on loan service and promotion to the Cyprus Police.)

There had been no great surge to join once the Drill Halls had been reopened, for there was an undoubted reluctance amongst the wartime veterans to don uniform so soon again after demobilisation. Likewise there was some understandable antipathy amongst the wives to see the Army as once more part of their lives. Additionally the young men were already committed to National Service and their mandatory three years with the Reserves – either the TA or the Mobile Defence Columns (MDC). All these telling factors had clearly mitigated against a rush to enlist. In time, however, a band of wartime stalwarts had rallied to the cause and had produced the cadre nucleus necessary to establish a skeleton battalion organisation on which to latch the ever increasing NS Intake. In time this had inevitably created a serious imbalance in the battalion structure in that by the time I arrived the true TA volunteers were outnumbered five to one by the compulsory NS element. This was something previously unknown in the TA and ran directly contrary to the true volunteer spirit and club-type atmosphere that had previously pertained in TA circles. It certainly bore no relation to my father's LRB experience when the establishment of the Battalion had been some 900 all ranks and yet over 1,100 true volunteers had attended their 1913 Annual Camp. Let there, however, be no misunderstanding about it. There was much valuable wartime experience within the TA Volunteer Cadre element and they were backed by a strong team of Permanent Staff Instructors (PSIs) most of whom had sent recent active service with the 1st Battalion in Malaya. Additionally there were some very good NS Officers (chiefly law and other students) to hand, mainly ex-1st Battalion too, plus a smattering of some very capable NS junior ranks from across all Regiments and Corps in the Army. On paper the Battalion was some 1,150 strong and was set to conduct a major divisional exercise (in a nuclear setting) on Salisbury Plain that summer, the first post-war Annual Camp at which they were to be committed to training at a level (and in a setting) not previously tackled. Following some weekend training at Crowborough and Shorncliffe I, however, sensed a feel that rather too much was about to be asked of an organisation that was then barely (and truly) capable of carrying out much more than basic Home Defence type tasks. In short, and despite the fact that both my parents had been 'Terriers', I felt I had come to the TA at the lowest ebb in its history. Sadly my misgivings proved factual later that summer. Sharing my unease at this time were the other members of the Permanent Staff. These were the CO, QM, RSM and the Company PSIs. Our leader (who arrived three weeks after me) was Michael Jennings. He had been a university entrant just prior to the war and this was to be his first command. He possessed great charm and an excellent brain. His last appointment had been as 'our man' at the Portuguese Staff College. Stanley Sellicks was a distinguished QM of the old school (not much moved off his shelves unless it had to) and this was his last job before retirement. Among the PSIs were old chums from the Berlin and Iserlohn days like Mr Davies (RSM), WO2 Elkins ('A' Company), Sgt Humphries (Support Company – he had been with 'C' Company, 1st Middlesex in Korea), and Sgt 'Dinky' Lampard ('B' Company – and our Littlewoods Syndicate Leader – but more of that later). We were all new to the TA and at one level or another, in those early days, relied heavily on the advice of two great Battalion personalities – Nick Nice (the Battalion Second-in-Command) and 'Smudger' Smith (a Company Colour Sergeant and Union leading light). I believe that 'underneath' they were as concerned as we as to how things would pan out at Camp. Just prior to Camp the CO and I were required to conduct a detailed reconnaissance of our new mobilisation area in and around Burgess Hill in Sussex, a pre-requisite before producing a new unit mobilisation scheme. We had taken over the area from another London TA unit together with a copy of their instruction. As if to confirm our feel that all was not well with the TA at the time, we found that most of the accommodation earmarked for billeting had either long since been demolished or built over.

The Annual Camp that year was based on a tented camp at Bourley, near Aldershot. The first week was spent in preparation for the Divisional Exercise – DOVER CASTLE. During that time whilst trying to fit faces to names and sub-units (most of the NSM had never been seen before) we drew up all the heavy equipment and vehicles necessary to put us on a war footing. This involved taking over such kit as Stuart Towers, 17 Pdr Anti-Tank guns, Rear Link half-tracks and the like from various Stores Depots. All the kit had for long been stood in the open on a 'Care and Maintenance' basis. It had certainly not been in use recently and this became only too evident as breakdowns littered the route to the Assembly Area on Salisbury Plain. Some of it I am sure had last seen action somewhere between Alamein and the Sangro. It was the hottest June in years and the exercise began in heatwave temperatures. By the third day heat exhaustion had begun to set in amongst the weary and generally unfit marching troops, to add to which there had also been replenishment problems in getting food and water to the leading elements under cover of darkness – breakdowns, bad map reading and the like. The Plain was by now littered with broken-down and abandoned vehicles of all sorts and sizes. Morale was ebbing fast when suddenly in mid-afternoon there was a cloudburst accompanied by torrential rain which drenched all and sundry. At that time the leading companies had just reached their objectives after a long advance to contact and were supposedly reorganising. They were, in fact, huddled together under every piece of protective cover available – towels and all. Out of the gloom there then appeared the GOC Eastern Command, General (later Field Marshal) Sir Francis Festing, mounted on his horse. He rode into the 'B' Company position and was immediately greeted with cat calls. A thunderflash was then thrown under his horse. The animal reared and nearly threw the GOC who then rode off as quickly as he had come. This was the scene that greeted me when I arrived some minutes later in the vehicle Nick Nice had sent to collect me. For my Rear Link half-track had finally 'given up the ghost' near Fox's Covert. By then he and the RSM had restored some semblance of order and the Regular Army Senior Umpire had come in 'out of the gloom'. I have yet to forgive him for 'ducking out' when firm action could have saved the day. Within hours the exercise was brought to a premature halt, the return to Bourley began, an inquiry into the incident was initiated and the entire Divisional Permanent Staff were left on the Plain to clear up the mess – it took us a week. This scale of TA exercise was never attempted again. It was way beyond the capabilities of those involved, even if one ever believed that they would arrive in time to actually take part in the nuclear battle on the West German Plain. Thereafter the emphasis switched to our Third Echelon Home Defence Role and, in particular, the Civil Defence aspects. As a prelude we Permanent Staff all attended First Aid and Rescue Courses at Storrington and Millom. Both were very good value and introduced a new and interesting slant to training at both weekends and on drill nights. Next year's Camp was held at Castlemartin, Pembrokeshire, and we took Volunteers only. We were able to sharpen up some basics within the cadre element. In 1957 we went to Fingringhoe, near Colchester, with one years worth of NSM as well. We did some valuable rangework. Never again were we invited to do the near impossible. Despite the trials and tribulations we suffered in those difficult TA times, we did achieve some success. We were granted the Freedom of the Borough and, when we exercised the privilege, the neighbourhood turned out in strength to give a big cheer to their 'Bermondsey Boys', as they regarded the Battalion. It was a highly moving occasion. We won the TA Cross-Country Championships three years running, took the London Scottish TA Rugby 'Sevens' in 1957, reached the TA Soccer Semi-Finals in the same year and, at the

At weekday duty with the Reserve Army – Bermondsey 1957.

first time of asking, won the Divisional Stretcher-Bearer Competition. We also established good working relationships with the local and famed Fisher Boxing Club and the London & Middlesex Rifle Association. This all served as some deserved reward for all the personal effort Michael Jennings had put into straightening out the Battalion. It is only sad that the 'TA Lobby', always very strong in the Palace of Westminster, managed to 'spill most of the gravy down his tunic', rather than those directly concerned, in the inquiry findings to the Festing incident. A career that I am sure had promised more finished at full Colonel. The Littlewood's Syndicate was not much luckier. After an early win in our first season, some £125 each, we never came near it again.

The TA provided no Mess accommodation for bachelors so I had to go necessarily on the Lodging List. The thought of a 'flat in Central London', however, sounded highly attractive. There was, though, the question of cost. There was also, in Mother's eyes, another important element – the neighbourhood. She accordingly entered the fray before I had even left Nairobi and 'turned up' a very pleasant 'bed-sit' in Sloane Gardens at a rental of £4 a week. It was very handy for the Tube and no distance from the Nuffield Club then in Eaton Square. At this time Chelsea very much reflected the 'fifties' image of London, with much activity centering about the Royal Court Theatre Club run by Clement (later Sir Clement) Freud. I can recall seeing *The Threepenny Opera* and John Osborne's *Look Back in Anger* from 'the Gods'. Just around the corner from the theatre was an excellent (and cheap) little restaurant (The Queen's) run by Field Marshal Lord Alexander's wartime House Sergeant, where one got a frequent sight of such as Augustus John, the artist, and Jill Bennett, the actress. In short, it was a neighbourhood that, at that period, had a great deal going for it. London is, however, a big place. At that time the population was around the seven million mark. If you didn't know the other 6,999,999 folk it could, though, be a very lonely place indeed. I didn't and thus I had no one with whom to exploit the Sloane Square scene. Before I had always had School or Mess chums to hand. The younger TA officers saved me. Some I had previously known from my Berlin and Iserlohn days and most were Kensington or Chelsea based. The party invitations came in and I never looked back thereafter. I shall always remain very grateful to such as Jimmy Parrish, Michael Konstam, David Hughes, Michael Mott and the like for their kindness in this respect. This was all long before the 'Sloane Ranger' tag somewhat tarnished the King's Road scene.

I enjoyed my social life. It had, however, to be heavily curtailed once study for the dreaded Staff College Examination had to begin in earnest. I had decided, on the advice of Michael Jennings, to take the February 1957 exam. This was the first year I became eligible to sit and whilst I might pass, and then be too young to gain an immediate nomination, the theory was that I would at least have success in the exam under my belt. I set to in earnest after Annual Camp at Castlemartin and to establish a proper work programme took the Correspondence Course then run by the Metropolitan College at St Albans. They covered all the seven papers then required to be taken – Tactics 'A', 'B' and 'C', Administration and Morale, Military History, Military Law and Current Affairs (a year later they added an extra paper, Military Science, so it was fortunate that I made the decision to sit when I did). Papers were corrected and commented upon by tutors who were retired senior officers. They knew their stuff but were perhaps a trifle prone to overmark. They also had a tendency to reflect on past memories with such additional comments as, 'Did I not meet your father on the Frontier in '37?' or 'I can recall thrashing your 1st Battalion in the Army Hockey Cup in '28.' All very touching and one went along with it – after all, one might finish up doing the same job some years hence. That November, at the then HQ Eastern Command, Hounslow, we candidates were required to attend a three-week Pre-Staff College Course, at the end of which there was a 'mock' examination and those who failed were recommended to sit for promotion only. In those days forty per cent was the pass mark in all subjects. To gain a Staff College Entrance pass, however, you needed not only to pass in each subject but to obtain an overall pass mark exceeding fifty per cent. I am sure today's candidates would wince at such thoughts. For, like the academic world in general, the Staff College exam has now been subjected to the 'not too difficult and no stress' approach. It was, however, in those distant days a real test of knowledge, nous and powers of application. In short, one really had to make a determined and prolonged effort and find *your* time in which to make it – no bad test of will in any walk of life. Alec Fearnside-Speed, my old chum who was Adjutant of our other TA Battalion (the 5th at Guildford), was also a candidate that year, as was Michael Hicks (later Major General), who had won the King's Medal (as the brightest student) in Intake I at Sandhurst. We all made it first time round. Whilst I, however, got a nomination in 1958, Alec sadly never did. He thus left the Army to become, in due course, a successful sugar broker; for at that time there was no compensatory 'staff-qualified' (or s.q.) label to be earned by those who failed to make it to Camberley. The 'one in four' club theory then very much prevailed. It still does to a very large degree, though there have since been some very distinguished exceptions to the rule – and notably a recent Master General of the Ordnance (General Sir John Stibbon, KCB, CBE). I was, therefore, now set to attend the 1959 Staff College Course. I remained, however, at Bermondsey until my three-year tour was up in March 1958. Despite all our initial teething troubles they had been happy years in the main. I had made some good friends in those cheerful parts. I still attend their Old Comrades Association (OCA) gatherings, though the faces I recall are sadly fewer these days. Even more sadly subsequent TA reorganisation severed the Regimental link with Jamaica Road except for the local Army Cadet Force (ACF) – a great pity Regular recruiting-wise since the true docklander remains a great character. I remained convinced, though, that we had not yet determined a truly practical role for the modern TA and this had been highlighted during the Suez operation when gaping holes in our essential Reserve Forces logistical 'Order of Battle' (ORBAT) had been uncovered. Our sole contribution to the crisis had been the 'donation' of all our medium machine gun (MMG) and mortar spare parts.

As I already had a nomination for the 1959 Course at Camberley, and had been 'selected' (or was 'available' as I was later to discover) for No. 14 General Staff Science Course (GSSC) at the Royal Military College of Science (RMCS), Shrivenham, in October, I was posted to the 'Held Strength' of the Depot in early April 1958. Rowley Mans (later Major General RSN Mans, CBE and my predecessor as Colonel of The Regiment) was the Depot CO and was himself headed for Camberley as a member of the Directing Staff (DS) prior to going on to teach at the Canadian Staff College. To bridge the gap he got me on to the RAC Squadron Leaders Tactical Course at Lulworth as the single Infantry student. I had a very relaxed six weeks during a glorious June sitting on my shooting stick as we were put through a series of TEWTS in and around such delightfully named villages as Piddlehinton, Piddletrenthide and the like. Whilst all the exercises had a distinct armoured bias, they had yet to be overrun with that BAOR 'make believe' mystique. I learned a lot under the excellent tuteledge of the Chief Inspector – Dick Vigors. In Desmond Langley (later Major General Sir Desmond Langley, KCVO, MBE, and Governor of Bermuda) and David Rowat I made a couple of chums who were, respectively, to accompany me to Camberley and Latimer. I had hardly returned to Guildford when on 4th July the Iraqi Royal Family were murdered in a Nasser-inspired coup and both the Lebanon and Jordan appealed for help from the US and UK. Jordan's cry was answered by flying into Amman the 16th Parachute Brigade plus some RAF Hunters from Cyprus. Out of the blue I was suddenly ordered to report to RAF West Raynham in North Norfolk to take over an Air Control Team (ACT) for probable follow-up air despatch to Amman. It seemed that 'somebody' had latched on to my Kenya experience. I arrived at West Raynham clutching my Khaki Drill (KD) and in my first car (an upright secondhand Ford Popular). I found that a Royal Signals Detachment from Catterick had already drawn up two rather aged half-tracks from a Vehicle Park and had fitted the required air to ground radio sets. All they were now awaiting was the 'expert' to teach them what to do. We were at forty-eight hours' notice to move and thus time was pressing. However, RAF West Raynham was then the Central Fighter Establishment and there was a nearby air to ground firing range on the coast. With

Hunters to hand we had it all there for the asking. During the next two weeks, whilst still on standby, and with tremendous co-operation from the Station we really slaved at it and achieved a very high standard of expertise – it was all very satisfying. I was, however, due to go to Shrivenham in early October as the prelude to Staff College. I have to be honest here and admit that I wasn't raring to suddenly find myself in deepest Jordan. The Lord was, however, kind and the crisis blew over. By mid-September we had been stood down. Whilst I was up in Norfolk I rather naturally took the opportunity to renew my friendship with the Chapman family. I hadn't seen them since those balmy days in the summer of 1945. They were now well into the evening of their years. They remained, though, the most generous hosts and I spent several days off in their excellent company.

I arrived at RMCS to attend No. 14 GSSC in early October 1958 for the three-month course. The aim was to make potential General Staff (GS) Officers more technically aware. Or, put more bluntly, to avoid producing another vehicle such as the Champ – the original Jeep replacement. The specifications demanded by the various Arms had been such as to develop a very costly 'monster' that was anything but driver proof. For example, the Gunners had said it must be capable of towing a 17 Pdr artillery piece down jungle track. The RAC had stated a requirement that, for reconnaissance purposes, it should be able to go as fast in reverse gear as forward. Somebody else had demanded that it have a flotation capability. I could, therefore, well see the point. However, we did seem to stray somewhat from this as it wasn't long before we were back to some basic instruction in the 'dreaded' maths and science. I 'fell' early on when the DS put up on the Blackboard ($a^{-6} + b^4 - c^2 = ?$) and then said, 'What is the answer, Charles?' Having met my 'Beechers' here he followed up with, 'But you must know this one, ($1° = ?$)?' I didn't. When we later got into discussion of such as the Doppler effect and torque then I really did know that I was sinking fast. I was, however, in good company since, as 'availability' had been the actual criteria by which the course had been filled, there were other Infantry 'heavies' in our midst – such as Tony Ward-Booth (later Major General), Alan Jones (another Queensman) and Ian Cameron (I was his bestman at Camberley). I can recall giving a twenty minute lecturette, aided by the latter, on 'screw-threads' in the presence of the Commandant (later General Sir John Hackett, GCB, CBE, DSO, MC) and drawing up the specification for a low-cost tubular collapsible stretcher. I doubt if the great man got very much out of the former. The latter, though criticised by my DS as 'highly unstable', was later to be viewed, almost in exact detail,

at a display of airportable equipment – I had to smile. The outside visits
were, however, very good value. My main memories are of a very sinister
visit to the USAF Strategic Air Command (SAC) Base at Greenham
Common, a South Wales trip that included both the Port Talbot Strip
Mills and a coal mine face (I have had an undying admiration for miners
ever since, despite Arthur Scargill) and a tour of a car body assembly line
in Swindon. I couldn't have been happier when the time came to shake the
Shrivenham 'mud' off my shoes and when I came later to be posted to the
War Office I sent for my P/File. There I found my RMCS report and was
not surprised to read the final comment, 'This officer should never be
permitted to fill a Technical Appointment.' He never was. These days all
those with a non-technical background attend the Division 3 Course (the
successor to the GSSC) prior to going to Camberley.

In 1799 a Staff School for young officers had been established at High
Wycombe. In due course it moved to Camberley and in 1858 became the
Staff College with a separate establishment. So just one year after its
centenary I joined the Student body in mid-January 1959. The Staff
College was, and still is much more than a training centre for the staff. It
is also, without doubt, the chrysalis for our future senior Commanders.
The syllabus is thus designed to cover both aspects of the student's future
career on the separate staff and command 'ladders'. Whilst, therefore,
there is much emphasis on the staff duties angle, a great deal of time is
also spent on practical TEWTS at Battalion and Regimental command
level. At that time the College was organised into three Divisions – 'A',
'B' and 'C'. The first two were based on Camberley and the latter out at
Minley Manor (now the HQ of an RE Training Brigade). We only saw our
'C' Division chums at such as centralised lectures in the then Rawlinson
Hall. The student body numbered 180, of which 120 were British Army.
The remaining sixty places were filled by the other Services, the Old
Commonwealth, the US Army, NATO, and a 'paying entry' (and far from
cheap) from Israel to Venezuela. That year the extras (or 'funnies' as we
knew them) included David Hallifax (later Admiral Sir David Hallifax,
KCB, KCVO, KBE and Constable and Governor of Windsor Castle) and
John Bennett (later Major General and Nixon White House Aide – he was
the first to notify me of Miffie's death). The Divisions were divided into
instructional syndicates. Each term you were in the care of (and were
graded by) a different DS. The DS, all Lieutenant Colonels and awaiting
command, at this time included Tim Creasey and such other future stars as
Dwin Bramall (later Field Marshal Lord Brammall, KG, GCB, OBE, MC
and Chief of the Defence Staff) and Dick Worsley, (later Sir Richard

Worsley, GCB, OBE, and Quartermaster General). Old Sandhurst chums
to resurface once again at the College included Roly Guy (later General
Sir Roland Guy, GCB, CBE, DSO and Governor of The Royal Hospital,
Chelsea), Dick Lawson (later General Sir Richard Lawson, KCB, DSO,
OBE and C-in-C Allied Forces Northern Europe), Ian Baker (later Major
General) and John Parry (with the Worcesters in those Berlin days).

The first two terms were tough and tedious going and a great leveller of
one's pride. I can recall my first military paper being returned with the red
ink comment, 'I cannot read a word of this.' I simply dotted all the 'i's',
resubmitted it and it was returned favourably graded. I learned the lesson
that it did not pay to be slapdash. Once we, however, got out into the
country to conduct the TEWTs then the pressures eased. There then
followed the Battlefield (or 'Bottlefield' as it was better known) Tour to
the Normandy Beachhead. This was designed to impart some real 'battle
atmosphere' to the course. 'Guest Artists', from both sides, and at all
levels of command, took us through a series of 'battle cameos' about Caen
and leading up to the final breakout. It was fascinating stuff and brought
to life the true realities of command. Despite events such as this the
pressures never completely eased since there was always a threat of
dismissal (two students had been sacked midway through the Course the
previous year) and one was competing for the best appointment one could
get and at nothing less than Grade 2 (or Major) level. This was all
exemplified towards the end of the Fourth Term when the 'brown enve-
lopes' were slipped into student pigeonholes. These advised them of the
appointments they had been selected to fill. The scene outside the College
that lunchtime always resembled something akin to a 'pithead disaster' as
the wives hung around in agitated groups waiting to learn theirs and their
husbands' fate. The sad thing was that some of the ladies whose husbands
had obtained good Grade 2 appointments tended, thereafter, to shun those
who had only made lesser Grade 3 (Captains) posts. They say men can be
mean – ladies can be beastly too. My slip showed that I had been appointed to be Brigade Major (BM) to the Aden Protectorate Levies – an
obvious bachelor selection. I was, however, courting hard at the time and
so approached Rowley Mans and inquired whether I could 'swop' it for a
home posting and preferably in London. A wildly enthusiastic Light
Infantryman (as I supposed he would) jumped at the Aden opportunity
and I was switched to a new and special appointment in the Personal
Services Department then in Lansdowne House, Berkeley Square. Having
'fixed' it all I then went up to London to tell 'Flossie'. Her immediate and
somewhat startling reply was, 'Well, now there is no frantic rush.' I

merely walked straight out; another relationship with a young lady who
did not understand the Army (nor really wanted to) had 'bit the dust'.
Sports-wise we had a very enjoyable year. I was the Hockey Secretary
and we had at Minley probably the finest ground in the South of England
(it's now a Barrack Square, believe it or not). All the major London Clubs
loved to play there (and enjoyed our hospitality) and so we maintained a
most impressive fixture list – Tulse Hill, Southgate, etc. Roly Guy was up
front again and John Parry and I resumed our RMAS full-back partnership. Giving our visitors about ten years we usually ran out four to five
goals down – it didn't matter. The same venue was used by the Owls
Cricket XI (the 'stiffs') during a lovely summer and I spent some pleasant
afternoons there keeping wicket and opening the innings with Rowley
Mans – our running between the wickets, however, left something to be
desired. All in all it was a happy year and once again one established solid
friendships which proved immensely valuable in the years ahead. It all
came to a sudden end with the traditional Staff College Pantomime. All
good clean 'in house' humour it tended to be a little lost on outside guests.
At that point in time I had no inkling that just over a decade later I would
return as a DS. In the leave period before Christmas I began to turn my
attention to my new appointment as Deputy Assistant Adjutant General
(DAAG) (PS10(a)) in the War Office in the rank of Acting Major. I made
contact with the chap I was taking over from and, after a visit to
Lansdowne House, agreed to take over his 'bed-sit' in Lowndes Street –
conveniently close to my old Sloane Square haunts.
   I took up my War Office post in the second week of January 1960.
Following a recent major study of pay and conditions of service the prime
task was, with the Manpower Planning Staff, to match the proposed new
career structure with improved pay and pensions. In PS10(a) we were
purely concerned with the 'New Deal' for Officers – PS10(b) handled the
Other Rank side. In short, we became largely responsible for the introduction of the Biennial Pay Review procedure and a revised Retired Pay Code
which made all service reckonable for pension from age twenty-one years
and produced a pension scale that began at the sixteen year point and
reached its maximum (up to the rank of Brigadier) at age fifty-five (the
new guaranteed retirement point). The only real 'foul' we committed was
to deny those like myself, who had joined at age seventeen and three
quarters, any pensionable service before their twenty-first Birthday. It
still rankles a bit. Every month or so one was required to spend the night
in Lansdowne House as the Adjutant General's Duty Officer. One took
over around 1700 hours and finished about 0800 hours the next morning.

With our worldwide commitments at that time one was hard at it throughout most of the night as one fielded everything from requests to notify Next-of-Kin (NOK) of casualties to arranging the return of bodies for family burial in UK. When really stuck (despite the excellent 'crib' available) there was, thankfully, a very helpful 'expert' to hand in the Main Building – the Resident Clerk (a middle rank Civil Servant) – who usually saved one. The cardinal error was to notify the wrong NOK, always possible if there were two lads in the same Regiment, with the same name and initials and only one figure different in their Army Number. It was not a duty many of us relished – interesting, though sad, that it often was. Before I finished my tour I had to quit Lowndes Street as the house was to be demolished for redevelopment. The Estate Agent, however, rented me the top flat over his offices in Ebury Street. It was a splendid retreat and as I ate my breakfast I often watched Roly Guy striding past to the Main Building where he was a Military Assistant (MA) to a member of the Army Council. Unlike in AG's Department one couldn't, in his case, follow the line 'that what we cannot do today we can always do tomorrow'. I did get a game or two of hockey, along with John Parry, for the War Office XI; otherwise 'trips', beyond excursions to the Main Building, were non-existent. I can't really say, therefore, that I loved my first Ministry stint. It was, however, good experience and I mastered the system if not the Civil Service 'Minor-Mandarins'. It also enabled me to enter for, and win, the 1960 George Knight Clowes Essay sponsored by *The Army Quarterly*. The subject covered a recent 'hobby horse' of mine on the future of the Reserves in the light of the Suez experience. I argued the case that they should produce rather more 'tail' than 'teeth' in the future ORBAT. Right up to the end of the Cold War we, however, retained a large TA element who, though committed to BAOR, were barely up to it training-wise and would probably never have made it in the warning time available. It had taken the average Korean War reservist up to five days to settle his affairs and family and report to his unit. What was there to suppose that the TA soldier would make it to his TA Centre any quicker against the background of a World War III nuclear setting? Or that he would make it at all?

I was not too unhappy, therefore, when Michael Jennings, then the Home Counties Brigade Colonel, got in touch to say that I was wanted back at Regimental Duty (RD) in April 1962. There being no Company available for command in the 1st Bn, The Queen's Royal Surrey Regiment (the Sandys-imposed amalgamation with the East Surreys had taken place whilst I was at Camberley) in Hong Kong I was to go instead to The

Queen's Own Buffs (the recent Kent amalgamation) who were then part of the 19th Airportable Brigade in the Strategic Reserve. The fly-any-where, do-anything 'fire brigade' – or that was the concept. Clearly my travels were to begin again and later I was to pick up a red feather along the Rajang River to stick in my developing 'colonial army' image cap.

The saddest event during this period had been the death of Grandma Bridger (or 'Bridgeman' as we affectionately knew her) in 1958. At eighty-two years she had had a very good innings and had lived through the Boer War and two World Wars. She had lost her beloved son, Harry, in World War I. She was a great character from a great generation and was as sharp as a needle, mentally, when she died. She had had a very big influence in my upbringing during the war years and when we had moved into High Wycombe in 1946 she continued to run the household until a few days before her sudden death. She had enabled Mother to enjoy a successful business career. I missed her greatly and always felt that she saw in me a second Uncle Harry.

Chapter 7

Here, There and Far Away

Early in the New Year I had visited The Queen's Own Buffs, then Shorncliffe based. The CO, Blick Waring, had explained that, as the junior Major, I would have to take 'HQ' Company, or initially at least. This had not thrilled me and I had the feel that he was not too excited at having to accept an 'outsider' under the Brigade Group system. Be that as it may have been, fate changed everything within a few weeks, for having just begun my post War Office tour leave Father suddenly died. He had had a poor winter, with his usual bronchial trouble, and eventually his heart could no longer take the strain. It was a harsh blow since we had been very close and he had taken great pride in my career to date. I somehow always felt that he saw in my way of life something he would very much have wished for himself. I was given some additional leave in which to settle his affairs and I took Mother down to Brighton for a few days break once the funeral was over. Whilst there we discussed the future and, particularly, continued occupation of the now far too large a house in High Wycombe. She came up with the idea of moving to Beechwood Cottage in Marlow (it had been the old gardener's cottage of Beechwood House where she had begun the War) and which she knew to be for long let. To cut a long story short she moved there in late April 1962 and remained there happily until she died in 1967.

The 1st Bn, The Queen's Own Buffs, were the recent amalgamation of The Buffs (The Royal East Kent Regiment) and The Queen's Own Royal West Kent Regiment. They were still in the throes of settling down after the unwished for merger of 'The Men of Kent' and 'The Kentish Men'. Most of the Company Commanders, such as Rusty Thorneycroft, Bill Macdonald and John Dent, had been with The Buffs during my Kenya days. This made it easier to settle into strange surrounds and where a rich

Sarawak and Confrontation

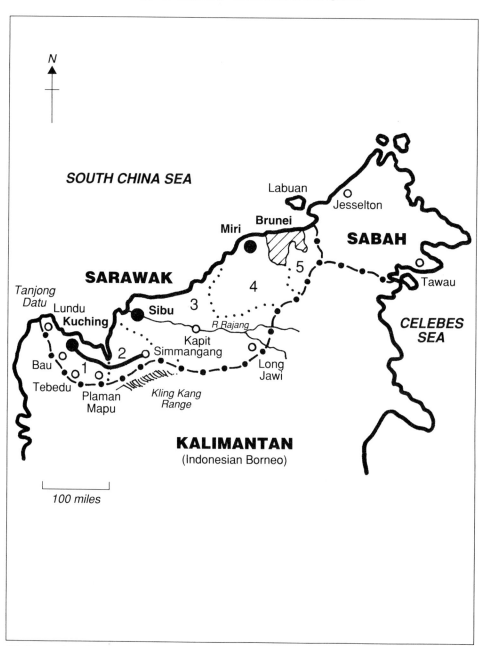

N

SOUTH CHINA SEA

Labuan

Jesselton

Miri

Brunei

SABAH

SARAWAK

5

4

Tawau

Tanjong
Datu

Lundu

Kuching

Sibu

3

R.Rajang

CELEBES
SEA

Kapit

Simmangang

2

Bau

1

Long
Jawi

Tebedu

Plaman
Mapu

Kling Kang
Range

KALIMANTAN
(Indonesian Borneo)

100 miles

III. Sarawak and Indonesian Confrontation, 1964–1965.

welcome had not been evident immediately. By the time I came to report to Moore Barracks fate had again played its hand and I was switched to 'B' Company to take over from Tony Franklin (later to command the Battalion). I shall always be grateful to him since he handed over a very good company as I was soon to discover. However, before I had time to really learn this we had to settle the little ceremonial matter of some new Colours. These were to be presented by the then Colonel-in-Chief of the Regiment, King Frederik of Denmark, on the Folkestone Cricket Ground. My part in the affair, as President of the Officers' Mess Committee, was simply to see that all went well at the 'posh' luncheon after the parade. To assist me I had an Annexure to the main Instruction which even set out, in exact detail, where every piece of Regimental Silver was to be positioned. It had been written personally by the CO and so I could hardly go wrong. A great man for detail was our Blick Waring but he taught me the value of considered decision. I can't say that I greatly enjoyed the splendid occasion and Bill Macdonald (the next CO and deputed to run the Other Ranks side of the affair) and I never even saw the actual parade. Mother, however, did and overnight I put her into the Imperial Hotel at Hythe – the beginning of a long association as future events will show. Once the parade was over then the move of the Battalion to Colchester began in earnest. There we were to join up with the rest of the 19th Airportable Brigade as part of the Strategic Reserve. National Service had now ended and this was the first all Regular battalion in which I had served. The different feel, and especially in the continuity of personnel, was very evident from day one.

The Strategic Reserve concept had had its first airing in the Sandys Defence White Paper of 1957. By 1962 it had become very much a fact of life with increased air and sea portability and established stockpiles of heavy equipment and stores near possible areas of operations. The Army element comprised the 3rd Division of which the 19th Airportable Brigade was an integral part. It was to demonstrate the viability of the concept that the Brigade flew into Cyprus on a major exercise in mid-July. On arrival in Nicosia we were transported to our camp site in the recently established Sovereign Base Area (SBA) at Dhekelia. The advance party had arrived a few days earlier to set up the camp. They had eventually just found sufficient serviceable tentage to meet our needs and a good deal of this was 'more holy than righteous'. The majority had simply fallen apart as they tried to erect it – rotted to hell. The rest of the kit we drew up was in no better state and especially the defence stores such as sandbags and barbed wire. Whilst, however, one lesson learned from the previous year's

Kuwaiti operation had only partially registered, the other clearly had, for no attempt was made to rush us out on serious training until we had had time to acclimatise. In fact, we were given a week to do just that trekking in the Troodos Mountains from company camps established on the coast just east of Kyrenia. Then, and only then, did we enter into a major exercise. We emplaned at Nicosia, flew round for an hour and then, on super light scales (one Land-Rover and trailer per company only) with everything else manpack, set out on an advance to contact way up into 'The Panhandle'. It was very hot, very dusty and very hard going with no shade for miles. We suffered some heat exhaustion casualties. We were later to discover that undissolved salt tablets had largely been the cause. I have never taken another to this day. I have, instead, simply taken a pinch of table salt with water at breakfast and put some table salt into my waterbottle. 'B' Company were in the vanguard most of the way and I had the feel that we were under test – the 'sink or swim' variety. We, however, did not 'drown' and the Company came out of the exercise with honour. They had supported me well during a difficult time. From Cyprus onward the CO began to recognise my existence. I felt I had finally been accepted and that the Brigade Group system did work if one actually gave it a chance. For, after all, we all spoke Southern English and came from the Home Counties. That autumn this feeling was confirmed when, having met either Mr Lea or Mr Perrins of Worcestershire Sauce fame at a party in Marlow, he offered me his estate near Stornoway in the Outer Hebrides for a fortnight's 'dry' training. It seemed a wonderful opportunity to build on the Company spirit and understanding established in Cyprus. So I approached Blick Waring and he gave his immediate blessing. There was a train from Colchester to Glasgow once a week and which connected to Mallaig. At Stornoway there was a Lovat Scout (TA) Drill Hall. Bob Johnson was then on the staff of HQ Lowland District. He fixed for a 'stop off' Drill Hall in Glasgow and for the use of the Stornoway one as our Echelon base. We had a great fourteen days in mid-November in very mild weather. From then on the Company never looked back and we became a very close knit team, something we could never have done during the days of National Service. We also all came back with some very nice Harris Tweed.

At the beginning of 1963 we began our first monthly stint as the SPEARHEAD battalion. We were at short notice to move anywhere about the globe from say, Guyana to Fiji. During this period an HQ Strategic Reserve (STRATCO) Team conducted a snap turnout designed to test our speed of reaction, load tables and general state of readiness. It was a pretty searching affair and went as far down as to ensure that all personnel had filled water bottles, salt tablets, foot powder and the like. It certainly ensured that units maintained a high state of readiness during their tour. We used the time in those early months of the year to improve our airportable loading skills across the then current range of transport aircraft from the Andover to the Britannia. We also made time to sharpen up our helicopter drills and, in particular, the underslung load techniques in respect of both freight and heavy equipment (especially our anti-tank guns) when operating with either the Whirlwind or Belvedere. Additionally we rehearsed our IS drills and counter-insurgency postures from riot procedure, through road blocks to cordons and searches. The pamphlet *Imperial Policing* was still our guide at this time. Despite the lessons learned most recently in Cyprus, we still, for example, retained the longstanding 'Amritsar' style approach to riot dispersal. This included the 'Disperse or We Fire' banner and the subsequent command 'No? Rifleman – one round at the man in the red tarbush – Fire!' It had indeed seen us safely through countless 'colonial' alarms and excursions but was perhaps wearing a little thin in changing circumstances – but more of that later when we come to the early days in Ulster a few years hence. This key period of 'master the trade' airportability apprenticeship culminated that Spring in a most imaginative and major counter-insurgency type exercise produced by our then Divisional Commander (later Field Marshal The Lord Carver, GCB, CBE, DSO, MC). It began with a seaborne landing in Lulworth Cove, was followed by a heliborne assault on the bridges over the Kennet and Avon canal and finished with a major cordon and search operation on the Standford Training Area in Norfolk. By this time we reckoned that we were a fully 'paid-up' member of the Strategic Reserve. It had all been very lively and refreshing training and the Company had sensed the real purpose behind it all. That's always a good thing if you want to keep the lads happy in peacetime. Or, put another way, 'variety is the spice of life' in soldiering as elsewhere.

That Summer we were flown to Canada to take part in Exercise POND JUMP III. We went to Camp Gagetown in New Brunswick in the Maritime Provinces. It was the home of the 6th Canadian Brigade. We were to take the place of the Canadian Black Watch on an eight-week exchange and whilst the Brigade was conducting its Annual Concentration. The Brigade comprised The Royal Canadian Dragoons, 1st Royal Canadian Horse Artillery, The Royal Canadian Regiment and a Battalion of the 'Vingt Douze'. For the period of the Concentration they had moved out into the adjacent training area to established log cabin style base camps on

high ground some twenty miles to the West. It was country in which the
Empire Loyalists settled after the American War of Independence and
founded such settlements (long since vacated) as New Jerusalem, New
Bethlehem and the like. We had the option to follow the experienced
Canadian example but our 'boss' chose to stay closer in so that we could
more readily meet our social obligations when the need arose. Our advance party literally, therefore, 'hacked out' our camp site from near
virgin forest and we soon learned, to our acute discomfort, why the locals
had chosen to get up into the hills; for the low lying area (bordering on
swamp) where we were sited was the breeding ground for every vile
insect species that inhabited those parts during high Canadian Summer –
and especially the voracious deerfly. To put it mildly we had a very
unhappy time in camp and, despite being bathed in insect repellent and
sleeping and eating under mosquito nets, were simply bitten to death.
Those with any sort of allergy had a very torrid time indeed. We were, in
fact, happier to be out on exercises than back in camp. We also had
another good reason to be happier ·in the Styx, for as we had plenty of
Duty Free 'booze' we drew 'callers' and 'guests' from all the Canadian
units at all times of the day and night. In fact, we came eventually to field
a 'host duty drinking team' each night of one Major, one Captain and
three Subalterns. They saw it out till the last 'guest', usually a well-
balanced Canadian Army Officer of the time (i.e. a chip on both
shoulders), had departed and hopefully before he unloaded the contents of
his revolver through the roof of the Mess marquee. The training schedule
was both highly imaginative and challenging. It began with a Platoon
Commanders Test exercise involving some demanding navigation and a
high level of endurance. Then we moved up one to Company level and,
with a supporting Centurion Troop of Canadian Dragoons, conducted an
'incident packed circus' over some thirty miles of varied terrain (and in a
quite terrifying electrical storm) and culminating in a field firing exercise
that included a creeping artillery barrage. It became apparent during both
these exercises that, at this point in time and nearly a decade after their
Korean War experience, our hosts' morale was pretty low as they still
sought a purposeful role for the years ahead. The spectre of unification
had yet to raise its ugly head.

    We next set about a counter-insurgency exercise written for the Battal-
ion by HQ 3rd Division. There was a sizeable and heavily wooded peaks
area within the Gagetown training complex. This had been selected as the
area of operations and the 'Vingt Douze' as the enemy. It was all over
within twenty-four hours. They had simply not appreciated how, with a

combination of slick helicopter drills and accurate compass navigation plus the fitness to 'leg it' fast, we would, from the outset, insert deep penetration patrols avoiding all tracks and other natural approaches. It was a great fillip for the Battalion and confirmed that lessons learned the hard way in Malaya, the Aberdares and Troodos had registered. We finished with a Brigade exercise in which we produced the umpires and a controlled enemy – my Company plus an experimental Canadian Anti-Tank Company largely missile equipped. I doubt if we proved, as was the aim, that such a screen could really contain a major armoured thrust even in such heavy scrub and difficult tracked terrain. Though it had mainly been work with little play there had been a lighter side to it all. I had rather hoped that there would be. Otherwise I believe we might all have gone home believing Canada to be one vast wood full of insects and other 'creepy crawlies'. One evening, for example, we went to the local Armoury (or Drill Hall) of our affiliated militia unit, The Royal New Brunswick Regiment, and had a fabulous meal of the largest lobsters I have ever seen. We also gave a very good farewell party in the main Camp Gagetown Mess before we departed. They almost drank us out of house and home. Just prior to that we were given four days R & R leave. It was arranged that most of the soldiers should visit Montreal. With the Adjutant (Maurice Dewar) and John Davison (who had done an exchange tour with our affiliated Queen's Own Rifles of Canada) I decided to hire a car and take a break in Boston. Our initial approaches to both Messrs Avis and Hertz in Fredericton (Fredsville to us) were met with the cry, 'We don't hire cars to soldiers.' It cut no ice whatsoever when we tried to explain that we were not 'soldiers' but British Officers. We finally went to the Beaverbrook Hotel and used the good offices of Reception to do the job for us. In next to no time a Hertz Pontiac was delivered to the door. We enjoyed the highly scenic drive down through Maine, New Hampshire and Massachusetts to Boston. With three drivers we did the some 450 miles or more comfortably in a day. We then spent the next two days based on the Marriott Hotel in Cambridge whilst we explored Harvard and the Boston scene in general. Refreshed and revitalised we made the return journey in good heart. A few days later we flew out of Fredericton via Gander to Lyneham. It had all been a worthwhile experience despite the deerfly. In our report we did, however, make the point that those who followed us should be given more time at the end to see something more of Canada than we did. The message was heeded thereon.

On our return to Colchester we first heard the news that the Battalion was to go to Guyana on a nine-month unaccompanied tour in March 1964.

There had recently been some unrest in the capital, Georgetown, culmi-
nating in some serious rioting. Whilst it would be essentially garrison
style duty, there would be a distinct IS slant. A month or so later I took the
Company to Jutland to act as enemy to our affiliated Royal Danish Life
Guards. Apart from an introduction to the hazards of Schnapps and the
Tivoli Gardens it was a pretty gently paced exercise. On my return I went
down to Folkestone with Roly Guy (then a Company Commander with the
KRRC in the same Brigade and Colchester based) to act as DS on the
Eastern Command Pre-Staff College Course. We had a pretty exacting ten
days in the Grand Hotel on the Leas marking some high grade offerings
mixed with a 'bundle of rubbish'. Little did I then appreciate that some
years hence I would be doing it for real at Camberley. Once back in
Colchester I learned that I was to be Brigade Major (BM) to the 99th
Gurkha Infantry Brigade in April 1964. I wrote almost immediately to the
chap I was to relieve and heard that, now back from Brunei, they were
again Nee Soon based in Singapore prior to moving across to Kuching in
Sarawak to relieve HQ 3rd Commando Brigade. The letter also contained
the advice that the Brigadier neither smoked nor drank. To which I ob-
served in my reply that, 'I did both and adored women as well – do you
think I should come?' I never received a reply to my question. I was,
however, delighted to get the job and especially as Confrontation with the
Indonesians along the Sarawak border had begun in earnest. I also had no
doubt that I had probably not been the first choice. In the final event the
'singleton' label combined with that increasing 'colonial army' image had
possibly carried the day. A year or so later when Confrontation was at its
peak it became very fashionable indeed to be Borneo based – even
amongst the 'Other Army'. Events in Guyana early in 1964 very nearly
required that I proceed via there to the Far East, for the Governor requested the despatch of a further battalion to bolster the garrison. With
most of the 3rd Division then deployed along the 'Green Line' in Cyprus
the Strategic Reserve was already overstretched. He was, therefore, asked
to confirm whether the additional battalion was 'essential' rather than
'desirable'. The latter was thankfully his reply. The Battalion thus departed as scheduled and I left for Marlow and some embarkation leave –
as it was still termed despite the demise of the troopship. It had been a
good two years with plenty of travel and varied and challenging training
to boot. I had earned a strong recommendation for Command and had an
exciting posting awaiting me in the Far East. Above all I had had the full
support of a super all Regular company who had helped to make it such a
memorable tour. I am happy to say that I saw many of them later make the

most Senior ranks within both The Queen's Division and The Ulster Defence Regiment (UDR) Warrant Officers' and Sergeants' Messes. After those two years in the then Strategic Reserve I had come to believe that we had established and proven a valuable role for the new and smaller all Regular Army.

I flew in late April by British United Airways from Stansted to Singapore. I spent one night in the Tanglin Mess there before flying on to Kuching in a RNZAF Bristol Freighter (or 'Frightener' as we later came to know it). Once the home of the White Rajahs, Sarawak had joined the Malaysian Federation in 1963. There was still some feeling amongst the indigenous Dyaks and Ibans that they might, in time, become the victims of Malayanisation by 'Big Brother' – and how right they were to be was proved over the passage of time. It was precisely this feeling that Dr Sukarno sought to exploit in his initial quest to secure what he described as 'North Kalimantan' (i.e. Sarawak, Brunei and Sabah). Indeed, he had a point since kith and kin-wise the villagers, for example, of Aruk and Biawak, some twelve miles apart across either side of the border, were essentially of the same stock. Colonisation not race had determined the borders. Having said that the real threat of subversion was posed by the large Chinese element of the population, and notably the sizable Clandestine Communist Organisation (CCO), which had established covert cells throughout the country. Some 1,000 young Sarawak Chinese had defected to Indonesia on the formation of the Federation. It was these renegades, who had since been afforded military training, that Sukarno used at the outset to promote armed insurrection. By the time I arrived a number of such incursions, some of considerable depth, had been defeated by the Security Forces. The problem remained, though the focus increasingly switched to the hunting down of the CCO military cadres. The task of coping with the internal threat had become primarily the concern of the then Sarawak Constabulary (to become part of the Royal Malaysia Police before I left) with an active and expanding Special Branch together with a now sizable Police Field Force. The main battle had now switched largely to the border where Regular units of the Indonesian Army sought to hinder and, if possible, dislodge the Brigade as it set out to seal the border in strength. The frontier in the Brigade Sector was that of the 1st, 2nd and 3rd Divisions (or Provinces) of Sarawak and extended for some 350 miles in all. Most of the country was lowland and there was a great deal of swamp. Inland, and notably towards the border, there were hills rising to fair-sized mountains up to 8,000 ft in the Kling Kang Range. The whole country was originally covered with jungle and there were many rivers and streams. The latter had in the past provided the key to both settlement and communications and remained the prime means of getting from one kampong or longhouse to another. This was the topographical background into which the helicopter was introduced and in which it was to play such a vital part in logistically maintaining the border defences.

By the time I arrived in Borneo Major General Walker, the Director of Borneo Operations (DOBOPS – and later General Sir Walter Walker, KCB, CBE, DSO), had established a command structure comprising three clearly defined brigade sectors. West Brigade (99th Gurkha Brigade) with 5 battalions held Kuching (only thirty miles from the border) and the three Western Divisions of Sarawak. Central Brigade (51st Brigade) with 2 battalions were responsible for the rest of Sarawak and Brunei whilst East Brigade (5th Malaysian Brigade) looked after Sabah with 3 battalions. The Special Air Service (SAS), the Guards and Gurkha Independent Parachute Companies and Border Scout sub-units were allotted to brigades to watch long sectors of the frontier which were not covered by military or police posts. This especially applied to the 3rd Division where there had been a deep incursion down the Rajang River the previous November. The main force had been deployed to cover the 1st Division which, with Kuching at its centre, might reasonably have been described (in best Churchillian manner) as 'the soft underbelly' of Sarawak. Our HQ was alongside that of the Sarawak Constabulary in Badruddin Barracks on the outskirts of Kuching. It had once been the home of the Sarawak Rangers, the pre-war Territorial Force unit. It was very much a Joint HQ and included both an RN and RAF cell. The former controlled the activities of Naval Party KILO. This was a Special Boat Section (SBS) type inshore patrol operation designed to combat any attempted seaborne incursion round Tanjong Datu at the western tip of Sarawak. The naval cell was also our liaison link with the minesweeper flotilla operating offshore to counter any Indonesian fast patrol craft naval activity. The RAF cell with the Forward Air Commander (Wing Commander 'Fearless' Foskett and later the Station Commander at RAF Muharraq during my Gulf command tour), had operational control over both the RAF (Whirlwind) and Naval Air Commando (NACS) Wessex Squadrons. The former was based on Kuching and the latter 'twixt Sibu and Nanga Gaat in the 3rd Division. He also had a tasking responsibility for the Army Air Corps (AAC) Scout Detachment and any Battalion Air Platoons (Sioux) operating in the area. With the Brigade logistic staff he was also responsible for air resupply with drops mounted from either RAF Kuching or RAF Changi. He also had a lien on some Singapore based Javelins for air defence and air escort duties. Up front we fielded a 'mix' of British, Gurkha, Malay, Australian, New Zealand, Royal Marine and Parachute battalions. At any one time five were in the line and, during my fifteen months in the theatre, some sixteen different major units 'passed through' the Brigade on a roulement programme involving Singapore, Malaya and Hong Kong. The Gurkha battalions did six months 'in' and four and a half months 'out'. The remainder played it the other way around. At one point the Royal Ulster Rifles (RUR) came out direct from UK on a nine-month unaccompanied tour – it was never tried again. Backing this formidable array were 4th Field Regiment RA with the new 105 mm pack howitzer (they also had a troop of 5.5 inch mediums under command), a Saladin equipped armoured car squadron from 4th Royal Tank Regiment (RTR) (their prime role was to escort daily convoys between Kuching and Simmangang and back and their OC was later Lieutenant General Sir Richard Vickers, KCB, LVO, OBE, a former Equerry to HM Queen). At one time or another 'B' Squadron, 22nd SAS Regiment under Johnny Watts (later Lieutenant General Sir John Watts, KBE, CB, MC, and Chief of the Defence Staff to the Sultan of Oman's Armed Forces), Lord Patrick Beresford's Guards Independent Parachute Company and the Gurkha Parachute Company were under command in the 'eyes and ears' role, and primarily, in the 3rd Division. At the airport we had a light air defence battery, equipped with Bofors and who also retained a 4.2 in mortar section for border deployment, plus a company of the Singapore Guard Regiment. This very sizable force, and possibly the largest Brigade the British Army has known, was supported by an equally large and varied Brigade Administrative Area (BAA) based essentially in and around the airport. Specialists here included air despatch teams and for a time, for use in the 3rd Division, a pack mule detachment borrowed from Hong Kong. At one point a hovercraft was brought over to assist with resupply up the Sarawak and Rajang Rivers. Sadly the quantity of 'flotsam' in both continually damaged the skirt and rendered the equipment largely useless. A bunch of thrusting and generally able COs included three who made it subsequently to the very top – Dwin Bramall (later Field Marshal the Lord Bramall, KG, GCB, OBE, MC, and Chief of the Defence Staff), David House (later Lieutenant General Sir David House GCB, KCVO, CBE, MC and Black Rod) and Ian Gourlay (later General Sir Ian Gourlay, KCB, OBE, MC, and Commandant General Royal Marines). There were, however, always the notable exceptions and I can recall one, who having been told not to come on what was considered a too early a 'recce', was found sitting in the Brigade Commander's Office clutching his Mk4 Rifle and with grenades liberally strapped about his belt. He remained a fairly good pain in the backside thereafter. We weren't sorry when he and his outfit departed. Around this time Tony Farrar-Hockley of Korean War fame (later General Sir Anthony Farrar-Hockley, GBE, KCB, DSO, MC) appeared on the scene as the new Personal Staff Officer (PSO) to DOBOPS. Thereafter he was to become a regular visitor to Kuching.

I served two Brigade Commanders during my tour. The first was Brigadier Pat Patterson (later Major General AG Patterson, CB, DSO, OBE, MC), another 6th Gurkha like General Walker. There was a distinctly old fashioned charm about him. He was, however, sharp as a needle, very lean and fit and he really knew the jungle. He had just two pet hates – to see an officer in dark glasses or carrying an umbrella (monsoon or otherwise). It was sad that he became somewhat disillusioned with Service life after a tour in the Ministry as Director of Army Training. Not surprisingly he and the Civil Service 'Mandarins' had very little in common. He was, though, precisely the man in the right place in 1964 in Sarawak, for under his astute direction West Brigade established a formidable forward defence along the border. Company bases were moved right up to the frontier and were heavily fortified. Every trick in the defensive trade was used to make them as impregnable as possible whilst ensuring that the attacker would have difficulty in avoiding the selected killing grounds. A combination of Claymore mines, panji mantrap pits, barbed wire and seismic detectors (like the Claymore obtained from US sources in Vietnam) were then linked to extensive cleared fields of fire. In addition, small 'car lamp' type searchlights were rigged up so that, at the flick of a switch, the immediate approaches could be fully illuminated and the enemy's night vision ruined. In the Bau sub-sector, covering the shortest approach to Kuching, we also had on standby proper Searchlight 'Battlefield Illumination' as had been practised in NW Europe during World War II. To add a bit of variety to the life of the AA gunners and the 'tankies', they were from time to time, deployed in forward bases with their respective heavy mortars and dismounted BESA machine guns. We also found a use for those two stalwarts of yesteryear – the 2 in mortar and the EY rifle grenade launcher. Both were invaluable in bringing down 'close-in' defensive fire support. It was, however, essentially an offensive defence posture in that each company remained responsible for dominating the adjacent jungle in its sector through a combination of offensive patrolling and ambush. In short, in no way were the Indonesians to be permitted to belong in the jungle. Despite a series of prepared assaults on the forward bases by such as their best Raider (or Commando) units, they achieved little. They did

A helicopter deployed mortar team go into immediate action – Bau 1964.

give an early and rather nasty dusting to a Gurkha company base that had been left with only a small rear party (thereafter it was ruled that the rear party should be at least one third of the company strength). From then on, and though Dr Sukarno had boasted that he would crush Malaysia by the end of the year, his Army had no real success. The larger the attack the more bloody the noses they got. During this time I can recall two such typical 'battles' – one by night, the other by day. The first concerns a night attack on a 1st Royal Green Jackets base at Stass in the 1st Division. In line with the policy outlined above the bulk of the company were out in ambush positions on the approaches to the base. David Roberts and his platoon had been left as its custodian. Around 8.00pm the enemy began their attack. Roberts, unable to raise his artillery support over the radio, rang the Brigade HQ Operations Room over the civil phone line, and called for defensive fire. Thereafter Tim Lloyd, the GSO3 (Ops), maintained contact with Stass and I with the howitzers at nearby Bau. Between us we managed to relay the necessary orders such as 'Up 50, Down 100' and 'Fire for effect' – all the gunner jargon I had picked up at Camberley and had never used before in earnest. We were learning every day and I am happy to say that young Roberts (now the No 2 at WH Smith Ltd) earned a much deserved MC for a very determined action. The enemy was driven off with heavy casualties. The second incident relates to a near last light attack on a Gurkha company base near Serian. Once more the attack was launched with only the rear party platoon *in situ*. There is little doubt that the enemy used their 'eyes and ears' intelligently too. The platoon was commanded by a Gurkha Colour Sergeant (or in Tim Creasey's famed words 'better a good Colour Sergeant than an indifferent young officer') and he immediately called for indirect artillery fire assistance from the neighbouring base. The problem was that his English was not up to coping with the fire order procedure. We, therefore, gambled on the fading light and tactically flew in Mick Cousins, (GSO 3 Int), by Sioux helicopter. It was a risky business but Mick was a 10th Gurkha and so once in the base he controlled the fire of the neighbouring howitzer. This was so effective that the enemy broke contact once darkness fell. They left several dead behind. Despite the protracted fire fight the 'home side' had only one rifleman slightly wounded.

There were inevitably some 'own goals' during this period amidst the plethora of anti-personnel mines and booby traps surrounding bases. These arose when units had not maintained an accurate record of 'what they had laid, where and when'. Whilst easier said than done in the circumstances that then pertained, it could present hazards on handover between units. Within twenty-four hours of taking over from a Gurkha battalion in the Bau area 4th Royal Australian had suffered their first casualties of the campaign from an 'unplotted' Claymore. All resupply was conducted by air and this included rations, ammunition and defence stores. We had our problems here too. Several of the Changi based Argosies overshot the border and attracted hostile fire from the Russian made 12.7 mm machine guns the enemy had positioned along the border. The customers too didn't always get quite what they expected. In one 'bad' week the RUR were twice dropped the neighbouring Gurkha battalions rations and vice versa. Around the same time David House, whilst visiting Stass, was 'showered' with corrugated iron sheeting (or 'Big Window') and angle iron pickets that came adrift of their pallets during descent. The CO 1st Green Jackets was not amused, I can assure you, and a delinquent logistician left for Singapore the same evening. Not long before the change of Brigadiers there was a brief truce following a peace initiative by President Macopagal of the Philippines. During this it was agreed that any Indonesian infiltrators within Sarawak would be permitted to withdraw through a number of specified check points. The operation was to be supervised by the Thais. In the final event only one check point was established at Tebedu and on 18th June, and for about twenty-four hours afterwards, some three or so bands of Indonesians, clutching olive branches and wearing orange armbands, paraded almost ceremoniously through the check point. I was there talking to the CO of 4th Royal Malay when one party went through. They were so clean shaven and well turned out as to suggest that they had probably been inserted less than twelve hours previous. Commenting on this the CO also said, 'I've seen the one leading that group before. He came through with the first lot. I'm also pretty sure I recognise him from the Congo when one of their Raider battalions was alongside us.' The Tokyo Summit that followed was no more than a charade. For Sukarno was still set on crushing Malaysia and to make his point he took immediate advantage of some serious inter-racial rioting in Singapore that summer to launch a seaborne landing at Pontian in SW Johore followed by an airborne assault at Labis. Both actions were a fiasco in every respect. Over the next six months attempts were made to land small saboteur groups in South Johore and on Singapore Island. However, the focus, thereafter, switched back to Borneo and the desire to secure 'North Kalimantan'. Incidentally, a 'spark' from the inter-racial riots did reach Kuching; a brief 'Show of Force' by the Brigade Gurkha Defence Platoon, however, and that was that.

The new Brigadier was Bill Cheyne. A Queen's Own Highlander he had had KAR connections in his time. Captured with the 51st Highland Division at St Valery he had spent most of the war as a POW. While he had something of a 'short fuse' he was as astute as they come and ideally suited to the more aggressive phase of operations shortly to begin. It is just sad that his tragic cancer death denied him the true desserts of his success. Before we, however, switched over to the offence we had to be prepared to meet the renewed threat posed by a now thoroughly frustrated Sukarno. Our intelligence had it that he was planning a major assault on Sarawak and notably against its 'soft under belly' or the 1st Division. It was thought he might try a major push directly on Kuching through the Bau Sector combined with an airborne assault on the airport. It was also felt that he might even attempt a seaborne landing near Lundu via Tanjong Datu. Summoned by the Commander early one morning I was given the major factors for the outline of an 'Appreciation of the Situation'. I was then despatched to DOBOPS's Kuching Office and told to get on with it. As I produced my draft the pages were collected by the Chief Clerk and taken across to Bill Cheyne. He then 'massaged' them to produce the final draft. It was the first and last time in my career that I ever wrote an

'Appreciation' in earnest. That evening our finalised offering was taken by special courier flight up to Labaun (an island off Sabah) where General Walker had his HQ. Our main bid was for two extra battalions: 1st Scots Guards, just finishing their Jungle Warfare School stint, and 1st/6th Gurkhas to be borrowed again from Hong Kong. We also requested an additional artillery battery, an extra armoured car troop (known to be in Singapore) and some RAF Regiment from Changi to assist with airfield defence. We also recommended that Central Brigade took over the 3rd Division from us. To our utter amazement some weeks later the whole of the 19th Brigade (my old outfit from Colchester) suddenly appeared and were deployed as Mid-West Brigade with responsibility for the 2nd and 3rd Divisions. HQ 17th Gurkha Division were also brought over to Labuan to form a separate Land Forces HQ – COMLANDBOR (the first time it came over the signal net it was corrupted to read 'COKLANDBORE', intentionally or otherwise). DOBOPS was not, however, promoted Lieutenant General and this inevitably drew some speculative comment – not all kindly. There was just the feeling, thereafter, that we had established one HQ too many and had created that most undesirable command structure of 'one, over one, over one'. This reinforcement had all been sanctioned by the new Labour Government. Dennis Healey (later Lord Healey) now Secretary of State for Defence, had paid us a very positive and recent visit and his attitude had been robust. No doubt with his strong support the new administration agreed DOBOPS's request to take the war across the border. The aim being to mount raids and ambushes against enemy bases on intelligence gained largely from radio intercepts. At the outset battalions were required to nominate one specific sub-unit to conduct these operations under the Codename 'Claret' – but better known in Brigade HQ and elsewhere as 'Harrow Football'. Initially operations were to be carried out up to a depth of no more than a mile. Later this was extended up to a distance of ten miles and force levels were increased too. All plans were jointly prepared with Brigade HQ and then were despatched by special courier to DOBOPS for final clearance. The only VC awarded during the campaign was won by Corporal Rambahadur Limbu of 2nd/10th Gurkhas inside Indonesia, as were several MCs and MMs by other individuals and units. In each case the citation related to action on or near our side of the frontier, as did the supporting SITREP and press release. An official Press 'Denotice' was applied to 'Claret' operations. Only one solider is, however, known to have written to one of the tabloids to complain. Thereafter most of the fighting took place on Indonesian soil, though friend Sukarno would never admit to it. Despite being now very much on the defensive, he never gave up his ability to strike back when the opportunity arose. Such a chance presented itself on 27th April 1965 at Plaman Mapu when a Parachute battalion base was attacked at dawn by what was rated an Indonesian battalion. No doubt the enemy were aware that only a weak rear party was in occupation of the base. In this instance it was dangerously near the minimum manning level prescribed. A 'Rorke's Drift' type defence under the Company Sergeant Major, however, finally drove off the enemy after three determined attacks, in one of which the howitzer pit was temporarily overrun. In short, the enemy retained a dangerous sting in their tail right up to the end.

Besides Dennis Healey we also had such distinguished visitors as Lord Mountbatten on his farewell visit to Far East Command as CDS. He was accompanied by his Chief Scientific Adviser, Sir Solly Zuckerman (later a Life Peer), and the C-in-C Admiral Sir Varyl Begg (my wicketkeeping 'oppo' from those far off Depot days). The party actually totalled twenty-four heads and some 185 pieces of baggage. Thankfully we had in Richard Vickers a 'tame equerry' to hand and we offered him the Gurkha Defence Platoon to assist with the task. He perhaps wisely decided that his own 'tankies' were more likely to be able to cope with the different coloured labels marked 'No 3 of 8' and so on. The Defence Platoon had, however, their morning of glory when they escorted the master and his more senior acolytes on a helicopter jaunt to see the famed Orang-Utans under the direction of the well known Kuching Museum Curator, Tom Harrisson (he had led an irregular force of some 4,000 Dyaks against the Japs). The visit, however, produced one major benefit – the 4,000 Armalite rifles we were so urgently seeking to support 'Claret' operations. Less profitably the 'Claret' planning preparations that Sunday afternoon were somewhat rudely interrupted when the MA rang to ask for some No 9 pills to be despatched immediately to the Aurora Hotel for a Wren CPO Writer in dire need. In contrast, the next visitor, HRH The Duke of Edinburgh, arrived with a party of no more than eight persons all up. On some of the lesser visits I was used as the main escort. This enabled me, coupled with frequent liaison visits to units and 'Hearts and Minds' projects (we must have built umpteen jetties along the Rajang), to see a great deal of this wild but lovely country. None was more beautiful than that along the Rajang River in the 3rd Division. A former High Commissioner had once described Kapit as 'Paradise' – I rather agreed with him. It all did much to dispel that 'head hunting' and 'Wild Man of Borneo' image that still prevailed at home. Having sent 'the red feather up the Rajang' we, in fact, recruited many as trackers for the British battalions. To further alleviate this notion I recall the regular sight of the Constabulary Band each Sunday afternoon on the Central Park bandstand. Their selection had by this time just got around to including 'Bless the Bride'. I also remember a dinner at the Astana (the former palace of the White Rajahs) amidst a welter of gold plate and the sight of the last Commissioner of the Sarawak Constabulary sailing away down the Sarawak River at sunset with both banks of the river lined by all ranks and with the band playing 'Auld Lang Syne'. It all had a distinct Somerset Maugham touch about it. There was just one hard and fast rule that the Commander and I never broke. That was that neither of us were out of the HQ at the same time. In his absence I acted for him and when an operational decision had to be made, and no radio or phone contact could be established, I made it. Just such an instance arose towards the end of my tour when a 'Claret' SAS patrol were jumped and dispersed. Their leader was wounded and did not make it out with the rest. I immediately put up a helicopter to search his last reported location. It picked up the NCOs Sarbre Beacon bleeps. Gil Hickey, CO 1st/6th Gurkhas, then agreed to put in a company to effect the rescue. Once safely in friendly hands another helicopter was despatched to casevac the SAS NCO. Throughout no contact was possible with either the Brigadier or the Forward Air Commander. Somebody had to make a positive deicison and one was clearly needed. One cannot prevaricate when it is a matter of life or death. There was a brighter side to life even at the height of Confrontation. I had two periods of four days, R & R leave amidst the bright lights of Singapore – Raffles Hotel and all (though I am told I would not recognise the city these days). We had a Nuffield Trust motorboat, which we brought across from Nee Soon (with my famous tin trunk), and used it for the occasional water-skiing recreational afternoon and picnic on a super beach down towards the mouth of the Sarawak River. Our Mess, Angby House, once the home of the Manager of the Sarawak Steamship Company, provided us with the means to host the odd Sunday curry lunch for our military and police associates. Every now and then we had a 'run ashore' to the Aurora Hotel – the then 'Ritz' of Kuching. I still exchange Christmas Cards with a very able and talented Chinese Special Branch lady who used to provide some light relief on these outings. We were grossly overcrowded in Angby House from the sleeping accommodation angle but, as most of the junior staff were on shift duty, we managed. Chris Bate (later Major General), the chief logistician, and I shared what had been a box-room. We became great chums and I lost a very true friend when he died suddenly of a heart-attack at his desk in the Ministry.

This had to date been the most rewarding, exciting and exacting appointment I had yet held. To this day I still regard it as ranking a narrow second to my Command tour. I truly felt that this was what real soldiering was all about. It was sad then when, a sudden change of terms of service, brought it to a premature end: for, with no early end to Confrontation apparently in sight, our masters decreed that, staff-wise, we should hereon follow what had been Korean War practice. In short, except for the Brigade Commander, who would do a two-year accompanied tour, the remainder would do one year only. The second year to be in the Far East too if a suitable appointment could be found. This meant that, on 1st April 1965, Chris Bate, and most of the staff who had come in to relieve HQ 3rd Commando Brigade the year before, upped sticks and departed. Not the best way to run a war, one might say. A relief was then fixed for me in early June and I received a Posting Order to be DAAG Singapore Base Area. To give him his due, Bill Cheyne nearly went mad and within days, and following a spate of signals 'twixt Kuching, Singapore and London, a more suitable slot was unearthed. This was as Deputy Assistant Adjutant & Quartermaster General (DAA & QMG or what Chris Bate had been to us) to the 39th Infantry Brigade. On inquiry I, however, discovered that they were currently engaged on operations in the Radfan. I saw myself leaving the jungle for the desert in one uneasy move. However, by the time I came to report they were back at home base in Northern Ireland. I left Kuching in early June. The Band of the Sarawak Constabulary gave me a great send off and I departed, like Brigadier Patterson as a special treat, by the evening Fokker Friendship to Jessleton and Singapore. The aircraft I had watched each evening fly over the HQ and which had so many times conveyed our special courier to DOBOPS with our latest 'Claret' plans. It had all been a great experience and it was perhaps sad that, throughout, all those who had achieved so much under the West Brigade banner had simply been described as 'Malaysian Security Forces' in all the press reports at home and abroad. For at its peak some 17,000 Commonwealth Servicemen had been engaged in operations in 'North Kalimantan' and the bulk of these had, at one time or another, been under our command. Confrontation finally ended on 1st August 1966, a great deal earlier than had been anticipated and no doubt due to the string of 'Claret' successes. The Gurkha battalions had taken most of the strain and had accordingly borne the majority of the overall casualties sustained – 114 dead and 181 wounded Let there be no mistake about it, the Indonesians had taken a hiding. Or, as Dennis Healey put it to the House of Commons on 27th November 1967, 'It will be recorded as one of the most efficient uses of military force in the history of the world.' Certainly it was a 'war' in everything but name and I remain of the belief that those who took part (our first all Regular Forces since the end of National Service) were as professional as any who have since performed, in far more public circumstances, in both the Falklands and the Gulf. This was essentially a junior leaders' war and the standards achieved were of the highest. They were also attained whilst retaining the ability to smile – end of message.

I arrived back at Heathrow one morning in mid-June via Eagle Airways. We had been delayed at Bombay due to engine trouble. Mother was, however, there to greet me. We were soon back in Marlow. Beechwood Cottage had been transformed and looked at its very best on a glorious summer's day. I was happy to be back, though full of great memories, and clutching my very special ceremonial Kukri presented to me just before I left. While I had been away I had paid for mother to visit the Rodes family and other chums in the USA and she had sold her interest in 'House and Gardens' in Marlow and was now a partner in a new enterprise, 'Farthingales', in Old Amersham. She seemed in good health and heart and there was no evident signs of the troubles that were to beset her two years on. A few weeks after my return I learned that I had again been Mentioned-in Despatches and had earned the new General Service Medal, with clasp 'Borneo', on which to wear that coveted oakleaf. I also heard that the Malaysian Government had awarded me their Ahli Mangku Negara (equivalent to our MBE) for my services in support of the Police and Border Scouts.

Chapter 8

Last Leg to Command

I set off for Belfast in the second week of July 1965. I drove up to Liverpool in my new Mini-Cooper with great pride. It had been largely purchased on my Borneo tour savings. In those days there was still no 'drive on/drive off' ferry service available, so one had to have one's car at the docks by 11am for crane loading prior to the evening sailing. A cradle net was used and I was only to discover how the ropes had 'savaged' the paintwork on my new 'Roller' (or that is what it seemed to me) when I got the other end. I had then to spend the rest of the day idling my time away in the city on a summer's day. In fact, after a good lunch in The Adelphi I went to the nearby Odeon Cinema to see *The Sound of Music* for the first time. Thereafter this became standard drill when awaiting the evening ferry. I arrived in Belfast on a Sunday morning and drove the short distance to Lisburn where the Brigade had its HQ in Thiepval Barracks. They shared an Officers' Mess with HQ Northern Ireland who were situated 'across a sportsfield' away. Other than a couple of subalterns in the signal squadron I had the brand new Mess Annexe virtually to myself and a very spacious flatlet within it. To add to the 'Luxury' there was also a garage for the car. Next morning I met the Brigade Commander – Brigadier Chan Blair (later Lieutenant General Sir Chandos Blair, KCVO, OBE, MC). Another Queen's Own Highlander, he had also been taken prisoner with the 51st Highland Division. He had, however, escaped through France and Spain to Gibraltar. He had commanded a KAR battalion and then the Brigade during the later phase of the Radfan Operation. He was a superb golfer, a keen fisherman and a natural leader. He also possessed a delightfully dry sense of humour. Under his guidance it became a very happy team and especially once we had taught the young new BM to relax a bit. Straight out of the Staff College he tended,

initially, to rather confuse the pace of Ulster life with that in Fallingbostel
in BAOR – his last posting before Camberley. He learned fast, however,
did our Jack Dixon, deftly moulded, no doubt, by Robin Merton. He was
the GSO3 (Ops) and had, in fact, gone from Borneo to the Radfan with his
squadron in one 'uneasy' move. I had last seen him on the Kuching to
Simmangang convoy escort run. We had a signal squadron but no integral
logistic units were under command. At the time the HQ had been deployed, at short notice, to the Radfan these had been cobbled, together
from resources within the Aden Protectorate. We were, therefore, somewhat surprised when it was mooted briefly that, if a force was despatched
to secure the Kariba Dam following Mr Smith's UDI Declaration, we
might be sent again. The political risks were, however, adjudged too great
for the government to play the intervention card. The logistic unit problem thus 'went away' and, in due time, the Ulster troubles committed it to
history. The Brigade 'teeth' comprised an armoured car regiment, The
Queen's Dragoon Guards (QDG) with Michael Mates (later The Minister
of State for Northern Ireland) as OC the airportable squadron. They were
based at Lisanelly Camp at Omagh, Co Tyrone; 1st Bn, The King's
Regiment at Ballykinlar at Co Down and The Middlesex in Holywood
Barracks, Belfast. This was, in fact, the paper strength. For at the time the
QDG had a full strength squadron under Maurice Johnston (later Lieutenant General Sir Maurice Johnston, KCB, OBE, DL) as part of Mid-West
Brigade at Simmangang in Borneo and the King's and Middlesex were to
follow each other in turn to Guyana for nine months. I took the opportunity to visit Georgetown during the changeover just to see what I had
missed by not going with the Queen's Own Buffs. Not much was my
reckoning. However, it was useful topographical background when, some
years later, I was faced with some logistic problems in the not too distant
Belize.

I arrived in time to view the Belfast parade associated with the '12th
July' and the Orange Order's annual celebration of the anniversary of The
Battle of the Boyne. I even heard the famous Lambeg Drum (the biggest
in Ulster) beating away when I awoke that morning. As I drove into the
City I could not fail to spot the now notorious divide between the Shankill
and Falls Roads. Above the former flew Union Jacks of all sorts and sizes.
Over the latter fluttered a variety of large and small Irish Tricolours.
However, the real depth of this divide did not truly reach me – then or
throughout the year I was at Lisburn. During the parade, which took some
four hours or more to pass me and contained some 200 plus fife and drum
bands, I was however conscious of a very considerable police presence

blocking off the side streets along the parade route. Likewise the following Easter, on the Fiftieth Anniversary of the Dublin Rising, and when we brought over two extra battalions to cover any possible trouble one was aware that some undercurrent existed. However, at that time, not long after the IRA border inspired troubles of the late 1950s when several police stations had come under heavy attack, the Royal Ulster Constabulary (RUC) still seemed focussed on a repeat of this sort of action as the real threat to Ulster security. Any joint liaison or study sessions concentrated on this aspect of the threat. Even when Dr Paisley began his public rantings in mid-1966, and just before I left, serious civil disturbance did not seem to feature as a possibility in the RUC mind. They were, in effect, and especially out in the country, almost a para-military force on French CRS lines supported as they were by their Shorland armoured cars and a sizeable and well armed reserve – the 'B' Specials.

That first summer and autumn we kept ourselves busy despite the lack of a brigade to train. Early on Robin Merton and I were despatched to Northumberland to arrange a three-week training session for Brigade HQ and the supporting signal squadron. Once established in that well-known hostelry, the Percy Arms, we set about a through 'recce' of the Otterburn Training Area. We finally came up with an HQ Command Post Exercise (CPX) and a field firing sequence for the signal squadron. On our return we all decamped to Magilligan Point (where there was a week-end training centre – now a prison) and ran a fourteen-day Combined Cadet Force (CCF) camp for the Ulster Schools. During it the Brigadier made a determined effort to introduce both Robin and myself to fly-fishing. Several evenings running he took us to his favourite stretch of river at Limavady and put us through our paces. Sadly, not being true countrymen by nature, we failed to latch on. Then with my SC'Q' (Punchy Lloyd and another 'Blackfriars Grammar' lad) and some borrowed hands from HQ Northern Ireland, I ran an airhead at Nutts Corner (a disused wartime airfield) to support a Strategic Reserve exercise. In this instance a Light Infantry battalion group were being flown into the Province to hunt down an enemy 'spetsnaz' party believed to have recently been parachuted into the Sperrin Mountains. This was my first feel of true logistic play and I can recall the Brigadier coming out to visit the airhead on the second afternoon. An Argosy had just completed its unloading. Entering the main hanger, where we were still 'breaking down' the load into ration, ammunition, POL and other stacks he suddenly said to me, 'How do you know, Charles, when you have got all you are likely to need?' 'Sir,' I said without batting an eyelid, 'I've told the SC'Q' to "switch off" once any stack reaches the level of the hangar entrance.' He didn't bat an eyelid either. In short, at this point in time my logistic 'know-how' relied simply on a combination of rule of thumb and practical commonsense. Despite all I learned later as a DS at Camberley concerning 'outloading', 'dumping', 'breaking bulk' and the like, I still relied heavily on a 'mix' of nous and experience. Come early October and we all went across to Otterburn to conduct the CPX and field-firing Robin and I had planned earlier. The weather was near perfect, we virtually had the area to ourselves and all seemed to enjoy both the change of scene and the training. Certainly the signallers revelled in the chance to field-fire, throw grenades and fire the rocket launcher, something they had never done before. It was a lesson I carried with me years later to the 4th Division – it produced Ex ICE BREAKER for the logistic units in 1975. Our final duty in 1965 was to run a three-week Pre-Staff College Examination course for all prospective candidates in Northern Ireland. This time the surrounds were not as plush as the Grand Hotel in Folkestone for we had to return to Magilligan Point. The chill kept the brain sharp, however.

After Borneo the pace of life in Lisburn was generally pleasantly re-laxed. I had the time and opportunity to get back on the hockey field and played a lot of tennis. Jack Dixon also introduced me to dinghy sailing on Loch Neagh. The wind on this large inland lake can, however, veer very suddenly and we were 'ditched' on more than one occasion. The hazard, thereafter, was not getting to the shore but fighting off the swarms of midges that swam along with you. Danny Cadoux-Hudson, who had been a Captain of Boats at Sandhurst, also persuaded me to join him on a number of afternoons on the River Lagan. We borrowed a skiff from the Queen's University Boat Club. We had, however, to be careful to choose high tide to avoid tangling with dumped bedsteads and the like. In short, they were happy and carefree days in what then appeared to be a happy and beautiful land. Though people still joke about the number of 'soft Irish' (or wet) days, the scenery is generally lush and lovely. I particularly enjoyed the Ards Peninsular; the Carlingford Loch surrounds, the Mourne Mountains (and especially when the gorse was in full bloom) and the north coast 'twixt Portrush and the Giant's Causeway. Many a quiet Sunday afternoon did I spend on the beach at Ballyhalbert with my latest Bond paperback. We also made the odd International at Landsdowne Road. Having said all that I have to admit that, but for a trip to play hockey at RAF BallyKelly and another to attend an RUC Passing-Out Parade at their Enniskillen Depot, I rarely crossed the River Bann. I, therefore, sen-sed no premonition of the troubles to come. Beyond what I had witnessed that day in Belfast, the only other clue was when I was advised one Sunday to make a diversion to avoid a big Nationalist Hibernian Order march just ahead. So much was I enjoying it all that I persuaded Mother to spend Christmas in Ulster. I put her in the Cadogan Hotel at Dunmurry (since bombed several times) and we had a very happy time. Mother became a firm Ulsterphile. Early on in 1966 I heard that I had been selected to attend Course No. 33 at the Joint Services Staff College (JSSC), Latimer, beginning that October. Before I left for the course I also learned that I was to be 2ic 1st Bn, The Queen's Regiment (we went 'Large' in 1966) then in Munster, BAOR. In the interim, and before I began to pack, we had another session at Otterburn. This time we even included a 'semi-TEWT' on the Otterburn battlefield of 1388. Another occasion when the 'old enemy' gave us a bigger hiding than they ever took from us at Wembley. On 14th August I finally crossed the Irish Sea for home. Four years later to the day I was to return in very changed circumstances.

The Joint Services Staff College (JSSC) was established at Latimer near Chesham in Bucks in 1947 by the then Chiefs of Staff, their Lordships Tedder, Cunningham and Montgomery. (It has more recently moved to Greenwich and is now known as the Joint Service Defence College (JSDC) The initial aim was described as 'To nourish and to disseminate amongst the higher commanders of all Services and their staff that mutual understanding and inter-Service comradeship-in-arms which, in war, were the very basis of our success and without which we should be in poor shape to face a future war.' Unlike Camberley to the Army, and Bracknell to the RAF, Latimer attendance was never a career 'must', though the RAF seemingly put rather more weight on it than the other two Services. To many of the naval students, to whom passing the naval staff course was then no essential career criteria, it was their first staff training experience. In short, the course was generally filled with those of some recognised ability who were between postings and appointments. The student body totalled some fifty or more overall. There were in those days roughly a dozen per Service, another dozen from the US and Commonwealth plus a handful of Civil Servants and Colonial Police. The DS appointment clearly did not carry the same cachet as at Camberley. It was, however, a very welcome change of scene plus being something of a necessary 'brain sharpener' after that relaxed Ulster tour. It was, of course, also only some sixteen miles from Marlow, though I chose to live in. It also proved a happy reunion with several chums and especially from Borneo. Max Tebbut, who had commanded 1st RNZIR was there plus Peter Welsh (later Major General) who had won a very good MC when with the

Brigade playing 'Harrow Football' across the border. Bruce Thomas (later
Commodore) who had commanded the offshore minesweeper flotilla also
identified himself. Our last contact had been over the phone one Saturday
evening following a disturbance in the Kuching Open Market involving
some of his sailors. He had rung to seek our advice as to the action he
should take. 'Sail,' I had said without hesitation and the only person who
looked a bit put out the following morning was the local police chief.
Others amidst the gathering, and whom I had not seen in ages, were John
Guy, David Rowat and David O'Morchoe (later Major General). John, a
Marlburian, I had first met in those wartime evacuation days and I can
recall him declaiming at length in the Memorial Hall there. Now a Royal
Fusilier he was later to leave the Army for a career in theatre manage-
ment. I hadn't seen David Rowat since those balmy Lulworth days and
David O'Morchoe (now The O'Morchoe) since Sandhurst. Amongst the
other students there were two who made it to the real corridors of power.
The first was John Fieldhouse (later Admiral of the Fleet The Lord
Fieldhouse, GCB, GBE and CDS) and the other Ted Anson (later Vice
Admiral Sir Edward Anson and Chief of Staff C-in-C Fleet). The former
was a submariner the latter a naval aviator. Both were Commanders at the
time and this illustrated one 'bone of contention' between the Services;
for whilst the Naval and RAF students held a rank equivalent to Lieutenant Colonel, the Army were all Majors. During a subsequent visit to HMS
Dryad we espied a Sub-Lieutenant, raised him on several Army shoulders
and paraded him to our coach to the chorus, 'Yes. They do actually begin
with one.' All I have subsequently discovered is that, when at sea, a Royal
Marine Major ranks equivalent to a Commander – but we were not at sea.
We didn't, however, try the same on the RAF for we felt that they 'might
not be amused'. The other thing that confused the issue was that the Navy
had fairly recently removed the Branch colours from between those
golden stripes. For example, the pursers had worn white. As a senior
airman put it to me some years later, 'You know, Charles, why there are
so many pursers in the Ministry – they're the only sailors known to be
able to read and write.' The chap who really threw me, however, was the
Commander who wore his cap at a distinct Beatty angle and whom I could
visualise on the bridge of a destroyer hunting the *Scharnhorst* in a North
Sea 'Force 9'. In fact, he turned out to be a 'schoolie' – at least our
'basketweavers' wore an obvious cap badge of their own.

  We spent a great deal of time studying the Sino-Soviet conflict in much
detail. We also listened to all the great men of the day from Dennis Healey
to the CDS. In syndicates we produced presentations to cover our

thoughts for the size and shape of the forces for the next decade. Most of the time, however, we were involved in a series of paper exercises based on a variety of joint operations scenario. Some came close to possible contingencies, and notably in the Caribbean. Others were more specious, with either a Middle or Far Eastern setting. All involved the seizing of an airhead, usually by airborne assault, a marine landing across the beaches from HMS *Intrepid* or *Fearless* (or both) and the steady build up of troops and supplies by air and sea. The whole supported by a naval task force including a carrier. One contingency we didn't study was any threat to the Falklands. It could have proved of value to John Fieldhouse years later. Whilst we were busy playing our war games and preparing our presentations, Dennis Healey was actively reviewing our national Defence Policy. We were, to put it bluntly, preparing to finally 'withdraw from empire' by the end of the decade or thereabouts. Interwoven within these discussions a fierce controversy raged 'twixt the Admirals and the Air Marshals over the future of the aircraft carrier. Despite years of jointery, at Latimer and elsewhere, there remained (and still remains I suspect) a single service blinkered urge or trait, to stubbornly and often unreasonably go down fighting one's corner to the bitter end – even if obviously dead wrong. Fortunately, as time has told, the carrier received another lease of life. Without it the Falklands could never have been recovered. Legend has it that during the in fighting the RAF even 'moved Gan a little' to suit their argument. 'Two is company and three is a crowd' so they say and when it comes to inter-Service relations there seems to be a natural affinity between the soldiers and the sailors. Perhaps it all has something to do with history. Certainly the best supported sports fixture is still the Navy versus Army annual Rugby match. Our time at Latimer generally reflected these relations and it didn't help that most of the RAF students took quarters at RAF Halton and were thus seldom seen in or about the Latimer environs after hours. As one senior sailor put it on the last day, 'I'm buying the Latimer Cormorant tie – not the Halton variety.'

We played a lot of squash in the evenings and some hockey on Wednesday afternoons. Bruce Thomas and I made up the full back partnership and we had notable victories over both the Staff College Owls and Sandhurst Occasionals. There were also some very good outside visits and events thrown in. Highlights were certainly a tour of the London Air Traffic Control Centre at West Drayton (how they keep all those 'blips' apart still amazes me), a sea outing in a submarine during a 'Navy Day' style visit to Pompey (like the miners the submariners have my undying admiration) and a most impressive 'Battlefield Firepower Demonstration' at

Warminster. The most memorable was, however, the trip to BAOR. We were based in and about Celle and were sponsored by 11th Armoured Brigade. Besides an evening in Hamburg, a sight of the East German border installations (sinister in the extreme) we spent a day amongst the soldiers and equipment of the brigade. It was an invigorating display. A lot of new equipment had recently been issued and notably the mighty Conqueror tank with its 120 mm gun and the Abbott self-propelled (SP) gun. The AFV432 armoured personnel carrier (APC) was also now in general issue, so morale was high amongst the operators and this certainly came across to our friends in dark and light blue. Early on I spotted Robin Merton grinning at me from the turret of a Conqueror. Now back at regimental duty, he was with the Royal Hussars to whom he had trans-ferred whilst in Ulster. Shortly after I bumped into Dick Worsley, the Brigade Commander and whom I had last seen as 'Exercise Controller' at Lulworth Cove as I and my company made our assault landing there. When next we met he would be Corps Commander. During the morning we were permitted to clamber over everything and drive or fire this and that. Perhaps the most entertaining sight was to see a future Sandhurst trained West African coup leader out on the cross-country vehicle circuit. At the wheel of a Saladin armoured car one could just see his broad grinning face through the driver's flap. As he whizzed by for the third time we were, however, assured that a highly competant NCO from the local armoured car regiment was at his elbow. He was later 'given the chop' by yet another Sandhurst trained coup leader. After an excellent lunch in a tented Mess pitched for the occasion, and with tables loaded with mess silver, we came to the climax of the day – a mechanised assault by 1st Royal Anglian battle group. For the purposes of the exercise we students were split about the group and, if soldiers, were given tasks unrelated to arm. I was made a Chieftain gunners mate. My role being to keep heaving 105 mm blank shells into the breech as and when required. Hot and heavy work I can assure you. My gunner was another naval 'schoolie'. Once we began the assault a combination of the cordite smell from the breech and the uneven motion of the tank turned his lunch over and he puked mostly over me. I was far from pleased but my humour was restored when I watched my most non-favourite RAF DS being given a real rollicking by a young Royal Anglian NCO as he stumbled on dis- mounting from the APC and had to catch up with the assault. All in all it was an excellent day and did the brigade great credit.

Back at the College, and as we settled in to 1967, one began to appreci-ate that time was running out on the course. It had been entertaining rather than highly instructive but one had certainly made some useful inter-Service contacts (and chums) for the future. Socially it had been nothing very outstanding since most of the sailors and civilians were weekly mess boarders and the RAF were mainly slanted towards 'JSSC Halton'. Amongst those wholly Latimer committed we did have some fun and I recall my thirty-ninth birthday party when we took over the Saturday second sitting at the 'Hare and Hounds' (the pub just below Beechwood Cottage on the Henley Road). Mother joined us since one of the couples lived over 'Farthingales' and most of the others had been customers at one time or another, gently persuaded, or otherwise, by Millman and especially in the lead into the Christmas just passed. Just prior to the end of the course, and some leave I had due, I received a letter from Toby Sewell, my new CO to be, indicating that he wanted me to report for duty the day after the course ended. I knew him to be keen (but not that keen) since he had been BM to HQ Mid-West Brigade in Borneo and we had together sought to ease the obvious friction between our Commanders. I had, however, always known where my loyalties lay and I think this had perhaps prevented a deep friendship from developing. He had a change of heart when I made the point that 'the Russians had not crossed the Elbe since 1945 and seemed most unlikely to do so within the next fourteen days.' He also indicated that as part of the Defence cuts 6th Brigade, of which we were part, were to be withdrawn to UK. We would be the first unit to move and were destined to 'mark time' in Hobbs Barracks, Lingfield, prior to going to Bahrain on a nine months' unaccompanied tour in January 1968. I would be taking the advance party to our hutted camp home base in late July. It seemed, therefore, that having last been in BAOR in 1951 I was to do only four months this time round. More importantly, as I was later to discover, I was never to get the chance to earn my mechanised spurs. At that point in time Bahrain was just a distant thought. From my limited knowledge of the Arabian Gulf it seemed then the ultimate '*terra incognita*' of our remaining overseas commitments. How wrong I was to be proved.

I had left the 1st Battalion in 1951 as the Senior Subaltern. I was now returning as the Senior Major or 2ic. During the JSSC visit to Warminster I had met a subaltern from the battalion who was doing a course at the School of Infantry. During a chat I asked him how long he thought it would take me from Ostend to Munster once clear of the ferryport. 'No more than four hours at the absolute maximum – I often do it at weekends,' was his prompt reply. So very early one April morning I set off from Ostend with the good intention of making my destination well before lunch. After I had been going hard for some three and a half hours I spotted an overhead autobahn sign that read 'Munster 154 kms'. I took it that I had either been conned by my young blade or that he had made it 'cross-country' in his Lotus Elan. For I really had been motoring. When I finally made it to York Barracks, after some six hours and ten minutes, I was assured by Bob Johnson, who was in the Mess to greet me, that my timing was a near record. The welcoming sight of Bob had been heartening and very shortly after Don Donaldson and Peter Clayton also turned up to greet me. We had all been subalterns together in those far off Iserlohn days. The disquieting aspect was, however, that as we fell into discussion it emerged that Bob was Families Officer, Don the President of the Regimental Institutes (PRI) and Peter, OC 'HQ' Company. Not exactly the key appointments in any battalion and yet in those early days they had all been bright lads with promising futures. Admittedly Bob and Don had very recently suffered personal tragedies in their families and Peter was now somewhat slanted towards the Technical Staff. Be that as it may I gained the feel that rather more had soured them off with Service life. This clearly wasn't going to make life any easier for me since when you find your chums are unhappy and 'sparkless' you hope it is not going to become infectious. As 2ic I, however, had plenty to get stuck into and especially on the training side now that our mechanised days were ended, and we were earmarked for the Arabian Gulf, we needed urgently to get off our backsides and on to our feet again.

Before I could set this transition in motion I did, however, have to bear with a bit of the 'mystique' that had overtaken life in BAOR those past sixteen years. First I was required to address the Divisional Study Period on the newly introduced KIP – or 'Kits Individual Protection'. At the briefing by the Brigadier I didn't let on that I had no idea to what he was referring. I was too much of a coward to do that. I just appeared intent, took notes and smiled politely here and there. On the way out I merely latched quickly on to the CO of the Devon and Dorsets (later General Sir John Archer, KCB, OBE) to obtain the answer. I got away with it on the day and even threw in a couple or so slides showing how best to use the sheeting with a variety of fire trenches. Next I got caught up in the Exercise QUICK TRAIN turnout procedure. Like HQ Strategic Command (HQ STRATCO), HQ BAOR conducted a test turnout on units from time to time. I had hardly been with the battalion a week when early one morning it was our turn. I just went with the system like a 'blind man' since noboby had felt it necessary to brief me.

That over, we launched into a visit from the then Colonel-in-Chief of the Regiment, HRH Princess Marina, Duchess of Kent. During it General

Sir Richard Craddock, then the Colonel, let it be known to me that he hoped I would succeed Toby Sewell before or during the Bahrain tour. I was heartened by this possibility since the age for promotion to Lieutenant Colonel had recently been dropped to thirty-nine years and some early Sandhurst 'fliers', like Roly Guy, were on that year's promotion list. Later the age was to be dropped even further to thirty-seven years. However, command was not generally given to the 'whizz-kids' until around age thirty-nine. Where it was it produced, and especially in Ulster subsequently, a disaster or two, for they do say that there is no substitute for experience. Against this background I viewed the forthcoming battalion training session at Vogelsang with increased interest. As the chap producing the programme, I agreed at the outset with Toby Sewell that the emphasis should be afforded to physical fitness, endurance and field-firing. We also agreed that we should finish up with a Platoon Commanders Test Exercise on the lines of that undergone at Camp Gagetown. So over the Easter Break I sat down and produced an outline programme and a skeleton exercise off the map. I then went up to Vogelsang to tie up the arrangements with the Belgians (they still ran the place) and to walk the proposed exercise course. The scenery was as beautiful as I had remembered it. Suffice it to say that we had a very good three-week session in near perfect weather. We all returned a good deal fitter, our feet hardened up and one or two platoon commanders a great deal wiser. We were now into June and one last task remained before I headed for Lingfield and the detailed reconnaissance of Hobbs Barracks and what it did, or did not have, to offer. That was to run the annual skill-at-arms meeting at Sennelager. Nothing very special one might say. When, however, Les Wilson (the RSM – and we had been near 'boy soldiers' together in the battalion) got up there to see how the preparations were getting along not one marquee had yet been erected. In short, not one NCO present had any idea how to set about it. So like two 'Works Foremen' we got the teams together, laid all the kit out in the correct order and then gently cajoled them into setting things up. I then told the RSM to ensure that marquee pitching be included in all of future NCO cadres. For we always still need tents – and big ones – for those special military occasions.

In the second week of June I drove home to UK to conduct the on-site 'sizing-up' of Lingfield and its problems. We were then some three months away from the arrival of the advance party. By mid-October the main body would appear – families and all. Hobbs Barracks fronted the A22 just to the north of East Grinstead. It was a pre-war militia style hutted camp and had last been occupied by the WRAC Depot whilst their 'Empire' at Guildford was being rebuilt. That had been some two years ago. It had not been permanently occupied since a transport regiment had left some long time back. In short, it was in need of major refurbishment. Whilst this was already underway, especially as regards floors, roofs and rewiring, I had that nasty feel that unless the contractors were kept under constant pressure the task would not be completed before the main body arrived. I earmarked the essential accommodation required by the advance party and made it clear that this had to be ready for occupation by 1st September. There were no sports fields, the nearest range was at Shoreham in Kent but there was a small and perfectly adequate training area nearby at Pippingford Park. I, however, gleaned from the local authorities at Crawley, just down the road, that I could hire sports pitches in their new sports complex. HQ 2nd Infantry Brigade at Shorncliffe, our new masters, agreed to make provisional block bookings for the range and training area. We then came to the vexed subject of married quarters for the families. There were none. So clutching the bill by ranks and family sizes I then met up with a Ministry team from the Quartering Directorate. From the outset they were able to state that they now had approval to go out into the civilian market to purchase the necessary houses. Not too easy a task in an area very much bordering the 'stockbroker belt'. But they acted fast and wisely. The eventual outcome was an officer 'colony' in Sharpthorne, a WO's and SNCO's 'patch' just outside East Grinstead and the junior ranks on a new housing estate on the edge of Uckfield. Only in the latter case did we meet any resentment from some residents, mainly 'first-time' buyers and understandable I suppose. It had been a useful exercise and I returned to Munster believing that we might must make it. But it was going to be a tight thing and we would be faced with a major problem of getting the 'pads' to and from work. The most disquieting feature of the trip had, however, been a visit to Marlow where I had found Mother in some distress with back pains. The initial diagnosis had been disc trouble – rest was needed. Thereafter a good break was suggested. I, therefore, proposed that she came out to Munster for a week prior to the departure of the advance party on leave. Then, *en route* for home, we would spend a long weekend on the Belgian coast at her favourite hotel, the St George's (now flats) at Le Zoute. I also promised to throw in an evening or two at the Knokke Casino – another great favourite. This plan seemed to meet with general approval and she was certainly in better heart when I left.

My short sojourn in Munster had not been all that happy. It had, however, drawn a few smiles. One of my duties as 2ic had been to chair (even as a 'singleton') the Parent Teachers Association at the local British Forces Education Service (BFES) primary school. Keen to show the right degree of interest and enthusiasm early on, I asked 'Fred the Head' (as he was known) if he would show me round. As we toured the establishment we suddenly came to a door marked 'Think Room'. I asked the significance and was told that any youngster with a problem or puzzle to solve could use the room for a little privacy and silent thought. We opened the door and there was a little lad, who had clearly 'misunderstood' the intention, and was quietly relieving himself against the wall in a corner. I next discovered that our 'Fred' had ordered a sizeable play pool and hadn't yet got enough in the kitty to pay for it. He was some £3,000 short and the pool was due the next week. My old chum Les Wilson (a real Mr 'Fix-it') came to the rescue immediately. That Saturday afternoon he arranged a battalion fête and advertised it all over the garrison. We made the target and more. In order to get my car British Forces Germany (BFG) registered I had first to pass the 'tick' test. This was supervised by the Motor Transport Officer (MTO), Frank Oram. In brief, one had to be conversant with the Bonn rules of the road, road signs, speed limits and so on. I took time out to study the BFG Highway Code and passed the test with a little help, no doubt, from Frank. Within a week I misread the speed limit coming back from the air display at RAF Gutersloh and received an on the spot fine. I remain to this day wary of the rule that all traffic from the right has priority. I am sure that my insurance company were happy that I didn't attempt to overplay my hand in this respect. Once I was BFG registered I was invited one Saturday evening to partake in a car Treasure Hunt around Munster. My partner for the evening was the unit SSAFA Sister, a very cute and petite brunette. I had been on station for three weeks, she barely a week more. Our knowledge of the City was thus scant and certainly we had no idea of the location of the main railway station where we were required to have a passport photo taken. Determined not to be last, we settled on those clues we could positively handle such as the 'pill' we obtained from the military hospital. We actually finished eighth out of the twelve teams. I cite this story since, whilst the breathalyser had not yet hit UK, in West Germany, it was already a feature at any road accident. One can imagine the reaction today if one attempted such a fun event in any BAOR garrison. Both the civil and military police would go mad.

Mother arrived towards the end of July and she had a week in a local and very comfortable gasthaus. We threw a party in the Mess and also did some sightseeing. She was still complaining of back twinges but aided by some pills seemed to be coping. But then she was not one to make a meal of anything. We enjoyed our time at Le Zoute, including a couple of evenings at the Knokke Casino. I then had a week or so of leave before assembling with the advance party at Lingfield on 1st September. By that time the camp was still not completely ready, though the quarters situation was well in hand. We kept the pressures on and by the time the main body descended upon us the place was habitable, the ranges, training areas and playing fields had all been booked and the recently purchased quarters were fully furnished. All that remained was for the vehicle party to draw up our allocation from the Depot. Since my original 'recce' one additional complication had, however, arisen. The hutted camp at Broadbridge Heath, Horsham, had been earmarked for the 2nd Battalion to stage in on their return from the Far East and prior to moving to Ulster. It was too small for them and so it was agreed that two companies should be Lingfield based. With a little bit of adjustment we found the necessary room. The Battalion adapted well to its temporary home and we soon got down to some useful individual training including some refresher IS drills. For the latter was to be one of our roles in Bahrain. A major outbreak of 'Foot and Mouth' disease about Kent and Sussex involved much of Support Company in manning control points. The remainder conducted some 'Keep the Army in the Public Eye' or KAPE tours about our large recruiting area in the Home Counties. All in all there was enough to keep all fruitfully employed as the January move to the Gulf steadily approached. It was, meanwhile, confirmed that I would be taking command in March 1968. So with Toby Sewell and the 2ic Designate, Noel Pepperall, we set to to agree an initial outline programme of events from the first day the Battalion arrived at Hamala Camp. Our only real upset at this time was when the Bandmaster's wife burned his uniforms in the hope that this would prevent him having to go to Bahrain. It did – he was sacked and Kneller Hall produced an immediate replacement. The big upset was to come. Suddenly Mother's back condition deteriorated so seriously that she had to be taken into hospital. The diagnosis wsa chronic pancreatitis. I drove over each evening to High Wycombe after duty, stayed the night in the cottage and drove back to Lingfield the following morning. Eventually it was decided to operate. She died some three days later still in obvious distress. It was a very sad end for someone who had always been such a live wire. She had been a wonderful mother and a really true friend to many. The funeral service at Little Marlow Church was packed out. Bob Johnson very kindly accompanied me to the final burial in the Camberwell New Cemetry at Forest Hill alongside both her parents and husband. I took some compassionate leave to settle her affairs and then awaited attendance on the COs Designate Course in early February. I also went to Gatwick to see the main body depart for Bahrain. It had been a rather tedious last leg to command which had ended in great sadness. Looking back, one wonders whether something could have been cut out of what was, essentially, a longish 'mark-time' period. Perhaps if I had had the chance to fully exploit my luck in the Borneo posting I could have gone to BAOR earlier as 2ic and earned those mechanised spurs. But what will be will be – or so they say. Instead I merely added to my 'old colonial' image. This time amongst the Arabs of the Gulf.

Chapter 9

Command
From Bahrain to Bermuda

Early in February 1968 I attended the CO's Designate Course. Largely based on Aldershot, a series of lectures, presentations and visits hammered home the line that in peacetime the CO bears an 'uncharmed' life. If there is food poisoning in the cookhouse it is his responsibility. If the barracks burns down it is nobody's fault but his. The same applies if the paymaster is caught fiddling the regimental accounts. The options for 'disaster and a shortened career' appeared very considerable indeed and across a varied range of possible pitfalls. I shared this tale of impending woe with some twenty others and notably such Sandhurst chums as Derek Bishop, Mike Hardy and Dennis Shuttleworth. It all seemed rather at variance with that talk we had had from the great Field Marshal just before we left RMAS. He had described regimental or battalion command as the most satisfying in service life; but then he was concerned with battle leadership not peacetime accounting. Thereafter one was encouraged, if time permitted, to visit units in the training organisation and notably, in my case, the junior infantry establishments at Oswestry and Shorncliffe. The former was then the home of the Infantry Junior Leaders Battalion and was commanded by my old friend Ian Cameron. I was impressed then by the high standards attained in these excellent units and the quality of the product they injected into the regimental system. I have never changed my mind since. Many made the most senior non-commissioned ranks and most quartermasters I knew had begun as 'boy soldiers'. Despite these plain facts I have never ceased to be amazed how the Army continues to 'blow hot and cold' over the question of the need for the junior intake. Currently we are going through a lukewarm phase.

The Persian Gulf

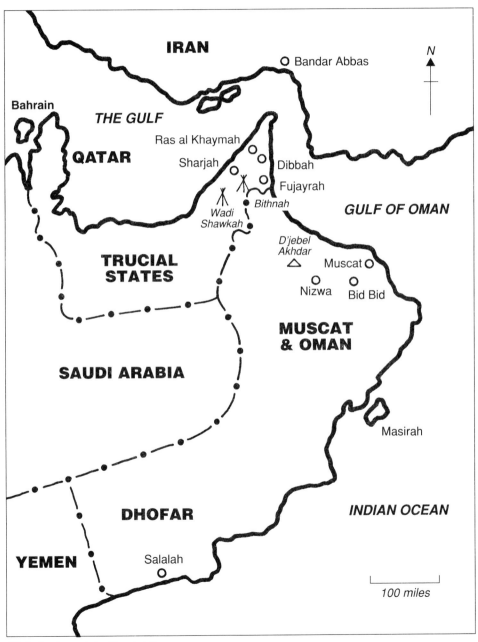

IV. Bahrain and the Trucial States.

Back from the course I began to prepare for the vacation of Beechwood Cottage. Mother and I had had some very happy times there. The owner would, however, never sell it to us since he had earmarked it for his retirement once he handed over his farm to his son. In any event it was thought most unlikely that I would ever be posted near enough to Marlow to use it again as a proper home, or that was the general viewpoint. As it turned out, my next posting after command would have enabled me to do just that. I moved all my furniture and boxed belongings to Hobbs Barracks for storage there during my Bahrain absence since I would take over the CO's quarter on my return. I then nominated an elderly but dear couple, who lived across the road, as my next-of-kin. I had no blood relations remaining. They had been very close friends of my mother and being ex-army they understood both me and my way of life. A retired Sapper Major General, he had been largely instrumental in building the Rheindahlen complex – or the HQ BAOR location once they quit Bad Oeynhausen. It was indeed 'Uncle George' Hatton who drove me to Reading Station that day to begin my journey to Bahrain in late March. It was not to be the most happy of experiences as I was soon to discover. The first indication that all was not well was when I arrived at Swindon station. For when I approached the RAF Movements NCO. I found I was not on his nominal roll for that evenings VC10 departure. I, however, joined the coach to RAF Lyneham where, on inquiry at reception, a highly attractive but rather officious young WRAF Movements Officer confirmed that I was not listed for the flight. At that point a distinguished looking naval Captain (later Vice Admiral Sir Cameron Rusby, KCB, LVO) joined in the rapidly overheating discussion. He was also to fly out to Bahrain that evening to take command of HMS *Tartar* – a frigate bound for the Beira Patrol. Despite our combined entreaties the young maiden stubbornly refused to budge and made it very clear that there could be no question of junior ranks being taken off the plane for our benefit. The intercession of the MOD Duty Officer also failed to move her. In short, due to inadequate documentation and thus no booking, we had definitely had the VC10 schedule that evening. The eventual solution was that we departed early the next morning on a Britannia freighter via Cyprus and Masirah for Bahrain. The load included we 'strays', fourteen guard dogs, thirty 'Irks' returning from leave to Masirah, plus some cargo. Some fifteen long hours later, after a very noisy and even more uncomfortable journey, a couple of rather bedraggled COs arrived in the early hours of the following morn at RAF Muharraq. Entering reception there was nobody to meet either of us. No message had ever been passed on indicating our amended arrival timing. When the VC10 arrived without us it was assumed presumably that we were either sick or AWOL. We both had to ring our respective Duty Officers for transport. It wasn't really the most auspicious way to begin a command tour.

After a quick 'wash and brush up' I joined Toby Sewell for our hand-over/takeover session. As that evening he was to depart for home. I had, I believe, the great advantage of knowing the Battalion. For I had been the 2ic in the lead into the tour. Some have since argued to the contrary. You cannot see the 'blindspots' so they say. I had also had a chance to prepare the outline training programme in concert with both Toby and Noel Pep-perall whilst at Lingfield. More recently I had prepared a families events programme with OC Rear Party on a visit to Hobbs Barracks. There was no doubt that the Battalion had settled well and had already established its presence at Hamala and about Bahrain in general. There had perhaps been a little of 'we'll leave that one until the new CO arrives' and, in retrospect, I am sure that Toby Sewell and I would agree that it would have been better had I been in the chair from Day One. MS were, however, quite adamant that it should be played their way. However, I did subsequently ensure that there was no such replay when I came to handover. Others will also say that I was extremely fortunate to have an all 'Passed Staff Col-lege' (p.s.c.) 2ic and company commander team. I will not deny this but, more importantly, it keeps the CO on his mettle. For there can only be one CO – or boss. That makes it one of the loneliest jobs in life since one cannot be seen to give fear nor favour to one rather than another. Yet they are all hopefully riding on that key recommendation for command.

Bahrain Island itself is about thirty miles long and ten miles wide at its broadest point. It is located about half way down the Gulf, just north of what were then the Trucial States and some twenty miles off the east coast of Saudi Arabia. The capital is Manama situated at the north shore of the island. The next largest town is Muharraq, where the RAF had a station and which was also used as an international airport. A causeway (the key to the IS problem) one and a half miles in length linked the two. At that time the population was estimated at around 350,000 and the main source of income was oil. This was centred on the Bahrain Petroleum Company (BAPCO) cantonment at Awali. The climate is humid all the year round, the coolest period being 'twixt December and March. I had arrived as it began to 'stoke up'. Politically we then had treaty obligations to both Bahrain and the Trucial States. In this respect the Foreign and Common-wealth Office (FCO) were represented by Political Agents (or advisers) throughout the Trucial States and Bahrain. They were headed by Sir

Stewart Crawford, GCMG, CVO, a most charming diplomat of the old school and, who having been previously in Baghdad, knew the Gulf scene well. He was titled Political Agent, Persian Gulf, and his brief extended into Muscat and Oman. The Political Agent in Bahrain was the sharp and ever helpful Tony Parsons (later Sir Anthony Parsons, GCMG, LVO, MC, of Falklands UN Assembly fame). The military were headed by a Commander British Forces Gulf (a Two-Star airman in our time) operating from a Joint Force HQ alongside the 'stone frigate', HMS *Jufair*. The naval element were headed by a great character – Commodore Tom Fanshawe. His base, in effect, supported the then Beira Patrol (usually a single frigate at any one time), a minesweeper flotilla committed to anti-smuggling and anti-piracy duties in the Gulf and any naval group, or craft, staging *en route* for the Indian Ocean and Far East. The US Navy then maintained an ancient cruiser in the harbour from which their local Gulf Commander flew his flag. As often as not he had no ships under command (rather different than in more recent times). Shortly after my arrival John Archer assumed the appointment of Commander Land Forces Persian Gulf (LFPG). Whilst he too was Bahrain based, the majority of what was essentially a brigade group was stationed down the Gulf at RAF Sharjah. There could be found 2nd Bn, The Royal Regiment of Fusiliers (later to be relieved by 2nd Grenadiers), a battery of 105 mm howitzers, a sapper squadron, a squadron of Saladins and an AAC flight. Additionally, the locally raised Trucial Oman Scouts (TOS), with seconded British Officers and SNCOs came under his command. The role of this force was to counter any possible insurgency inspired from within or without the Trucial States and Muscat and the Oman. There was always a threat from dissidents in the Dhofar promoted by the Yemen. In our case we had the additional task of supporting the Bahrain State Police should the need arise in aid to the civil power. Whilst in the Gulf the Battalion establishment included an air platoon (3 × Sioux helicopters) and the Vigilant wire guided missile as an increment to the anti-tank platoon. One of the helicopter pilots was, incidentally, the young blade who had owned that Lotus Elan in the Munster days. An interesting statistic rank-wise was that there were on the island another twenty-seven Lieutenant Colonels with not a soldier to command between them. The immediate RAF support element was divided between the stations at Muharraq and Sharjah. The mix of aircraft included Hunters in the ground attack role, a Whirlwind helicopter support lift and Argosies and Andovers for air movement and resupply. The staging post at RAF Masirah, in the Indian Ocean off Muscat, was almost administered from Bahrain.

In framing our outline programme for the tour, our prime aim had been to vary the pattern whenever and wherever possible. What we were seeking to avoid particularly was 'stagnating' in Hamala Camp and especially during the very hot season in July and August. In short, we hoped that we could genuinely match the adage that variety is the spice of life. That is not to say that Hamala Camp was not well found. We had our own swimming pool, tennis and squash courts, football and hockey pitches and the like. We even had our own range. Canteen facilities were provided by NAAFI, the Mission for Mediterranean Garrisons (MMG), the PR1 and the camp contractor. To supplement all this we established a variety of interest and hobbies club activities from model aircraft to art classes and philately. We allotted each company a worthwhile project to improve some feature in the camp on a self-help basis. We also encouraged them to do a bit of gardening and soon periwinkle and oleander were sprouting everywhere, for there is nothing the good cockney soldier cannot put his hand to given the necessary encouragement. The daily routine we followed was that long established in such parts. We worked from 7.00 am to 1.00 pm 'made shade' between 2.00–4.00 pm and then 'resurrected' the Battalion for organised recreation from 4.00–6.00 pm. We set out, for example, to ensure that all could swim at least a length of the pool before we left – and very nearly succeeded. Once a fortnight or so companies would organise a novices boxing competition as the evenings entertainment. In a battalion with a fine boxing record this was also popular. On other occasions the band would give an evening concert of popular music. The accommodation though hutted was air-conditioned and spacious. We could have been a great deal worse off. However, we clearly needed to produce a change of scene from time to time plus a varied challenge.

Our first venture off the island was to the Wadi Shawkah on the edge of the Jebel some thirty miles inland from RAF Sharjah. We flew in by Argosy and then motored out to a tented base camp we had established in the foothills. Having been delayed on take-off by engine trouble, I was soon to earn (after several such sagas) the title 'The Albatross of the Gulf'. The camp was maintained daily with fresh rations, water and ice by our echelon in Sharjah. Over a period of three weeks we conducted some very varied company training, much field firing and an advance to contact battalion exercise. Above all we concentrated on those ancient military skills of picketing the heights along the line of advance and the construction of rock sangars in the defence, features of those now distant days of actions on the NW Frontier just prior to World War II. The field-firing was an experience. There were virtually no limitations on arcs of fire and so on. The Fusiliers provided an enemy for the battalion exercise. They were perhaps too vehicle bound to provide realism and so I took note next time to try and get some TOS. By this time the Battalion were fully acclimatised. Having said that, it was very hot and humid and except for the battalion exercise we stuck by our Bahrain daily routine. Despite this we did have the odd heat exhaustion case, including one company commander who was overcome during an exercise 'recce' and brought round by his driver and signaller. One soldier became mentally unstable and left a message in his bivouac to say that he was leaving the camp to 'finish it all'. Fortunately we were alerted in time and a prompt air 'recce' sortie spotted him some three miles to the north. In another incident one of the QM's staff fell asleep in the back of a ration truck returning to Sharjah and was tipped out of the vehicle. His absence wasn't noted until the truck reached base. A helicopter search back along the route was then instigated and his red PT vest was some time later spotted as he crouched in the shade of a thornbush. Without even a water bottle he was no worse off than being somewhat dehydrated. We all learn by experience.

The next event in our variety sequence was a Searchlight Tattoo designed to mark the Battalion Day – 'The Glorious First of June'. Noel Pepperall, Les Wilson and I had originally planned the outline back at Lingfield. Thus by the time I arrived companies had been allotted their scene, costumes were being made by 'Ginger', the contractor and his team, and rehearsals had begun. The event spanned the history of the Regiment from its formation on Putney Heath in 1661 to the Salerno beaches in World War II. The climax was to be simulated guard mounting ceremony *à la* 'Buck House', for I already knew that we were down to do a public duties stint sometime after we got home. We now had ten days or so in which to add the final polish. On the evening in question I was in my room dressing when I happened to glance out of my window towards the main road from the City. There was a solid stream of cars for as far as the eye could see. In all some 4,000 and more attended and everyone who was somebody in Bahrain, including the Ruler, was there. It was adjudged a huge success and we never as a Battalion looked back from that day. It was a personal triumph for Les Wilson who, as RSM and co-ordinator, had persuaded the soldiers to give of their best to it. The following week we were invited to repeat the performance in the setting of the Awali Club grounds.

We now had a couple of months to fill in before our next scheduled major training event in Masirah in August. This was also the period we had set aside for adventure training and anything else on offer in the variety field. We had, however, to bear in mind that, strictly speaking, we were not permitted to have more than a company group in strength away at any one time. When we were all away, as at the Wadi Shawkah, a company group was always flown in from Sharjah to meet the essential IS need. We had already agreed around this time to conduct a series of OMEX patrols in the mountain fastness of the Djebel Akhdar in the Muscat and Oman. Back in January 1959, 22nd SAS, on their way back from Malaya (and possible disbandment believe it or not), had scaled the Djebel and finally crushed a rebellion against the Sultan. Ever since one of the Gulf-based battalions had mounted periodic ten-day patrols of the area in a combined 'shewing the flag' and 'hearts and minds' exercise. We were also committed to produce, on roulement, some instructors to assist at the Sultan of Muscat's Armed Forces Depot. The Kuwaitis also wanted the short term loan of a team to help them convert to the new 81 mm mortar. With the assistance of the RAF and Navy respectively, adventure training parties made it to and from Madagascar and Iran (via Bandar Abbas). A frigate, *en route* for the Far East, was required to conduct a series of formal visits to ports up and down the Gulf. The Captain very kindly agreed to swap his Marine detachment for an equivalent one of ours. Meanwhile the minesweeper flotilla maintained a steady stream of requests for small parties to act as gunners' mates and duty buglers during their patrols. One such party got as far as Singapore and back. For those who didn't manage to make one or other of these openings we set up a tented R & R camp on the southern tip of the island. This was, of course, with the Ruler's blessing. However, having recently been loaned some of his horses, and granted permission for the officers to use his private beach, we were not surprised when he agreed to our request. We christened the site 'Riviera Beach' and it could take up to a strong platoon for four days. The facilities on offer included swimming, water-skiing, canoeing and, of course, idling. Barbecues featured each evening. It was generally popular (there are, however, some soldiers you can never please even if you played snap with golden coins) and served its purpose at that time.

For some reason best known to the RAF they suddenly cancelled our impending session on Masirah. I believe it had something to do with them now wanting the accommodation for the staging needs of others on a more important exercise. Be that as it may or may not have been, we clearly had to think again. A few evenings later I was dining at the Crawfords and asked Sir Stewart if he could recommend anywhere we might now go at short notice at this time of year. He came up immediately with Bithnah where he said he had camped himself some time back. But not in August.

It was high up in the Jebel about forty miles due west of Fujayrah on the
Gulf of Oman. There was an airstrip nearby and he described the scenery
as near breathtaking. In this respect I was reminded of that former High
Commissioner's description of Kapit. If it did prove suitable then we were
'off the hook', since Support Company were already scheduled to go to
Yas Island, off Abu Dhabi, to fire their weapons (including Vigilant)
around the same time. Noel Pepperall, I and the doctor flew down within
the next few days to conduct the 'recce'. It was indeed a beautiful spot
deep in Bedouin country. The wadis were alive with oleander and every
now and again one came across a thornbush hutment and adjacent compound in which a few goats were searching for nourishment. Early on we
encountered a Bedouin family on the move; a yashmaked lady in brilliant
blue astride a scruffly looking camel being led by the husband with two
small kids at his side. Like all true males in those parts, he was sporting a
rifle across his shoulders and a bandolier of ammunition about his waist.
In those days it was the SMLE that was the prize possession rather than
the Kalashnikov. We took all the necessary wet and dry bulb temperature
measurements and concluded that a useful period of company training
could be conducted provided all were sensible and we adjusted the daily
routine hours of work. We settled on 4.00–11.00 am for one session and
4.00–8.00 pm for the other. Each company would do ten days in turn and
the last thirty-six hours in each case would be devoted to a Test exercise
set and controlled by Bn HQ – the camp to be properly found for main
tentage and gas refrigeration; and fresh rations, water and ice to be flown
in daily from Sharjah. Whilst it was hot and very humid, there were less
flies around than there had been at Wadi Shawkah. They had been so bad
there that we had had to eat under mosquito nets. Here the main hazard
appeared to be an attentive hornet 'dressed' in Middlesex Regiment rugby
colours – maroon and yellow stripes. During our formal visit to the
Sheikh, which included an 'hors d'oeuvres' of sheeps' eyes, he had
stressed that during the next two months or so freak thunderstorms were
always a possibility high up in the Jebel, followed by flash floods in the
wadis. There had, he said, not been one in the Bithnah area in recent
years. He, however, advised us to ensure that we pitched camp on high
ground and avoided positioning equipment and stores in neighbouring
wadis. We accordingly chose a site above the main wadi and adjacent to
the airstrip. It was later set up by Noel and a small QM's administrative
party. All companies, in turn, were reminded of the possible storm hazard.
Two days after the leading company had begun their stint, Noel and I were
preparing to dine with BAPCO friends at the Awali Club when a FLASH

signal came in from Bithnah saying that there had just been a tremendous storm and, that in the subsequent flash flood, the Sioux helicopter (for casevac purposes) and an administrative three-tonner had been swept away, and two soldiers were missing. Later, when calm had prevailed, it was determined that both the helicopter and truck had been found seriously damaged. No soldiers were missing. Noel and I flew down the next morning and it was obvious that the Sheikh's warning had gone unheeded. Both equipments had been parked in the main wadi. Enough said other than to add the rider that when the RAF tried to lift the Sioux back to Sharjah, as an underslung Whirlwind load, they dropped it some miles out. It then became a total loss. Despite this poor start the training period went well. We did plenty of uninhibited field-firing with the local Bedouin to be seen, at maximum range, collecting up the lead bullets for subsequent sale. Our medics also did some worthwhile 'Hearts and Minds' sorties about the neighbouring area. The Test exercise helped me to sort the 'wheat from the chaff' in the potential command stakes. It comprised a fifteen-mile advance to contact followed by the night occupation of a defensive position. I, Noel, Les Wilson and the Corps of Drums/Pioneers were the enemy. We taught some a few lessons in anti-ambush drills, picketing, mine clearance and, above all, that it is the chap who is on the highest ground at dawn who is the winner.

Our grand finale training-wise was in late September at Dibbah just south of Ras al Kaymah on the Gulf of Oman. There was a major airstrip just inland and we had cleared the use of the area with the Sheikh at the same time as the Bithnah 'recce'. Based on all that splendid joint services teaching I had garnered at Latimer I then wrote and ran an exercise which I doubt whether any battalion commander will ever have the chance to follow; for there will, I am sure, never again be the scope, money, manpower and equipment on hand to repeat it. It basically involved the relief of an 'oil prospecting party' (represented by 4th Royal Tanks personnel) at Tayibbah some twenty-five miles to the west. It began with a heliborne assault to secure the airstrip, followed by a landing across the neighbouring beaches to secure a pontoon site for the transhipment of the heavy equipment from a Landing Ship Logistic (LSL). In Phase 2 the remainder of the battalion group were flown in from Sharjah. Fighter ground attack sorties were available on call and later, during both the advance and withdrawal, air alert cover was constant. The enemy were provided by the TOS and were controlled by an umpire team fielded by 2nd Grenadiers. Once we had relieved the 'oil prospectors' we reversed the procedure and finally left Dibbah as we had found it – peaceful, dusty and hot. We had only one 'ugly' incident where a TOS patrol got slightly over enthusiastic and drew their knives. In another incident a Land Rover strayed across the Ras al Kaymah border and drew some hostile fire. It had been a great ending to a thoroughly enjoyable and profitable tour from the training angle. We were now all very fit, well acclimatised and ready to conduct serious operations about the theatre. In fact, as we returned to Bahrain one company was stood by to proceed at short notice to Salalah to assist the Sultan of Muscat and Oman.

During our nine months in the Gulf we had both worked and played hard. There had been some good laughs and no doubt Tony Tippet, a distinguished purser who commanded HMS *Jufair* (later Vice Admiral Sir Anthony Tippet, KCB and organiser of the Great Ormond Street Hospital Appeal), won the 'man of the match' award in this respect. His fancy dress donkey polo and donkey derby events were both outstandingly memorable occasions. We won the former and Cameron Rusby the latter – perhaps not quite to the liking of the noble Commodore who was, maybe, one who rather preferred to win. BAPCO were very generous hosts at the Awali Club where I sought to master the art of tenpin bowling, only to be banned for 'throwing' by the Arab manager. Each Sunday after Church the senior management set sail in their respective 'barges' for a picnic lunch on one of the small islands offshore. The Commodore possessed the Admiral's barge from Aden days, the Brigadier had an RASC converted fast launch and the RAF an air-sea rescue craft. I usually got an invite on one or other as they all vied for the best beach. Otherwise I joined the Mess Dhow party for the day. Both the Serjeants' and Corporals' Messes caught on here too. Some families also enjoyed the fun as we managed to negotiate caretaking 'leases' with Service, BAPCO and Foreign Office families proceeding on leave. We got them to and from Bahrain on RAF indulgence flights (spare seats to the uninitiated) and all ranks benefited to some degree. A twenty-eight day stay was the maximum I would sanction. I only had to 'deport' one officer's lady who had overstayed her welcome. The Ruler gave the Battalion a most sumptuous banquet out at his palace. As we left the retainers descended like a pack of hungry wolves to clear the 'unexpended' portion of the evening's feast. We responded by inviting him to lunch with us. We scored a 'bullseye' when, on the advice of Tony Parsons, we included lemon and meringue pie – his favourite. Unlike the FCO at their Queen's Birthday cocktail party, his staff did not flick the lights three times when they required their guests to depart. Besides the traditional mess dinner nights, we organised a monthly roulette evening open to all expatriates on the island. The Field Officers and I financed a syndicate to run the evenings. We set the stakes at rather less than Monte Carlo so as to ensure that we didn't meet the chap who had broken the bank there. It was all very professional with the croupiers white tuxedo clad, sporting carnation buttonholes and the like. Supper and drinks were included with the ticket and the Regimental dance band did its stuff in another room. They were very popular occasions and it was all good clean fun. I am happy to say that the syndicate did not finish up out of pocket. I acted as 'Chef de Casino'. It is sad, however, that there is always somebody who has to spoil the enjoyment of others, in this case a couple of officers, who should have known better, had finally to be warned off.

As we settled back in Hamala for the final weeks before going home there was time for reflection. It had been a good tour for the Battalion and John Archer had told me so. It was one soon never to be repeated. The soldiers had responded well and despite the 'bird vacuum' had given little trouble. The hobbies exhibition, judged by Lady Crawford, had borne witness to their enterprise and endeavours out of hours. All but a handful had failed to pass the swimming test and the 'self-generated' boxing evenings had undoubtedly established the firm foundations of which the Regiment was to build, with such great success, in the decade ahead. I had enjoyed the hockey despite the humidity but, like Noel, had decided that once back at Lingfield it would probably be time to hang up one's boots. There is little doubt that it helped that John Archer had known the Battalion from Munster days, that we had strong naval ties through our HMS *Excellent* affiliation and 'The Glorious First of June' and that 'Fearless' Foskett, the headman at RAF Muharraq, had been a good chum during those Borneo days. Having said that, especial praise was due to the personal contributions of Noel Pepperall, Les Wilson and Duggie Fraser, our QM. Whilst the latter two received both promotion and honours in due course, the former sadly did not. A natural trainer of men, and an able staff officer, he had been tremendously supportive of me. All I can say is that sometime after a reporting injustice must have been perpetrated against him. Such 'fouls' do occur, from time to time, under the Confidential Report system and usually where a personality clash arises. Come the end of October and the Cheshires advance party arrived to begin the handover. Known as 'The Athletes Foot', from their track prowess, they had somehow avoided amalgamation to date and had just got back their old cap badge. This all caused a little feeling amongst a Regiment which had taken the step to go 'Large' in what was then thought (and still is by many) to be in the best future interests of the Corps of Infantry. The week prior to their arrival I received an invitation from Brigadier Corran Purdon (later Major General), the then Sultans Armed Forces Commander in Oman, to spend a few days with him. As he put it in his letter, 'you will not want to be involved in counting the socks and empty cartridge cases.' We had known each other well in Borneo when he had commanded the RUR with great élan. Having cleared the visit with John Archer I flew down to Muscat. Thence, with an escort from the Muscat Regiment based at Bid-Bid (another scenic 'masterpiece' for the budding artist) I drove up country, via 'Windy Corner' (the perfect ambush) and the main track, to Nizwa (it's now all tarmac, so they tell me). I then had a scenic forty-eight hours mini-battlefield tour of the 1958 Rebellion highlights. This had been Saudi-inspired and much of the fighting had taken place in and around the old fort at Nizwa. It still bore the pockmarks from Vampire rocket and cannonfire. Looking around the fort I ran into a small boy heavily shacked about his ankles. I was told he was being punished for begging. The scenery was even more eye-catching than Bithnah and the mix of little forts, lush wadis and the craggy Jebel skyline made one appreciate why some who have served there never quite get it out of their system. By the time I returned to Hamala we were in the last throes of the pack-up. Whilst we awaited the arrival of the Cheshires main body we began the basic training of a selected cadre of potential officers and SNCOs for the proposed Bahrain Defence Force. They were eventually to take over Hamala Camp. Later still they, and the army of the United Arab Emirates (with the former TOS as their kernel), were to earn their spurs during the Gulf War. By 1971 we would have left Bahrain and it would become a fully independent state under the Ruler – HH Shaikh Isa bi Sulman Al Khalifa, GCMG. Many doubted that the ruling family would survive the pressures of such as internal unrest, Communism and increasing Muslim fundamentalism. They did and today, whilst the largest sources of revenue remain oil production and refining, the state has developed into an important financial centre. So much for the prophets of doom.

We flew home by Caledonian Airways charter to Gatwick in late November. I came in on one of the later 'chalks' (or flights) and it was then that I first truly appreciated that I was now alone in the world, for as we entered the air terminal building there was just my driver to meet me. The families were there in strength and clearly in tremendous heart. A lively wives' club programme, the monthly *Braganza* Newsletter from the Gulf and first-hand visit knowledge and messages from the 'caretakers' had all helped in this respect. To assist OC Rear Party we had also had, for the first time, a designated Families Officer. They had made a bold attempt to move my furniture and other stored belongings into the CO's flat on the top floor of the old house that adjoined the Officers' Mess. I had, of course, taken a great risk in storing it all for so long in a partially occupied hutted camp. However, in those distant days it was still assumed that, as in Wellington's day, the 'singleton' officer or soldier, owned only what could be contained in his pack and kitbag. Unlike the 'pads' therefore, he could claim no allowance for storage charges in a repository. Likewise whilst I was occupying a tied quarter as the CO, as a 'singleton', I was not entitled to any of the issue domestic 'frills' such as a fridge or washing machine. I had to go out quickly and purchase same. With leave I soon settled in and it was lovely to have many of the 'treasures' from the Marlow days about me again. On the anniversary of Mother's death the Wards (he had been the Adjutant in Bahrain) asked me over to Reigate for dinner and to stay the night (the drinking and driving law had just come in). I remain eternally grateful to them for their thought and kindness, since once darkness came an eerie silence and strange feel fell across the flat.

A year later in Londonderry I was to experience another strange phenomena. I don't believe all that psychic stuff but we had, of course, been very, very close. I spent Christmas with the Hattons. Early in the New Year Mike Reynolds (now the 2ic) and I headed for Otterburn for a detailed 'recce', for I had booked the training area for early March. From the soundings I had made in Bahrain it was clear to me that most would be strangers in those parts. Variety would once again be on offer to most. At this point I should perhaps digress a moment to remind the reader that on returning to Lingfield we had rejoined 2nd Infantry Brigade. A sort of 'holding' formation it generally contained units marking time '*en route* to' or 'just back from' somewhere. Most of us were in temporary occupation of some aged hutted camp about the Home Counties. Jack Fletcher had just taken the 2nd Battalion from Broadbridge Heath to Belfast. Robin Carnegie (later Lieutenant General Sir Robin Carnegie, KCB, OBE) had The Queens Own Hussars at Maresfield Camp (the old Intelligence Corps Centre) awaiting a move to BAOR; and Terence Holloway, an old Latimer chum, was based at Gravesend with 4th Royal Anglian. They were scheduled to relieve the Cheshires in Bahrain. The Commander was a signaller by breed – an unusual appointment even at that time. In his other hat he acted as Deputy Constable of Dover Castle. Against this background we headed for Otterburn in the first weeks of March. We should really have been all right bad-weather-wise. However, as we drove up we began to hit a heavy snowfall line just south of Newcastle. We just made Otterburn, as did the special train the following day. It then snowed hard for virtually the next forty-eight hours, by which time everything on the training area was either knee deep in snow or frozen solid. As fast as we cleared access to the ranges, and defrosted the range electrics, more snow fell that night and set us back to square one. After the fourth day, and we had nearly lost a couple of drummers in a snow drift during a fitness march, I began to feel that we were wasting our time. I even got Paul Gray, a keen military historian, to give the Battalion a lecture on the famous battle – I was that desperate. Up my sleeve I had an inter-company group defence exercise which I had written for Otterburn but was fully aware could be adapted with ease to other equally suitable ground. When on the fifth morning we were still to be denied any profitable training I rang the Brigadier and said that I was cutting my losses, reordering the special train and switching Ex DUFFERS DRIFT to the Pippingford Park Training Area. I hoped he would come and visit the exercise. This he did and was witness to a very useful three-sided company group exercise deploying basic defensive and patrolling skills, something we needed to adapt to soonest after our desert sojourn. To this day I don't believe he would have been as flexible as we had been. As it turned out, the ranges remained inoperable for up to a week after our departure. As it was, we did get in some profitable training. However, from that day on I began to feel that our new 'boss' was not quite on our infantry wavelength – nor I on his; all in very sharp contrast to what had been my recent Bahrain experience.

Over the 'Glorious First' we dug out the Bahrain customes and repeated a slightly modified Tattoo in the mess gardens for the benefit of our HMS *Excellent* and other guests, including the Colonel of the Regiment. Two days later we took over as the SPEARHEAD battalion and were promptly put to the turnout test. I can recall being awoken by a phone call around 11.45 pm from HQ STRATCO and, as dawn broke about 3.45 am, standing on the square beside my laden vehicle with all the Battalion to hand and set for despatch to RAF Lyneham. There was nothing to be seen of the adjudication team. About an hour later they appeared in some disarray. They had gone to Broadbridge Heath by mistake. There then followed a short notice summons to the Ministry. I was required to attend an urgent and top secret operational briefing. As I sat in the outer office awaiting my turn Richard Dawnay, CO 2nd Parachute Battalion, emerged. He and his battalion had recently been despatched to Anguilla, a small coral island dependency to the north of the Leeward Islands group, in the West Indies. There had been some unrest amongst the native population – around some

7,000 persons in all. Perhaps they were to be brought home and we were to replace them? I hoped not, since we did seem to have launched a 'sledgehammer to crack a nut' in that instance. I am happy to say that commonsense finally prevailed and they were replaced by a detachment of volunteer seconded British 'bobbies' – much more appropriate.

My briefing was concerned with the Island of Bermuda in the western Atlantic some 570 miles off the coast of North Carolina and with a total population of around 56,000. The economic structure of the island, some twenty square miles in all, was (and still is) largely based on tourism. The capital, Hamilton, with some 1,500 local residents, was the main tourist centre. It was here that Senior Naval Officer West Indies (SNOWI) then had his HQ and where the waterfront had been burnt down by rioting 'Black Power' youths the previous year at a cost of some £4 millions. The Police Commissioner had been sacked as a result of the troubles and the then Governor and Commander-in-Chief, Lord Martonmere, was concerned that there should be no repetition this year. Rumour had it that this was a distinct possibility and it would be damaging to the economy at the peak of the tourist season. Certainly the briefing was such as to suggest that a mini-explosion, akin to the recent Detroit riots, was festering. However, one felt that there was a need to maintain a sense of proportion. The population of Detroit was then some one million – that of Bermuda no more than 56,000. To combat any such civil disturbance the Governor had immediately to hand the small local police force and the Bermuda Regiment, a TA type unit around some 300 all ranks (and races) on paper. The latter's permanent staff were all provided by the Royal Anglians. Neither the police nor the Bermuda Regiment were IS trained or equipped. The Regiment could, however, be realistically deployed to 'shew the flag' and to guard VPs and KPs. My task was to assess how we might ensure that the waterfront was not burnt down again and to advise the Governor, SNOWI and London as to what steps should be taken to do this. The thought was that at least Bn HQ and a lead company should be deployed somewhere about the island as emergency back-up to the local security forces. It all had that Anguilla over reaction feel about it or as if we were clutching for straws in our search for a continuing overseas role (1968 was, in fact, the only year since the war in which no British soldier has been killed on active service).

The next day I flew with Mike Hare, OC 'A' Company, to Hamilton. Only Mike Reynolds knew what we were about. The remainder believed we were flying to Fredericton for me to write a major STRATCO exercise based about the Camp Gagetown training area I knew so well. This was the cover story and when we returned, heavily bronzed, with appropriate baggage labels the mission was accepted as such – by most at least. We travelled in civilian clothes as Mr Millman and Mr Hare and were put up in the Yacht Club. I don't think we fooled anybody in such a close-knit community. Within forty-eight hours we had done our 'recces', seen the Governor, Acting Police Commissioner and the CO Bermuda Regiment. SNOWI was, however, down visiting Anguilla and we could not depart until we had made our recommendations to him. So we had some four days idling our time away beside the Yacht Club pool and elsewhere. The Governor even took us in his motor yacht for a day trip round the island. Maintaining a sense of proportion, and bearing in mind the impact of a disciplined and impressive show of force by the Gurkha Defence Platoon riot squad during the Kuching riots, I was convinced that the solution to the problem lay in having to hand a similar such deterrent: in short, a highly trained and disciplined military riot squad detachment, skilled in the appropriate drills, and on short notice call to the Governor. The presumption being that at the first sign of trouble the police and Bermuda Regiment would be deployed, under emergency powers, to guard VPs and KPs, to secure the airport and to maintain a visible security force presence about Hamilton. On SNOWI's return we recommended to him that a sizeable Royal Marine detachment be maintained on his station and that, in case of alert, it be brought ashore covertly at St George's. We also added the rider that his HQ with his Lieutenant Colonel Military Assistant (MA) as the lead man, should form the basis of any emergency joint force HQ structure should the need arise. A longer term recommendation was that both the police and the Bermuda Regiment should receive instruction in anti-riot drills and that any necessary equipment should be purchased forthwith. I finished up in the CGS's Office, then that charming and distinguished gunner Sir George Baker, for the debriefing. Our recommendations were accepted, a sense of proportion was retained and the waterfront remained intact that year – and since. The following morning we drove up to the Stanford Training Area to join the rest of the Battalion. I was glad I had seen Bermuda, where so much history had been made between Churchill and Roosevelt in those early and difficult days of World War II. To this day a part of the island remains leased to the USA, for it was there that the famed 'Lease-Lend' policy was negotiated and our war fortunes took on a more favourable complexion.

Chapter 10

Command
The Bogside to Buckingham Palace

The first major civil rights march in Ulster was held in Londonderry on 5th October 1968. Thereafter the movement had mushroomed and there had been an ugly confrontation with the RUC in mid-April the following year. It had been centred about the Bogside and the neighbouring Creggan Estate – the Catholic 'strongholds' in that divided city. The next day the wave of disorder had spread to other parts of the Province. A bomb explosion at the Silent Valley reservoir in the Mourne Mountains cut water supplies to Belfast and County Down; an electricity pylon near Armagh was sabotaged; nine post offices, a bus station and other buildings were set on fire in Belfast, some by petrol bombs. These acts of sabotage and violence were never pinned on anyone. The most popular theory remains that a Paisleyite element was responsible, with the aim of drawing more troops into the Province to counter the mounting civil rights campaign. If they were IRA inspired then it is surprising that they made no positive move to support the subsequent 'Battle of the Bogside'. Whatever the case, the 1st Bn, The Prince of Wales's Own Regiment of Yorkshire, was despatched to Ulster on 23rd April 1969 to reinforce the garrison and to counter any further sabotage attempts. A few days later, whilst visiting HQ STRATCO, I was advised that if it became necessary to relieve them then 1st Queen's would be required to complete a four-month unaccompanied tour in Ulster from mid-August. It was considered at the time, and even later, that the need for such a relief 'was most unlikely'. However, during the period of training at Stanford we took the opportunity to brush up our ambush drills, cordon and search techniques and the like. In late July, following the Orange Day (12th July) distur-

121

Londonderry
(not to scale)

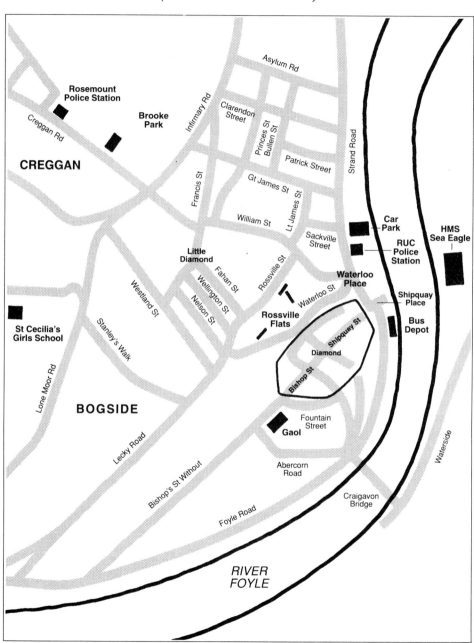

V. Londonderry, 1969.

The Derry Cohort

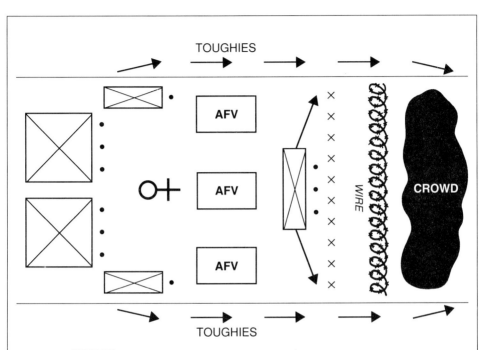

NOTES

1   Ideally a complete Coy Deployment.
2   Leading Pl shoulder to shoulder behind movable wire.
3   "Toughies" Snatch Squads on flanks.
4   Comd. in rear of AFVs.
5   Ideal AFV the SARACEN (FERRETS have been used).
6   Use of AFVs in back up provides:
    a. a deterrent effect.
    b. a tactical shield behind which troops can withdraw and
    regroup in the face of a hail of missiles and snipers.
    c. a means of producing a hasty road block in an emergency.
7*   Gas Cannon would replace central AFV.
8   Rear pls get to cover in doorways if sniper fire encountered.
9   Once under fire selected marksmen in Rear Pls get straight
    on to rooftops.

*An item of US eqpt and a proven winner

VI. The Derry Cohort, 1969.

bances and whilst the Battalion was on Block Leave, I received a further warning order. I was again advised that the move was 'unlikely'. By early August, however, a possibility had become a probability and within days orders were received for the relief to be conducted. There was still no hint of the dramatic circumstances into which we were soon to be pitched, or that we were about to enter another phase in that long and historic Anglo-Irish struggle.

The Battalion 'recce' party, having been recalled from leave, was despatched by civil air to Ulster under Mike Reynolds on 6th August. Their task was to tie up the detail in relation to the then proposed deployment plan. That was Bn HQ plus a company at RAF Ballykelly, another company at Lisanelly Camp at Omagh and the remainder at Magilligan Camp. The 'recce' was conducted under the auspices of HQ 39th Infantry Brigade now commanded by Brigadier Peter Hudson (later Lieutenant General Sir Peter Hudson, KCB, CBE, DL), and under whose command it was proposed we should come once in the Province. It had a decided training and administrative slant against the background to the task then still being painted. We were, for example, at this stage concerning ourselves with completing annual classification on Magilligan ranges, planning for an exercise in the Sperrins and preparing for the Army Boxing Championships. We had already 'thumped' 1st Staffords by ten bouts to one in the Open competition. Following the riots arising from the Apprentice Boys March in Londonderry on 12th August, the proposed deployment plan was modified in that the Omagh company was switched to Ballykelly. There was still no hint, even at this point, of what was to come, though I began to sense that action in aid to the civil power was an ever increasing possibility. On 14th August the Battalion advance party of some sixty all ranks, and headed by myself, flew into RAF Ballykelly. The troubles had begun some forty-eight hours before and by this time the Bogside was a barricaded fortress, the Rosemount police sub-station had been seized by the rioters and the police, heavily reinforced, had been defeated in the battle for the Rossville Street flats.

On arrival I was met by Bill Todd, the Prince of Wales's CO, and it soon became apparent that within hours he and his experienced battalion (they had Aden service to call on) would necessarily be deployed on the streets of Londonderry. In fact, by mid-afternoon they were on their way and their timely entry had almost certainly prevented a blood-bath developing in or adjacent to the Bogside. A 'peaceline' had quickly been established and the 'B' Specials, who it is said were about to assault the Bogside, were instructed to return to their Whitehall armoury. That evening Mike

Reynolds and I joined Bill Todd in the streets of the city. A heavy pall of smoke hung over the place, parts of William Street adjacent to the Bogside were still ablaze and there was a strong whiff of CS gas in the air. Below the Rossville Street flats the road was ankle deep in spent CS cartridges. Victoria Barracks, the local police HQ, resembled a casualty clearance station after a major disaster. The police had, in effect, been driven off the streets and all the public utilities had ceased to operate. A city of some 73,000 (or within the Londonderry Development Commission boundary) was in virtual limbo and law and order no longer pertained. A very basic appreciation there and then led me to the obvious conclusion that the relief would now clearly be conducted on the streets, and that ideally we should establish a main base nearer the city. This prompted short notice 'recces' of HMS *Sea Eagle*, HMS *Stalker* and the TA Centres at Caw Lane and Duncreggan. A revised reception and deployment plan was then finalised and I wrote the only for-real operation order I ever did in my service. Meanwhile, the main body who had set sail from Marchwood on 16th August aboard the LSL *Sir Tristram* (the sister ship to the *Sir Galahad* lost so tragically at Bluff Cove during the Falklands War) complete with all our equipment and vehicles, was diverted from Belfast to Londonderry. Certain signals were directed to the LSL to apprise those aboard of the changed situation and some necessary internal regrouping to meet my outline deployment plan. The main body arrived during the morning of 18th August and were quickly established in HMS *Sea Eagle* (now Ebrington Barracks). The next forty-eight hours were spent in preparing for the task, briefings and detailed 'recces' of the 'peaceline'.

Before we proceed further with the story, I believe it would be appropriate to acquaint the reader with a little background knowledge as to the City of Londonderry. The city lies astride the River Foyle in the NW corner of Ulster. Once a flourishing port, it had for years been a depressed area with unemployment running as high as eighteen per cent of the male working population. In recent years some new industry had been attracted to the neighbourhood, notably the Du Pont plant, but the textile trade remained then the community's lifeblood. The main part of the city, including the old walled centre of historic fame, lies west of the river and forms a small enclave jutting into Donegal and the Irish Republic. The Craigavon Bridge linked this part with the Waterside District (and the HMS *Sea Eagle* Compound) on the east bank. The ratio of the population was then some sixty per cent Catholic, forty per cent Protestant and the combined Bogside/Creggan Estate ('Free Derry') area housed some 25,000 persons in what had been described as a 'Catholic Ghetto'. The main Protestant equivalent was in the Fountain Street area, a semi-slum district adjacent to the East Wall, and the old city centre – The Diamond. There was another strong Protestant community in the Irish Street Estate in the Waterside. A ready demarcation line could in fact be determined between the two opposing factions, namely the line:

Bishops Street Without – The West Wall – Waterloo Place – William Street

The normal city police establishment had numbered some 103 all ranks, including Special Branch, Accident Prevention, Women Police, etc. In addition, the local 'B' Specials then mustered some 400 all ranks divided into two districts – City and Border. There had not been an RUC Station in the Bogside in twelve years and the force was entirely based about Victoria Barracks and the Rosemount sub-station. The 'B' Specials had their HQ in the Whitehall Armoury. Whisper had it that only mobile police patrols had entered the Bogside in recent years. On the evening Mike Reynolds and I had first gone into the city we had agreed to meet up with Bill Todd at Victoria Barracks. Picking our way through the chaos we had opened an office door to inquire where we might find the CO. Instead we had been confronted by a martially clad individual in Sam Browne and side hat who said something like, 'You've got the infantry and I've got the armoured cars – now we can sort them out.' I hastily withdrew and by the time I came to move in my Tactical HQ he had gone forever – thank heavens. His successor was Mike McAtamney, a tremendous help in those early days, and later the Deputy Chief Constable.

The relief of the Prince of Wales's was conducted in the streets beginning at 4.00 am on the morning of 20th August. At the time the 'peaceline' ran along the ready demarcation line described above except that, since the 'battle' had ended on the line of the Strand, the right flank rested there. As soon as was practicable we did a left form to secure William Street north to the Rosemount police sub-station. We also made a small tactical extension in the lower region of Bishops Street Without. To meet this requirement the initial Battalion deployment was as follows:

Tactical HQ - Victoria Barracks
'A' Company (+ Defence Platoon) - Strand Sector
'B' Company (+ 'X' Platoon) - Waterloo Place Sector
'Sp' Company (+ 'Y' Platoon) - Bishops Street Sector
Border Group - Recce Platoon + 17th/21st Lancer Troop
Forward Echelon - HMS *Sea Eagle*
Rear Echelon - Caw Camp TA Centre

The additions to companies had been initiated during the LSL voyage to take account of manning strengths and the 'peaceline' duty task. 'X' and 'Y' platoons had been raised from within Command and Administrative Companies (as they were then). They included such as the PT, PRI and Officers' and Sergeants' Mess staffs. The famous photograph of the soldier on the wall overlooking the Bogside, and which later became the Army Benevolent Fund (ABF) logo, was that of the Dining Hall NCO – a member of 'Y' platoon. This deployment allowed for no reserve and an early request was accordingly made for the provision of an additional rifle company. We had hoped to get one from the 4th Battalion, then the demonstration unit at the School of Infantry, Warminster. Instead we got 'C' Company, 1st Duke of Edinburgh's. They arrived by air on 26th August and remained with us thereafter. Hugh Canning and his excellent team could not have done us better. They were based on the Duncreggan TA Centre. Once established this 'peace-line' was manned twenty-four hours a day, for sixteen weeks in all weathers. The sectors each equated to a single company task and were manned on a roulement programme cycle of nine days 'in' and three days 'out'. When on the ground each company generally deployed three platoons manning barriers, check points and OPs, and the other on immediate reserve standby. The Queen's company 'out' remaining in battalion reserve in HMS *Sea Eagle* unless specifically deployed west of the river to meet some forecast contingency. Within days of being so established the Battalion came under command of HQ 24th Infantry Brigade. With Brigadier Peter Leng (later General Sir Peter Leng, KCB, MBE, MC) at their helm, they had on arrival taken command of all troops now deployed in the newly created Western Zone (west of the River Bann). I later learned, from a former Colonel of The Regiment, that some forty-nine years previous the forbears of the Battalion had stood in precisely the same streets in much the same deployment. They do say that history has a way of repeating itself and especially in the Emerald Isle.

On 14th August as the troops moved into the streets there had been a general sigh of relief within the City. To most it meant that bloodshed had been averted and peace, if only an uneasy one, had been restored. The soldiers were well received by both communities but it was soon evident that the 'honeymoon would be short-lived': for whilst the Bogsiders regarded the military as their 'saviours', the Protestants considered them the means by which the 'rebels' would be finally subdued. Against this background of hideous misconception it was painfully obvious that it would be difficult to please many much of the time. It did not take long for these misconceptions to be punctured and for realisation to hit home to the extremists in both factions. In the case of the Bogsiders the message was soon hoist in that, whilst the military were prepared to negotiate a return to normality, they were not, in the final event, prepared to dismiss the use of minimum force to achieve this end. Whilst this message was a necessary expedient its frankness inevitably produced a hostile reaction from the extreme elements (including the 'Foreign Legion', a collection of foreign students, anarchists and others) then still holding some considerable sway behind the barricades. Using the young hooligan element as their medium, they were quick to attempt to provoke the military whenever possible. On the other side of the city the failure to force entry into the Bogside had led to equal disillusionment and denigration from the more volatile so-called 'loyalists'. We were in their eyes reduced to the ludicrous level of 'Dad's Army'. To all intents and purposes 'a tale of two cities' pertained. Additionally we were faced with what amounted to a virtual collapse of the recognised civil administration and, initially at least, were seemingly responsible for everything from traffic control to conservancy. Pitched in at the deep end, we found ourselves rapidly involved in such diverse promotions as the restoration of the bus service to the Rosemount, the renewal of conservancy to the Creggan, the repair of GPO lines damaged in the Bogside and the return of football to Brandywell (the Derry City ground).

The task, however, seemingly, bore little relation to certain standard drills laid down in *'Keeping the Peace'*, Part 2, our IS 'bible'. The successor to *'Imperial Policing'*, it still contained, for example, the eventual 'one round at the man in the red hat' riot control sequence, something of a non-starter, or so I felt, in this setting. Some techniques had to be developed, and fast, whereby UK crowds could be dispersed with minimum force by soldiers acting as soldiers in a formed and disciplined body – something hitherto unknown in recent history within our green and pleasant land. Above all, was we stepped on to the streets, there were as yet no clear 'rules of engagement'. Later a 'Green Card' was issued to all soldiers laying down when a firearm might be used in self defence. In the interim I laid down my own rules well within the minimum force guidelines. A study of crowd and RUC tactics during the August riots helped us to develop a tactical concept around the following basic principles, namely:

a. Secure - The need to get up on the rooftops at the first smell of trouble.
b. Seal - The need to close one's barriers and seal off the crowd/riot from further reinforcement as soon as possible.

c. Separate - The need to move in quickly, in strength, and to get troops and wire between the rival factions physically to force them apart. (The 'Derry Cohort' (see diagram) became our tried and proven solution in this respect.)

With these principles as our guidelines the following standard drills were adopted:

a. An extensive and linked rooftop OP network was established throughout the city which could be full manned or reinforced in an emergency.
b. A linked barrier and wire 'Cut-Off' system was set up about the city with particular reference to known flashpoints and potential rioting lines of advance.
c. Immediate reserves were positioned adjacent to 'Black' areas and lived there ready to turn out at a moment's notice.
d. The barrier chain was permanently manned at all times to effect a rapid closure plan.
e. Strong reserves, including AFVs, were held west of the river to effect a prompt display of force.
f. The Recce platoon was deployed at the first hint of trouble as a mobile early warning screen and radio network.
g. A timely show of maximum force once trouble had begun.
h. Command and control was exercised by the CO or 2ic, in the streets, once more than one company had been committed.
j. Once trouble had started the RUC were withdrawn completely from the scene and future action became a purely military concern.

This concept abided by the theories that prevention is better than cure, minimum use of force equates to the maximum show of force, and that physical presence, in this setting, is better than mobility. In short, the writer considers that a sizable presence on the ground, immediate reserves at hand and the ability to react there and then prevented several disasters. It could be criticised as being too reminiscent of 'Cromwell and his Ironsides'. However, it paid off in that a tight grip was kept on things and, in consequence, a major degree of normality was restored to the city with the minimum of injury to civilian and soldier alike, minimal damage to property and the minimum physical display of troops on the streets. In meeting something new in the IS field, contrived protest supported by mass violence, I believe we achieved these aims.

We could clearly not have done so without the stirling efforts of the 'man on the street'. In this case the infantry private and junior NCO whose ready wit, patience, politeness and firmness earned him the respect of the vast majority of the thinking people in either community and brought a degree of sanity back into their lives. We needed to ensure that he was as best found, equipped and looked after as was humanly possible in the adverse circumstances that then pertained. Thanks to the kindness of Captain Tony Morton (later Admiral Sir Anthony Morton, GBE, KCB) we had early on established a firm base in HMS *Sea Eagle*. Besides providing accommodation for our reserve company and Forward Echelon, the excellent galley there helped feed the remainder on a container basis. We were, however, anxious, if possible, to get the soldiers seated for a proper meal in relaxed surrounds. We were thus fortunate to be able to enlist the services of HMS *Stalker*, a laid-up submarine depot ship, moored alongside not far distant from the city centre. A couple of companies could be fed in these civilised surroundings, and so we ran a roster related to the roulement programme whereby everybody had a share of '*Stalker*' feeding as well as a spell on containers. An emerging Gloria Hunniford conducted many of her earlier 'Ulster Calling' interviews in the 'luncheon club' setting of HMS *Stalker*. The '*Stalker*' example caught on and eventually produced the depot ship, HMS *Maidstone*, in which Admiral Sir Varyl Begg had once flown his flag on a visit to Murmansk, as the temporary home base for a couple of battalions on emergency duty in Belfast. Or as the locals used to say, 'What Derry does today, Belfast does tomorrow.' We had literally taken over from the Prince of Wales's in the streets. I slept my first three nights on a camp bed on the wall. Clearly one could not survive long on that basis and so we set to work to find everybody shelter adjacent to their task on the streets. The priorities were a roof overhead, toilets and a power plant for heating. With a great deal of help from locals, the staff of the 24th Infantry Brigade and the Property Services Agency (PSA), we eventually finished up with everybody reasonably housed on the job in accommodation ranging from Twynham huts to factories and the old jail. All were warm and dry, and all boasted proper lighting and toilet facilities. The soldiers themselves added the frills such as carpeting (no questions asked) and hired TV. However good the billets may have been, we were unlikely to survive long on the streets, and beside the barriers, unless there was both warmth and shelter. A combination of the brazier, the sentry box and the workman's hut helped to see us through the Irish autumn. Both the Church Army and NAAFI ran a mobile canteen service.

Troops manning the 'peaceline' had helmets and respirators to hand. During the recognised 'crisis' hours these were affixed to the person. The '1st XI' were always at duty during the 'crisis hours' (as the pubs tipped out in this 'drinkers' paradise' and on Saturday afternoons). All pickets and sentries mounted with a charged magazine, in pairs and with the weapon firmly secured to the person. 'Toughies' (or the Londonderry snatch squads) only were baton equipped. We dispensed with their shields since if carrying this they had no hand free with which to effect an arrest. We found the 'flak' vest an admirable piece of equipment. It looked fearsome and provided good body protection against the punch, brick, stone and slate missiles. It was worn by all sentries and pickets after dark. One thing we would have liked in those early days would have been a plastic helmet visor for facial protection. Most of our casualties received facial or eye injuries. CS gas was always 'on call' though none was used (not, contrary to popular belief, because the CO could never find his respirator). We dispensed with automatic weapons early on as a dangerous adjunct to our IS armoury and we likewise dropped the bayonet once we determined that the sight of it tended to incite hostility rather than deter it in this setting. The jersey heavy wool made its first appearance and was an absolute godsend. The combat suit, parka and poncho also proved their worth as the weather deteriorated. At this point in time the rubber bullet was not on issue.

The first phase of our time on the streets of Londonderry we christened the 'Negotiation Period'. This really began on 16th August when Bill Todd and I were invited by a Mr Green, a local trade unionist, to cross the barricades and meet the people of the Bogside. Near 'Free Derry' corner we encountered Bernadette Devlin. 'What are you doing here?' was her pert greeting. To which I promptly retorted, 'We might ask you the same question since you live in Cookstown.' We moved on and generally got a good reception. It was, of course, still the 'honeymoon' period. The area continued to reek of CS gas. From this small beginning a liaison was established with The Derry Citizens Defence Association (DCDA) and subsequently a meeting was arranged for 23rd August to discuss the removal of the barricades and the interim policing of 'Free Derry' pending publication of the Callaghan Reforms and the Hunt Report. The DCDA were apprised of the protective measures the military could guarantee along the 'peaceline' and the ultimate necessity to accept an interim police force. Negotiations along these lines, and headed by Brigadier Peter Leng, continued for some fifty hours, at all times of the day and night. Other useful contributions were made by John Hume, then only the

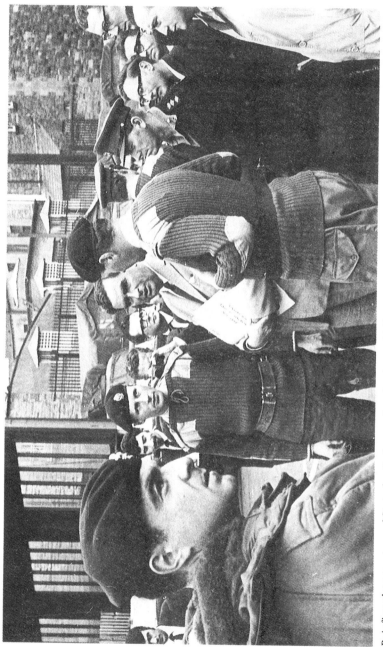

Briefing the secretary of State for Defence – Londonderry, 1969.

locally elected Stormont MP, and a Father Daly (later Bishop of Derry). Eventually the DCDA agreed to remove the barricades on 24th September. Throughout this period no troops entered 'Free Derry' and there was no hint or sign of any IRA interference in the affair – covert or otherwise. The DCDA were, however, under no misapprehension as to the outcome if the negotiations failed. Despite their ultimate agreement to the removal of the barricades, the DCDA remained temporarily reluctant to accept the interim policing proposals which centred about the introduction of a temporary military police post into the area. Here I should just digress to explain that the Hunt Commission had a remit to make proposals as to the future of the RUC. During their visit to Londonderry we had made some 'off the record' suggestions to them and especially to their police member, Mr Robert Mark, the former Chief Constable of Leicester (later Sir Robert Mark, GBE, QPM, Commissioner of The Metropolitan Police). From the grass root soundings we had made we recommended, in the short term, a detachment of loaned British 'bobbies' in blue uniforms and big helmets to man a Bogside police post. In the long term we advocated the establishment of a separate City force within the framework of the Northern Ireland Police Authority. In short, we were out to remove that 'dreaded green' tunic from the streets of Londonderry. Something registered since the blue tunic approach was followed up. Sadly, however, instead of producing new uniforms a batch of shoddy secondhand tunics with mixed buttons from various forces were despatched in lieu. Mike McAtamney and his lads had their hackles raised, and rightly, and that was the end of that – something so terribly simple which could have eased the tension if properly handled. Protestant leadership remained largely dormant during this negotiation phase. There was, though, continued criticism of the military for failing to occupy 'Free Derry' by force.

On the 11th September we had had a brief but ugly affray with the young hooligan element in Waterloo Place. It was our first experience of handling civil disturbance in a UK setting; very different from those rehearsal riots we had conducted under training at Lingfield and in Bahrain. To many of the younger soldiers it was a nasty shock though, once baptised, they rapidly grew from boys into men. On the evening of the very day the last Bogside barricade came down there occurred a short-lived but violent riot in the Diamond. Rival factions clashed initially in the Technical College grounds and, thereafter, splinter groups of supporters infiltrated the city centre. There followed a major confrontation which quickly developed into a brief episode of vicious sectarian close combat with petrol bombs and all. Forceful military action quickly separated the factions and casualties and damage were fortunately light. In this action the Battalion sustained three casualties all hit about the head or face by flying missiles. Following the riot immediate action was taken to impose semi-curfew conditions within the city and these measures, coupled with the arrival of long sought after reinforcements and the issue of powers of arrest to the military, brought the temperature down and prevented a replay. This period, or the 'Post Diamond Riot Aftermath', culminated in the acceptance by the DCDA of the interim policing proposals, the export of the 'Foreign Legion' from the Bogside and the abdication of the DCDA itself. The Brigade Provost Unit established the 'Bogside Police Post' at St Cecelia's School and were later administered by 2nd Grenadiers. Inkerman Company from 2nd Grenadiers were put under our operational control (a Line Regiment cannot have Guardsmen under command – we live and learn) as an additional reserve company and were permanently based on the Sailor's Rest Home west of the river. We were also given a troop of 60 Squadron, Royal Corps of Transport (RCT), with Saracen APCs, to assist with Craigavon Bridge guard duties. The vehicles also proved invaluable as an adjunct to the 'Derry Cohort'.

The publication of the Hunt Report, and news of the proposed Callaghan Reforms (he was then Home Secretary), prompted a more active display by the Protestant leadership. The 'Protestant Backlash', as we described this next phase, began with virulent denunciation of both sets of proposals in the local Press and elsewhere. In more extreme Protestant quarters, and notably the Fountain Street area, they were seen as nothing less than a sell-out to the Bogsiders. The military, as instruments of Westminster, were identified with this sell-out and there were threats of terrorist-type attacks on isolated pickets and sentries. Appropriate precautions were taken but thankfully, unlike in the Belfast Shankill Road, the extremists did not show their hand. Their less militant associates were, however, quick to stage a series of protests in the form of civil rights in reverse. The first of these, a sitdown on Craigavon Bridge on 18th October, proved largely a non-event in that, whilst the upper tier was temporarily blocked, traffic was quickly switched to the lower deck. On 25th October, after considerable publicity, a more determined effort was made on both tiers and hooligan elements, mingling with the demonstrators, were clearly intent on 'making a party', out of the afternoon's proceedings. After a brief fracas in the Diamond area, supporters of both factions rallied in strength about the city and only deliberate and forceful military action prevented a replay of the August riots. A couple of solders were injured during the afternoon and for the first time the 'Derry Cohort' tactic was employed. Using Inkerman Company personnel as our 'Toughies' (they were all over six feet tall), a number of arrests were made. A helicopter was also used, for the first time, as an airborne CP/OP. Precautions were taken the following Saturday to prevent a repetition of the trouble, and after some preliminary military manoeuvres near the bridge and about the Diamond, trouble was snuffed out before it had time to kindle into a bonfire. On 8th November a further preplanned show of force brought home to the organisers that this form of protest was no longer a worthwhile proposition. Apart from a short sharp affray on Hallowe'en Night, prompted by the hooligan element, we entered the final phase in comparative peace.

With the DCDA in suspended animation, the Civil Rights Movement watching and waiting on the progress or otherwise of reforms and the Protestants seemingly disillusioned, we had a largely uneventful last few weeks. Our main tasks during this period were to continue to keep the hooligans off the streets, to foster community relations and keep a watchful eye on parties of placard-carrying pickets who suddenly developed as a new sort of rash. Like the Windmill Theatre in World War II, 'we never closed', for at all hours of the day and night individuals and groups of people sought audience with the 'new administration'. Some were cranks, others mere troublemakers, but the majority were honest genuine folk anxious for an early return to normality. They ranged from such diverse organisations as the Strand Traders Association to the Creggan Tenants Association and the Waterside Young Unionists. As the months passed we increasingly involved both the RUC and Development Commission through the workings of a tripartite Security Committee. In this way it was possible to show to all that each and every decision was a joint one and that all agencies were combining in the common cause – a return to normality. Right up to the end of our tour we faced the odd deputation of protestation.

From the outset it was evident that in order to maintain the impartial image community relations could not, initially at least, get much beyond the open display of politeness and friendliness in the streets, a helping hand for the aged and an open heart for the children – a display designed to show that, whilst we had a difficult and tiresome job to do, we were still human. This simple approach produced its dividend in that before long kindness and friendship grew up beside the barriers, the girls (including the then youthful and lovely Dana, who was later to win the Eurovision Song Contest) came to the reserve company 'jump-ups' in the Foyle Club, the kids became regular camp followers and regular sports fixtures were in being. A limited start but certainly progress in the right direction. As tension eased, limited walking out was allowed and soldiers were permitted to accept invitations from across the barriers. We remained reluctant, however, to permit 'aimless' walking out in sensitive areas where a misplaced word, a drink too many, or a deliberate attempt to provoke or embarrass could have led to a fracas and an inevitable crack in the image. Finally in early November, encouraged by those above us, we found both the time and energy to tackle, in a small way, what we regarded as the city's chief problem – bored youth. All the troubles we had experienced had largely stemmed from this section of the community and each night they roamed the streets with little object in view. Their ages ranged from six to twenty-two and all, as the history of the August riots will relate, were potential petrol bomb or stone throwers. The young lady who lobbed a petrol bomb (fortunately it failed to ignite) on to my left boot toecap during the Diamond riot was aged no more than sixteen years. Investigation determined that some Youth Clubs did exist, that they generally lacked instructors, had lost their grip in recent years and never offered any facilities at weekends. We accordingly set about the task as follows:

a. Loaned instructors and equipment to established clubs (the Boxing Team who had had to be withdrawn from the Army Open Championships were particularly popular).
b. Established the 'Redcap' Club alongside the Bogside police post.
c. Set up the 'Braganza' Sports Club in HMS *Sea Eagle*.

The 'Redcap' Club opened twice weekly and the 'Braganza' Club sponsored a variety of events midweek, but was primarily concerned with emptying the streets on Sunday afternoons. The instructors were all found on a voluntary basis from within the Battalion group. The response was both gratifying and terrifying since, within a month, the 'Redcap' Club was playing to regular packed houses of 180 (others had to be turned away on a ticket basis till next time) and the Sunday turnout at HMS *Sea Eagle* had topped the 450 mark. Nobody would suggest that we had found the answer to the problem, were providing the challenge necessary to attract the older boy or that we had solved the sectarian issue. We have no doubt, however, that this venture achieved the following limited aims we set it, namely:

a. It brought home to the Development Commission the crying need for a properly sponsored Youth Organisation in the city.

b. It awakened Church leaders, on either side of the divide, to the fact that 'silence on the Sabbath' was an archaic approach to life where the modern young Irish were concerned.

c. It achieved a limited gathering of mixed sectarian youth without discord, something regarded as near impossible at the time. Yet we had no idea who was 'left' or 'right' foot.

d. It kept a lot of would-be miscreants off the streets and did marvels for the Army's image amongst the young.

e. It opened up to the RUC, who were encouraged to assist at the 'Redcap' Club, a chance to display their new image amongst the younger section of the community.

We should have liked to have done more, but tied to the streets as we were, and as a single battalion group, there was a limit to what we could do. We achieved something useful I have no doubt, even if we did but scrape the surface of a major Ulster problem. Just before Christmas and our departure we managed to produce 'Santa Claus' in Shipquay Street by helicopter and on a 'snow covered' Ferret scout car about the Bogside. Both these simple ventures were worth the effort, if only to witness the joy they brought to the kids. You can, however, never please all and the writer was confronted by a small girl in the Diamond who said, 'It's not 'Santa Claus' – it's only a soldier dressed up.' Our final gesture in this field was to present both Churches with a sizable cheque to back seasonal good cheer for the old people and the children, the two sections of the community we judged likely to have the leanest Christmas as a result of the troubles. The donations were made up from voluntary contributions from the soldiers as a means of saying 'thank you' to the many persons, of either sect, who in all weathers, and night after night, had out of their own pockets had the kindness to provide hot drinks and snacks for the sentries and pickets about the city.

We had plenty of visitors in those early days. Jim Callaghan (later Lord Callaghan) came twice and Dennis Healey and Roy Hattersley also appeared. Service-wise twenty-six star rating visits were conducted in the first fifty-two days. After that the tempo eased somewhat. CGS, last seen after Bermuda, had Roly Guy in tow as his MA. This was just before he took command of 1st Royal Green Jackets in West Belfast and earned an excellent DSO). Quite astonishingly the only person who did not visit us was Commander 2nd Infantry Brigade. We had been 'borrowed' from his formation. The Battalion never quite forgave him. Whilst these visits may have put something of a strain on the management, they were appreciated by the rank and file, for tucked away as we were on our own in London-derry it helped to dispel any notion that we were the 'Forgotten Army'. The media were also very much in evidence. In the search for news and a story (plus those 'action' pictures) it was perhaps a pity that they took too many interviews from 'Indians' and presented them as 'Chiefs'. Likewise in a 'rent a crowd' atmosphere it was only too easy to provoke a minor affray for camera purposes. Certainly some of the foreign pressmen were guilty in this respect. I believe we would have done better in those early days to have played the whole thing down media-wise. As it was we encouraged the DCDA and others to believe they were 'big fish' rather than 'small fry', an error of judgement from which we have suffered ever since in media cover of the Ulster troubles. Every little incident is still seemingly newsworthy in the nations parlours.

Despite having done thirteen of the past twenty-four months on unac-companied tours, and under a bachelor CO (a rarity in itself), there had been no major welfare problems. We stuck by some leave guarantees, notably in respect of childbirth, and the speed of welfare reaction was such that no problem developed into a drama. Anne Reynolds (it was 'all good practice' so she said) and the Families Officer had kept the wives and children happy. The '*Braganza*' newsletter was resurrected for the families at home and, of course, it helped that public telephones were available for the frequent call home. Our four-month contract was hon-oured and the soldiers appreciated that they had a worthwhile job to do. Likewise, they had been promised better living conditions and saw the day-to-day improvements going on before their eyes. HMS *Sea Eagle* had proved an admirable firm base and we were perhaps guilty of hastening its eventual demise, for later it became Ebrington Barracks, the home of the resident Londonderry battalion. The head *Sea Eagle* Wren, Mary Ames, and later Deputy Director WRNS, remains a firm friend to this day. Throughout I had been well supported by Mr Lewis, the new RSM. Once a Welsh Guards drummer, he had later transferred to the Royal Sussex. A very smart little man, he came very much into his own during our subse-quent Public Duties stint. One night he and I would visit all the pickets and sentries. The next Mike Reynolds and the Provost Sergeant would do likewise. It was, however, one morning in early December when Mr Lewis and I were walking up Shipquay Street that I spotted the Green Mini coming towards us with a grey-haired lady (with a slight blue rinse tint) at the wheel. I could have sworn it was Mother. Some fifteen minutes later we encountered the same car and driver coming the other way up Fountain Street. I could once again have sworn it was the 'old lady'. I had never seen the car before in all my time on the streets of the city and I never saw it again. It may all have been just auto-suggestion. I have since sometimes wondered as mother had a green Mini and always sported a blue rinse tint.

At the outset of the tour we had floundered in a totally new situation without very clear political, military and social objectives. Mistakes were made but fortunately we were able to benefit from these without disaster. By the time we came to hand over to the Gloucesters (or the 'Glooms' as they are sometimes known), a very considerable degree of normality pertained. The RUC were even back in the Bogside on shared foot patrols with the RMP. The Development Commission was back in full business. The Border Group had from the outset assumed responsibility for the road block/check point programme in the border enclave. They had also regularly patrolled the otherwise unguarded western Creggen perimeter. They were also very much our 'eyes and ears' from the intelligence angle. Like me they had been surprised that, at the height of the August riots, the Irish Army (or some renegade element of it) had not attempted to nip out the enclave by closing up to the Foyle and 'saving' the Bogside. This would have suited our Bernadette Devlin and there would have been little to stop them other than the 'B' Specials. I must also repeat here that as we came to leave there was simply no evidence that the IRA were yet exploiting the situation or were about to attempt to. Frankly I believe they had been completely taken by surprise with the course and speed of events that succeeded the ill-fated Apprentice Boys March. When, however, they did begin to react it was disappointing that Special Branch intelligence was so pitiful that most of the internment arrests were of 'yesterday's men'. I did not return to Londonderry till 1979 in my then capacity as Divisional Brigadier, The Queen's Division. From then, until I gave up as Colonel of The Queen's Regiment at the end of 1988, I was a frequent visitor. Each time I left I could never resist asking myself the question, 'What went wrong?' It was always a problem that only the politicians could solve. Having said that, I believe we may just have put on the military kid gloves a little too early, have seriously damaged our 'Hearts and Minds' image with misguided internment arrests and have permitted a too rapid an IRA 'build-up' through lack of adequate intelligence. It is always easy to be wise in hindsight. However, it is always sad to see your battalion's good work all come to nothing.

We departed the way most of us had come. By LSL, this time it had been *Engadine*, back to Marchwood and a welter of pleasing plaudits as to the Battalion's performance. What, however, had been the greatest compliment was the large number of folk who came down to the dockside to wave us away. They came from both sections of the community. As the ship eased its way down the Foyle to the sea the Drums and Fifes played the 'Londonderry Air'. One could not fail to be moved by the occasion. Back at Lingfield it was confirmed that we were down to do a six weeks' spell of Public Duties beginning in early March. We also learned that, on handover of command later in the year, I was to go to the Staff College as a DS. However, Mike Reynolds was not to be my successor (as the Divisional Brigadier had suggested during his visit to Londonderry – he did come) but Tony Pielow, the CO (Designate) of the 4th Battalion. The sad fact being they were to be disbanded and their posting to Berlin would now be taken by 1st Queen's. To avoid another Bahrain type saga it was agreed that Tony should take the Battalion to Berlin from day one and that I should go to Camberley early. This sound arrangement suited all parties except poor Mike. We eventually got him a Grade I Staff appointment (Lt Col) at HQ Allied Forces Central Europe (AFCENT) and he went on from there to command successfully the 2nd Battalion in BAOR in the mechanised role. He never looked back thereafter. We also discovered that the Brigade Commander was about to change. A born and bred infantryman was soon to take his place. To set things in motion for Public Duties I obtained, through contacts in HQ London District, the early loan of an Irish Guards (or 'Micks' as they are sometimes known) Drill Sergeant. He was a splendid fellow and knew exactly how to get the lads to respond. This was not before, at my behest, he had 'sharpened up' the Officers a couple of times on the square; for it has always been my experience that the officers personal drill is generally in need of more care and attention than the soldiers. Especially when it comes to sword drill (as it did in this instance) and where I was keen to overcome any tendency towards 'toasting fork' type carriage. Only one rather stuffy field officer had taken exception. We promptly dropped him from any further thought. Meanwhile, the ever-wily Duggie Fraser had discovered, and got his hands on, the pool holding of a proposed Atholl Grey overcoat awaiting troop trials. This would ensure that we did not look like the poor relations outside Buckingham Palace. The only problem was that, in selecting our guards, we had to find the men to fit the greatcoats rather than the other way about. We got round this one by allotting the smaller sizes to the Bank of England and Tower of London guards. They did not mount in broad daylight in the Palace forecourt in full public view. We also picked up a useful tip off the 'Rockapes' (or the RAF Regiment in tri-service slang) and that was to ensure that each soldier had a second chinstrap, for the wind in the forecourt is prone to gusting and flat dress hats, unlike bearskins, had been known to 'take off' at unwanted moments. Once we had done all this we produced three guard detachments based about 'A', 'B' and 'Sp' companies. We then rehearsed them in the mounting and dismounting procedures on a 'forecourt' and 'Friary Court' pair of sets we had created on the Lingfield Square. We did likewise with the 'babes' who were to carry out the 'Ceremony of The Keys' at the Tower.

In the week prior to the assumption of duties we took all the 'key' personnel up to London for two days to 'walk the course' as understudies. We were to share duties with the 1st Irish Guards and our recent Sharjah and Londonderry associates, 2nd Grenadiers. The latter had been pitched into the streets of Ulster straight off Public Duties and rather understandably it had shown. However, it seems we never learn since we did much the same at the time of the Falklands. Whilst they were London based, we, except for the Band and Corps of Drums, were required to motor up from Lingfield and change in Wellington Barracks. Fortunately there were no breakdowns or major traffic 'snarl-ups' during those six weeks. The Band and Drums were housed throughout in Chelsea Barracks. On our first morning, a Sunday, I invited the Colonel of The Regiment to attend the mounting. He was slightly taken aback to see the Drum Major resplendent in his new 'State Helmet' (a recently purchased pickelhaube and the forerunner of a subsequent purchase for all regimental bandsmen and drummers) and was somewhat concerned as to what Her Majesty's reaction might be if she spotted it from a Palace window. I hastened to explain that Line Regiments were generally only invited to assist with Public Duties when the Monarch was away on tour or on some long holiday break at Balmoral, Sandringham and so on. Suffice it to say that the soldiers enjoyed it. They loved showing themselves off, knew they looked good in their smart new overcoats and they gave it everything they had. They also felt it was a just reward for that difficult Londonderry tour they had just so successfully completed. It is, of course, one thing to do duty over a six-week period, quite another to do a two-year stint as a Public Duties Battalion. The Battalion drew considerable praise from a discerning section of the public and none more so than the Drum Major who regularly threw his mace in the Mall; a sight rarely seen since the Guards don't do it – perhaps they are frightened of dropping it. The irritating quirk was that only Guards bands were permitted to play in the Palace forecourt during the mounting ceremony. Ours had to remain silent. They, however, made up for it as they and the Corps of Drums headed the St James's Palace guard down the Mall to that then splendid new Regimental

March – 'Soldiers of The Queen'. The Bank guard (now no longer) mounted at Wellington Barracks and were then taken by coach to duty. In the old days, when I was at the City of London School, they used to march to and from the Bank via the Embankment. The Tower guard were also coached to duty. However, each evening around 10.00 pm, they conducted the short 'Ceremony of The Keys' in concert with the Yeoman Warders. Only the Buckingham Palace and St James's Palace guards mounted ceremoniously in full public view. It was my privilege to be permitted to invite a number of regimental and personal guests to view the ceremony from within the forecourt before lunching in the St James's Palace Mess. The guard commander hosted such occasions and had really only one decision to make thereafter – the choice of wine for dinner. The Bank guard commander received a free bottle of wine with his dinner and the Tower guard commander was allowed to invite a dinner guest. We left a suitably engraved silver wine cooler as a mark of appreciation to the St James's Palace Mess.

Once Public Duties were over, we settled back at Lingfield to await the arrival of some seventeen officers and 250 soldiers from the 4th Battalion. 'C' Company was reactivated and John Pollard, an old Middlesex chum whom I had known since my first Ulster tour, was their leader. The remainder, mainly specialists, were slotted into the support platoons. The officers were spread about the battalion. There was, however, one problem and that concerned both the Officers' and Sergeants' Messes. Since the Battalion would shortly be moving to Berlin, the families of the newly joined Officers and SNCOs remained in quarters at Warminster. Out of hours both messes were swamped, therefore, with 'weekly boarders' and the 1st Queen's 'singletons' felt 'unwelcome' in the new surrounds. This produced some friction and Mr Lewis and I took early and sharp steps to stamp it out. Sadly, however, as my time drew near to depart I began to appreciate that it was not the same battalion that had supported me so nobly through those difficult days in both Bahrain and the Bogside. It was clearly time for me to move on. I know that I was criticised by some for being 'too close to my Battalion'. During the varied and sometimes exacting tours we had conducted together, I don't believe we would have achieved so much had I not been seen to be a thoroughly approachable, strict but honest broker who enjoyed a beer and a joke with all. I am sure it was this relationship that was the strength of the Battalion and the one that earned me the OBE, on their behalf, in the Birthday Honours List, one of the first awards made in respect of the Ulster troubles. The great Monty had been right. Regimental or Battalion command, to my mind, remains the most satisfying level of command in Service life – and always will. For you are still in real touch with the Army's 'shop floor' – the soldiers. After handover I avoided any ritualistic-like send-off. It simply wasn't my style. Next day I just drove across to Camberley in my new Mini 1275GT followed by a Pickford's van with all my furniture and so on. For due to the kindness of Rowley Mans, then Deputy Commander Aldershot District, I had been allotted an unfurnished quarter – No 9 Everest Road. The day after Lance Corporal Brill, as he then was, came across to put up the wall cupboard, fix up some shelves and to adjust any electrical fittings. We had a beer before he departed and, as has always been traditional in the Regiment, I stayed away from the 1st Battalion during my successor's tenure. The Uganda Asians were the next and final occupants of Hobbs Barracks. It is now part of an industrial estate. The quarters were later sold on the civilian housing market.

Chapter 11

A Staff College Sequence Camberley to Khartoum

I was delighted to be going to be a DS at Camberley. I was also very happy to be afforded something of a break after what had been an enjoyable but exacting command. They, in fact, let me have some three weeks of complete peace in which to settle in to No 9 Everest Road. This gave me a chance to tackle the garden which had developed into something of a wilderness with the grass knee high. Not before I had purchased a mower and some garden tools, for being 'unfurnished' these were not provided. The house had in fact been unoccupied for some time since Everest Road was generally used by DS families as transit accommodation as they awaited a 'posh' house up in the College grounds. I took to the Commandant from the moment I met him. Probably the most senior 'singleton' in the Army at the time, he loved golf and fast cars. As sharp as they come, he was highly erudite and possessed a ready wit. In short, Major General Allan Taylor (later Lieutenant General Sir Allan Taylor, KBE, MC) was what both DS and students alike always believed the Commandant should be – an able and positive character. Though officially down to replace David O'Morchoe (he was to be promoted to Colonel GS of 'A' Division), I was, in fact, to take the place of Tony Ricketts on the Command and Training Team. He was off to command a sapper regiment. The General explained to me that the aim was now to have up to six DS, who had commanded, on the College establishment. David had been one of the couple presently on strength. The other, Paul Travers (later General Sir Paul Travers, KCB) was also off soon to become Colonel AQ of 1st Division in BAOR. Though this would leave me on my own there were another five ex-COs in the pipeline. In any event he felt sure that I, too,

The Sudan

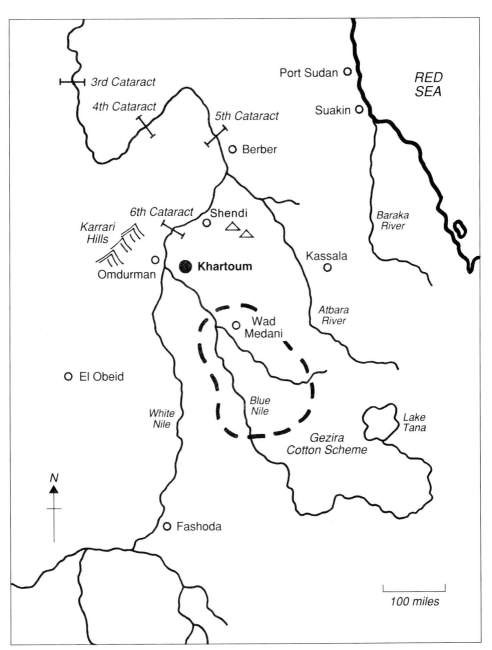

VII. Northern Sudan, 1972–1973

would be picked up early for the 'Blue' List. Here I did have to point out that I had never had an 'Outstanding' (or 'O') confidential report in my life and felt sure I would do a full two-years. As it turned out, the others did not come until a good year later. The first was Mike Gray (later Lieutenant General Sir Michael Gray, KCB, OBE) and we had known each other well in those early Ulster days. He had then been commanding the 1st Parachute Battalion in Belfast. At the first Study Period held there by General Sir Ian Freeland he had been required to talk on 'Public Relations' whilst I covered 'Community Relations'. He was followed quickly by Derek Boorman (later Lieutenant General Sir Derek Boorman, KCB), John Chapple (later Field Marshal Sir John Chapple, GCB, GBE), Mike Swindells (later Major General) and my old Borneo chum from the SAS – Johnny Watts. They were all three to four years my junior in age and, led by Mike Gray, christened me 'Uncle'. We all came up together in the same list for promotion to full Colonel in mid-1972. Or put another way, they had perhaps benefited more than my age group when the promotion 'goal posts' for Lieutenant Colonel had been adjusted rather more generously in their favour. This is not to say that I would ever have kept pace with them. I did just feel though that, thereafter, the 'playing field' was not quite as level as it might have been where I was standing. However, that's life and I never let it spoil my DS days at Camberley. They were happy and fruitful times and I enjoyed the excellent company of those about me. Many remain very good friends to this day.

I next learned that in September, and before I got into the DS teaching cycle, I was to attend a Senior Management Course at a well-known Management Consultant's in nearby Slough. It appeared that RMCS Shrivenham were particularly concerned at the time that, we in the Army, might be missing out on something associated with the then very fashionable management training cult. I believe General Allan had yet to be convinced. I certainly had some misgivings and needed no reminder that the Sandhurst motto remained 'Serve to Lead' not 'Serve to Manage'. It was further thought somebody with recent command experience was the fellow to send. I later called on the Command and Training team and swapped a few 'war stories' with my old friend Peter Welsh, the team leader. It was then that Tony Ricketts first acquainted me with Ex BLUE LAMP. This was an aid to the civil power exercise he was currently preparing for the Post-Staff Course (or Fifth Term). It was being written at the request of the Home Office and was to be a joint affair with the Bramshill Police College, much against the wishes of their then Commandant – John Alderson of subsequent 'community policing' fame.

However, after events the previous year in Grosvenor Square and elsewhere, it was thought high time that the Police College addressed the subject. I expressed very considerable interest and learned that, on the actual day, I would be the DS sponsor. In the interim I was invited to address the Bramshill Senior Command Course on my Londonderry experiences.

I was called in to understudy Peter Welsh during the final week of the Third or 'Overseas' Term and just before the summer college break. It enabled me to get the syndicate feel from the DS angle and I sensed that, as a former CO, I would find it not too difficult to say, when necessary, something like, 'You're talking nonsense lad – I've actually done it.' Then came the US Army visit. This was to Graffenwohr, a major US Army training area, close to the Czech border. There followed an amazing forty-eight hour 'fantasia' of modern military technology coupled with a display of awesome firepower. What was, however, far less impressive was the state of training and morale of those on view. The former, at squad or platoon level, would barely have matched that at an average school CCF Field Day. The latter was evident each evening as we walked from our barrack block accommodation to the Officers' Club. *En route* we stepped round, or over, individuals and groups clearly high on drugs, drink or you name it. US fortunes in the Vietnam war were at low ebb at the time. If this was a sample of what was fighting the Viet Cong then no wonder. On our return the College dispersed for the four-week summer holidays. I went down to Cornwall and discovered a sanctuary I have visited every year since – the Meudon Hotel near Mawnan Smith. Situated between the mouth of the Fal and the Helford River, it is, and remains, the near perfect setting for a truly 'switch-off' break.

After three glorious and very restful weeks I returned to Camberley to prepare for the course at Slough. Those attending would, I suppose, these days be described as 'Yuppies'. There were certainly all thrusting young executives hoping for subsequent stardom in various sections of commerce and industry. They drove executive range company cars and had expense accounts which covered their mid-week residence in Maidenhead's better hotels. Those controlling the Service purse strings demanded that I drove in and out daily. We were clearly on rather different wavelengths and this did not take long to manifest itself. For an early lecture was concerned with 'Industrial Relations' (then at very low ebb about the country) and, after a brief introduction, the speaker invited his audience to raise their hands if 'they had not had a strike in the past six months'. I shot up my hand only to find that I was in splendid isolation.

The lecturer was 'not amused', though I am happy to say that most of the 'Yuppies' were. Soon after we began an examination of the behavioural science approach to the technique of staff selection. At that time it was highly fashionable in the USA. From the outset I had some doubts about the true value of this proforma style selection process and reckoned it a very poor substitute for the board or panel approach. My misgivings were increased when I was handed a form to complete in no more than twenty minutes. It contained twenty somewhat strange (or plain odd) questions on the lines of that below:

Ques 1 – What would you rather have been:
A General   ☐
A Bishop   ☐
Don't know   ☐

One was required to tick (✓) one's answer in the box provided and was discouraged in the 'Notes' from making too many 'Don't know' entries. In short, you were encouraged to be positive. The second question, I recall, concerned your relations with your father, and, in particular, whether you had 'ever hated him'. I doubt very much if I would have chosen to select my company commanders by such methods – let alone my lance corporals. Not too surprisingly I came out in the selection ratings as a near 'psychopath' and a virtual cross between Hitler and Richard III.

There then followed a major business 'war game' in which, by syndicates, we were all allocated parts to play in some crisis management type setting. In my group I was the 'personnel manager' of a north country foundry which, following recent heavy investment in new plant, now had a 'new deal' to put across to its some 180 or so workers. There was also a need to refurbish the canteen. I suggested to the 'managing director' (being played by a young senior executive in a big biscuit firm) that the following morning he should get down on the shop floor and put across the 'new deal' personally to his employees. I also said that I felt that he and I should set a good self-help volunteer example by beginning the painting of the canteen that coming weekend. He could call for staff volunteers once he had finished putting the 'new deal' across. Having said my piece there was a pause and I thought that at any moment he and the DS were about to 'throw wobblers'. The 'managing director' had paled visibly. The DS accused me of 'throwing the welfare book at him'. At that point I simply had to explain that I had addressed my battalion regularly when in command so as to ensure that they were always in the overall picture. I likewise pointed out that when we had had to refurbish the PRI Canteen at Lingfield Les Wilson and I had been among the first unit self-help volunteers. We had certainly lost no face in so doing. All this really did convince me that we were living in different worlds. It also, to my mind, highlighted what was then so wrong with industrial relations. Or, in short, that there was far too little regular contact and chat between management and labour. The strength of any unit lies in its Sergeants' Mess, or the 'engine room', as we have come to term it. It's this supervisory level which has the close feel of the 'grass roots' and which any CO ignores at his peril. At the time I attended the course we had seemingly yet no similar working relationship between the shop floor, the foremen or supervisory element and the senior management. Cries like 'Management by Objectives (Mbo)' and the 'mumbo jumbo' associated with the behavioural sciences were, in my humble view, never going to produce the practical answer – good communication between all levels in business and commerce. I came back and wrote a report which the Commandant seemed to enjoy. With it I produced a DS guide to current management parlance (with tongue firmly glued to cheek). RMCS Shrivenham, always a bit short on humour, didn't quite appreciate it.

I then became a proper partner in the Command and Training Team – initially Peter Welsh and myself. On his departure to command 2nd Royal Green Jackets they drafted in Patrick Palmer (later General Sir Patrick Palmer, KCB) as his replacement. Within months the Argylls were resurrected and he was off to command. Johnny Watts then came in from 22nd SAS and the partnership developed which later became known throughout the College as 'The Morecambe and Wise Show'. My relief was Dick Vincent (later Field Marshal Sir Richard Vincent, GCB, GBE, DSO) straight from the streets of Belfast with a richly deserved DSO. The team was the smallest in the college, and besides producing the material to support instruction in leadership and training, was specifically responsible for the conduct of the then Post-Staff Course (of Fifth Term). We masterminded Training Exercises 1 to 3: in turn, the production by student sub-syndicates of a study period, a TEWT and a two-sided BAOR type exercise at brigade level. We invited such as General Sir Anthony Farrar-Hockley to support the leadership discussions. To back the general tone and tenor of the Post-Staff Course, we filled the Alanbrooke Hall with a succession of speakers ranging from leading trade unionists, such as Vic Feather (later Lord Feather), to the President of the National Union of Students (then Jack Straw and now the Labour front bench spokesman on the Environment). We did all this and taught as well. Out of the ten terms I spanned at Camberley I taught for eight of these. Not surprisingly, the only couple I didn't perform in were the Fourth, or 'Nuclear Warfare' Terms, in either year. They were no doubt reckoned to be slightly above the head of one with such an 'old colonial' image. The marking could really be a strain and especially during the First and Second terms. A pile of ten Operation Orders for correction, and which included at least one offering from an overseas student, could prove a long and painstaking exercise. It could take, more or less, a whole weekend to complete if one was to do real justice to the students work. I was always at particular pains to ensure that our overseas friends were made to feel that one had properly assessed their efforts. This could prove excruciatingly tedious and the sight of a syndicate student, striding towards the golf course while you toiled, never helped. I know that when Johnny Watts came to join me he found this aspect of Camberley life the most difficult to adjust to after command. I had been through the same experience so I didn't offer him much sympathy. Early on I picked up a very useful tip in the battle of wits 'twixt the DS and students. I found it particularly useful during the first week of any new term with a fresh syndicate. This was to open the day's proceedings with some 'Golden Shot' questions, such as, 'Tim, the mornings news headlines, please?' or 'David, the test score, please?' and 'John, what is the name of the new College Librarian?' Pretty simple stuff but it certainly achieved the aim. You were leading 'fifteen-love' at the start of the day. One student later admitted to me that when his bedside radio batteries went flat he had, one freezing February morning, to go down to the garage in his dressing gown to listen to the early news on his car radio.

I particularly enjoyed the TEWTs out in the local countryside and especially those along the Thames. Johnny and I used such occasions to conduct a little barter, or 'horse trading', with our Logistic Corps DS compatriots. We added a little tactical 'flesh' to their DS 'Pink' notes in exchange for the 'magic' associated with some of the calculations arrived at in their dumping and outloading programmes. It was a fair swop and it certainly eased us through some of the more difficult logistical studies and discussion periods. They were happy times and particularly during high summer. Memories abound and there were gaffs and laughs galore. Amongst the best was during a river crossing TEWT at Goring. The DS had assembled his syndicate at Stand 2 for the discussion of Problem 2. Turning to an Australian student, whose sub-syndicate included a WRAC officer, he said, 'Digger, can I please have your night deep penetration

patrol programme, please?' to which the unabashed Wallaby dryly replied, 'Certainly, Sir, Sarah, our tame Matilda will give you our agreed
solution.' Without blinking an eyelid the young lady stepped forward and
began, 'I'll start with the listening patrols.' The highlight of the course,
however, remained the Battlefield (or 'Bottlefield') tour. I missed the
1971 one to re-write Ex BLUE LAMP but more of that later. The next
year, however, Johnny Watts and I were invited to join a party being
organised by Ronnie Laughton, the Naval DS, to sail across to Deauville.
The yachting fraternity, both DS and students, generally followed this
practice. Ronnie, a cheery salt, described our craft as a 'small naval
tugboat' and said that the student crew he had assembled would do all the
work and we DS would simply enjoy a gentle cross-channel cruise with
plenty of good cheer to hand. To our horror we discovered too late that we
were to conduct the crossing in one of the tiny tugs that normally ply
regularly across Portsmouth harbour 'twixt those well known 'stone frig-
ates' – HMS *Dolphin* and HMS *Vernon*. It was by then impossible to retreat and so we duly boarded the craft to be greeted by our tame
'Hornblower' with a dry martini in either hand. We set sail almost immediately. It was a heavenly June day and the Channel was like a millpond.
However, the tug could not exceed eight knots even flat out. So some nine
hours later, very tanned and with several (and more) dry martinis taken,
we made Le Havre. Next morning we moved along to Deauville. A week
later we set sail for Pompey. The weather forecast had not been encouraging and there was clearly no millpond awaiting us. Fourteen very long
hours later, near green with '*mal de mer*', soaked to the skin, hungry and
wondering how we had survived that severe buffeting as we had crossed
the Channel's main shipping lanes, we crept into Portsmouth harbour. A
year later I visited the Staff College on leave from Khartoum and shortly
after the Battlefield Tour. Over coffee in the DS Ante-Room I asked
'Hornblower' if he had sailed again across to Deauville. His reply was
brief and to the point; 'Not bloody likely.' It seems we all learn by
experience.

   The Americans, Australians, Canadians, French and Germans all field
DS at Camberley. The Australian, Laurie O'Donnell (later Lieutenant
General and Australian CGS) became a particular friend. I was even
invited to be godfather to his lovely young daughter. He had commanded
in Vietnam and hadn't gone much on either the US strategy or tactics. I
sensed also that, like most Australian servicemen, who had answered our
call for assistance in Borneo, he had been a little disappointed when we
had not responded with some nominal contribution in Vietnam. Rather

naturally he ran the College cricket. Having made a good score in the DS versus students game, and which we won for the first time in years, I was appointed to take over the Owls XI. In our second season we had a new Commandant. Major General Pat Howard-Dobson (later General Sir Patrick Howard-Dobson, GCB) was a keen cricketer of some repute. An enthusiastic all rounder, he also liked to win. Suffice it to say that following the 1972 DS versus students match the following entry appeared in a version of 'Snakes and Ladders' in that year's copy of the College magazine, *Owl Pie*:

'Square 16.   Run-out Commandant at cricket. Sent to Afghan Staff College. Out of game.'

In short, there had been a misunderstanding between the wickets, no doubt attributable to differing prep school backgrounds. Be that as it may, all has long since been forgiven and I later came to work under the great man when he was Quartermaster General (QMG). This episode will shortly lead into the final section of this Staff College sequence – Khartoum.

Before that, however, I should just come back to the comment I made earlier about the re-write of Ex BLUE LAMP. As an initial means of breaking the ice between Camberley and Bramshill it had been an obvious success. It, however, clearly needed more body and substance before next time round and the Special Course was the wrong level of participation. These youngsters, even if potential fliers, had barely more than minimum beat experience, and were obviously no match maturity-wise for our students. So I set about producing something in which, against a topical scenario, civil disturbance problems could be discussed in depth. We also introduced the 'third force' issue or the need for something between the traditional British policeman and the military – the French CRS approach, for example. I also suggested that next time we try the level of the Inspectors' Course. We eventually got it right when we settled on the Bramshill Intermediate Course – generally Superintendents. It was my first real experience of close working contact with the police outside the Ulster and old colonial settings. I found them a little touchy on rank. They were also hyper-sensitive over the continued absence of any Hendon type officer entry as had been introduced by Lord Trenchard prior to the war. Having said that, they ran dinner nights that rather aped Service Officers' Mess traditions and practice. Some forces, and notably the Metropolitan, had even begun to introduce mess kit. I was also a little surprised that the

DS had been selected on the basis of open application rather than nomination by something akin to our MS system. This seemed to me to encourage the 'butterfly' mentality (so much denigrated by the Police Federation and others) whereby the scramble to compete for advertised senior career appointments (or flit anywhere for promotion) cannot altogether be in the best interests of either force senior rank continuity or loyalty. But then that is the humble view of one who was but briefly a 'fly on the wall' at the then Bramshill. I have to say that I met some very good police officers, both male and female, during my Bramshill connection. One, Brenda Chicken, QPM, recently retired from the Humberside Force as a Chief Superintendent, remains a friend of long standing.

It certainly wasn't all work. There was plenty of play and we had much fun within the DS fraternity itself. We got on well and the slightly over ambitious kept themselves generally in check. Perhaps they didn't need to behave otherwise since some twenty years on the majority were filling the top posts in the Army both at home and overseas. No doubt the happy atmosphere all stemmed from the top since both Commandants in my time were relaxed individuals. This is not to say that you could play it too casual. For your marked work came in for frequent scrutiny and added 'green ink' comment, likewise the 'headman' was always a likely visitor during a syndicate discussion period. We, the ex-COs, tended to pull the legs of the young 'whizz-kid' DS whenever the chance arose. Getting our Colonel GS (later General Sir Richard Trant, KCB) to sign it, Johnny Watts and I circulated a 'spoof' notice to all DS at the beginning of the then Third or 'Overseas' Term. This indicated that for those DS and students lacking jungle experience a familiarisation night was to be held in the nearby Windsor Safari Park some fifteen days hence. Those wishing to attend were invited to submit their names to their DS and were instructed to ensure that they brought a sleeping bag, gymshoes and mosquito repellent. To our pleasure the nominal rolls contained the names of several we had been after. They were in the event let down 'lightly' as they stood waiting in vain for the coach to Windsor on the evening in question. The great social events of the Camberley year remained the Summer Ball, the Drag Hunt Ball and the Pantomime. There were usually, interspersed between these highlights, a couple of divisional ladies' dinner nights, to one or more of which Mary Ames (now down the road at HMS *Dauntless*, the then WRNS 'flagship') came. Each term the syndicate party remained a regular feature. The best of these were an outing to the Windsor Theatre followed by local Chinese 'nosh'. The worst were those like that one of my US students masterminded where, in introducing us to 'manhattans' and 'sidecars' he had mixed too strong a blend in each case. Most of the guests were accordingly forced to depart before the party had barely begun.

Early in 1972 the Colonel of the Regiment, then the Lieutenant of HM Tower of London, had approached me concerning the post of Secretary to the Lord Mayor of London. Aware of my connections with the City of London, and my disappointment at not making the 1971 'Blue List', he thought I might be interested in applying when the vacancy came up in the spring. I gave it some thought but decided that I did still want to 'break the red hat barrier' to full Colonel and, hopefully, beyond. Within a couple of months it was confirmed that I had won a 'red hat' in the annual MS 'Blue List' lottery. Almost immediately after this news I was advised that I had been selected to be the Chief Instructor at the Sudanese Staff College. The initial job specification required an ex-infantry CO and ex-Camberley DS. Suffice it to say that it took some digesting since I had felt sure that, on promotion, my time had surely come to renew a rather long overdue acquaintance with BAOR. 'So be it' was, however, the cry. Just a little more sand in those already overloaded shoes. There followed a session in the Ministry at which I began to garner the extent of the task ahead.

Before I, however, expand on the requirement, and how we set about meeting it, the reader is in need of some background. The Sudanese Command and Staff College at Omdurman had been established initially by Brigadier Leo Plummer (later Major General) in 1964. The Chief Instructor had remained British and the courses had been British orientated until 1969. At that point in Sudanese foreign policy there was a pretty drastic swing towards all things Eastern Bloc and the College was accordingly taken over by the Russians and became thoroughly Soviet orientated. It is sufficient here to say that during the Soviet regime all instruction was conducted in Russian, through an interpreter, and that tactical doctrine was geared entirely towards the Soviet concept, and notably relating to the Warsaw Pact and Western Europe. A glance at the course syllabus indicated that War Studies included the Defence of Stalingrad, the crossing of the Dnieper, the assault on Berlin and partisan operations in the Balkans. No serious attempt had been made to adapt instruction to the role, organisation and equipment of the Sudanese Forces nor to the varied terrain over which they might have to fight. Instruction had laid great stress on the mass use of armour and artillery, neither of which equipments the Sudanese were every likely to possess in any quantity. Likewise the techniques of counter insurgency and IS operations had been totally ignored, yet at the time a major insurgency was aflame in the

Southern Sudan. The Soviet Advisory Staff had comprised seven officers – a Colonel Senior Adviser, three Colonel Instructors/Lecturers and three Interpreters. They had not worn uniform and the general medium of instruction had been the straight lecture followed by a quiz type question and answer period. No précis had been issued and students had been required necessarily to take notes. Practical-type TEWTs, as we know them, had not been conducted and there had been little emphasis on staff procedures. The Standard Staff Course had run for nine months and two and a half courses had been completed. The 1972 course had been terminated about the midway point. Following the unsuccessful Communist-led coup in July 1971, when President Numeiry had been temporarily deposed, the Soviet influence had gone into sharp decline. In the Sudanese Forces this decline had been further hastened by ever increasing problems with aged Soviet 'gift' equipment and a lack of any proper spares backing. It was perhaps, therefore, not altogether surprising that in mid-June 1972 had come the first Sudanese request for the revival of British military assistance – a return to the Plummer-style era at the Command and Staff College.

After my Ministry session there followed briefings from both Leo Plummer and Tony Uloth, our Khartoum Defence Adviser (then fortunately visiting UK). Then came a fourteen-day visit to Camberley by a couple of the Sudanese DS. By this time, around mid-August, I had gathered a fairly precise picture as to the requirement, namely:

a. A four-week Re-orientation Briefing for the current staff course who had parted with their Soviet advisers in midstream. In the limited time available it was agreed that the emphasis should be on Staff Duties, Operational Staff Procedures and Training. The briefing was planned to take place during the period 18th November to 14th December.

b. An especial thirteen-week Senior Command Course for selected senior officers to cover as above plus Basic Tactics and Logistics. The course would begin on or about 10th February 1973.

c. An annual thirty-two week Senior Command and Staff Course (SCSC), the first to begin in August 1973.

d. An annual twelve-week Junior Staff Course (JSC), the first to start in February 1974.

From the same sources of information I had also established that all instruction was to be in English (then the common language 'twixt the

Arab north and African south); that, though three Sudanese DS were available to assist, none were '*au fait*' with current British staff procedures and tactical doctrine, no current British training manuals were held and very limited 'English' clerical back-up was to hand. I was also very clear in my own mind that we should not repeat the Russian mistake and that all instruction should be related to the role, organisation and equipment of the Sudanese Army and the terrain over which they might have to operate and fight – desert, mountains and jungle in that vast country. Likewise I was convinced that the medium of instruction should follow the Camberley syndicate approach and its associated précis discussions. One did not, however, have to be a clairvoyant to appreciate that this would demand a major adaptation of both Camberley and Warminster (JDSC) précis, presentation and exercise material. It also led me to the rather basic conclusion that the task was one for more than a 'one man band', since the Chief Instructor could not clearly compete with the instructional and adaptation writing load single handed and certainly not within the limited time available. Thus, at the next big gathering in London (and I had never imagined so many could be interested in the project) I played my hand and made a firm bid for two British DS, an author each for the senior and junior courses, a superintending clerk and some short term clerical back-up. To both my relief and amazement no objections were raised and the bid was met in full.

Clear now in my mind as to the full scope of the project, the next task was to set about framing a master Block Syllabus in relation to both the Camberley and Warminster Courses. The latter could clearly wait a bit and the priority was obviously the Senior Command and Staff Course. In effect we settled, in broad terms, on the then first Three Terms at Camberley with certain specific additions from the Post-Staff Course. Bearing in mind the likely English comprehension problem, and our Camberley experience in teaching overseas students, we rather arbitrarily doubled the time allotted for periods in the Camberley programme (we found this rather basic ploy produced a near ideal answer). A week's hard grind in the garden of my favourite Cornish retreat produced the Block Syllabus and on my return to Camberley it was despatched to Khartoum for agreement and clearance. This was forthcoming within days. We then set about earmarking the relevant 'model' précis, presentations and exercises for adaptation. To assist me I was given Peter Dell (later a highly successful businessman) and David Goodman (later Major General). They were both DS at Camberley awaiting command. In addition WO2 Ingram, S Sgt Sheppard and Sgt McCaffery were 'borrowed' from local RAOC establishments. This was the temporary 'loan' team that were to see me through so excellently till just before Christmas. We actually first got together on 14th September and spent the next four weeks or so collecting up our 'model' material, ordering pamphlets, 'raiding' the map depot at Guildford (a good thing we did since the Sudanese had none to provide), assembling stationery, packing, being inoculated and so on. By the appointed date, 5th October, we were set to go. A slight hiccup over the Agreement (we needn't have worried as it was eventually signed eighteen weeks later) delayed our departure for a week. However, on the evening of 13th October, accompanied by our precious 'model' freight and following some self-help porterage at Heathrow, we departed by British Airways VC10 for Khartoum. Many sceptics reckoned we would be back in a week and we won a crate of champagne off a group of student wags when we weren't.

Khartoum was designed by Kitchener and the roads were laid out in the form of a Union Jack. It lies between the White and Blue Niles and the ancient city of Omdurman is across the Nile just north of the junction point. In more recent years the 'New Extension', as it is termed, has been 'blistered' on to Khartoum near the airport like a great big 'carbuncle'. It was here where we were to be accommodated in houses rented by the Sudanese Army. I had one, and remained there throughout my tour, Peter and David another and the WOs and Sgts a third. Some pretty basic barrack style furniture, used previously by the Russians, was all that was to hand. We also all had a local cook and houseboy. Despite the fact that the Foreign Office had been the prime movers in getting us there, they hadn't done much to see to our welfare. We even had to get our Ministry to 'buy' some surplus Embassy furniture to improve our initial accommodation lot – enough said at this point. The week's delay meant that we had precisely five weeks in which to produce the précis/exercise material for the Reorientation Briefing. After forty-eight hours initial briefing on the role, organisation and equipment of the Sudanese Forces, and a quick aerial 'recce' (by Russian HIP helicopter) of the neighbouring Karrari Training Area, we set to with pen and paper. We achieved the aim (or just) and at the same time managed to finalise the TEWT series for the SCSC course. We had many laughs amid the frustrations and perhaps it was this good humour that finally saw us through. I can recall the laugh we had over the 'night attack' TEWT. Standing on the start line I had queried the distance to the objective. Peter had said, '800 yards or thereabouts.' I had replied, 'It can't be – just look at the size of that lone tree there alongside the track where it dips over the hill.' At that very moment a gallabiyahclad local had ridden over the hill on his donkey and passed by what was no more than a knee high thornbush. Thereafter in Camberley DS folklore Millman's Bush became almost as famous in legend as Gordon's Tree. The Re-orientation Briefing began on 18th November and Peter and David quickly established that syndicate rapport that remained a glowing feature of the DS Student relationship – certainly in my time. There were some English comprehension problems but interest and enthusiasm abounded. Whilst they held forth in syndicate, I and the clerks continued the writing and production schedule, the aim being to hand over to the relief team at least the first six weeks' worth of the succeeding Senior Command Course. This we did not quite achieve as we handed over half a week's worth short. It had, however, been a major achievement on some pretty ancient typewriters and a hired early model photo-copier. The briefing ended in a spate of glory on 14th December. The day began with breakfast with the President followed by a picnic lunch on the president's barge on the Nile, tea with the Ambassador and sundowner drinks with the Chief of Staff. Finally on 19th December the temporary 'loan' team headed for home with many memories, a fund of stories, with everybody's best wishes and laden with farewell gifts. They had done both me and the College very, very well – and I really mean that. They were a very high grade bunch and I was lucky to have had such backing to launch the project.

I then had ten days alone in which to find suitable accommodation for the 'long term' team. By good fortune I fell, early in my search, upon a modern flat block close to where I lived. I christened it 'Knightsbridge' and allotted one floor each to the Tremellen and Wellings families and one to the 'singleton' authors. With the furniture left by the previous team, some more I obtained through the embassy and a container load 'borrowed' from the Forestry Department, the end product was comfortable if not exactly luxurious. We were, however, on 'Loan Service' and were being paid a healthy rate of Local Overseas Allowance (LOA). In addition, we were receiving a secondment credit (I bought a brand new MGB with mine). Both the new DS had come straight out of the National Defence College (NDC – and the successor to JSSC Latimer) on promotion. Their ladies were new to the rank too. I did once have to say 'lump it and like it or go home'. Thereafter a sense of proportion pertained. Christmas was saved by the kindness of such as the family Furness who took me under their wing. They were Shell expatriates and, together with some other oil families, did us proud. On 29th December the relief team arrived as scheduled. They were a welcome sight at Khartoum airport, despite the early hour. In addition to Colin Tremellen and Mike Wellings they included Brian Forsyth and Angus Fairrie, the two authors, and Mr Smith the Superintending Clerk (ex-JDSC Warminster). I had hung on to the WO's house for Mr Smith and his family if he subsequently brought them. We had six weeks left before the especial Senior Command Course was due to begin. To the credit of all concerned, and notably the authors, the writing programme was virtually complete by the time the course began. Mr Smith was, however, still struggling tirelessly to beat a major typing and reproduction problem. We got over this one eventually by sending our précis scripts back to Camberley via the diplomatic bag, having them reproduced there and then sent back weekly by the good offices of British Airways. Each Saturday morning one of us would go down to the airport to collect from the VC10 pilot.

The course began on 10th February with a complement of twenty-two students – four Major Generals, six Brigadiers and twelve full Colonels – a quite unique student body and a rather awe inspiring introduction to DS work for Messrs Tremellen and Wellings. The experience and background of the students was indeed varied. On the one hand we had the QMG, the Director of Armour and General Lagu (the former commander of the Anyana rebels plus three of his battalion COs) and on the other the Chief Director of Music, the head medic and the Air Force Chief Engineer. Be that as it may, the same excellent syndicate rapport was soon established. In essence, the course was a concentrated thirteen-week sample of the SCSC syllabus. As such it afforded us the opportunity to conduct a practical trial of the more complex instructional material such as the model presentations, the TEWTs and the Telephone Battle. We even included an 'outside visits' week in which we had outings to the Gezira Cotton Scheme, the Sudanese Navy and Air Force. During the former I encountered my first Voluntary Service Overseas (VSO) worker, a young lady taking a class outside a mudhut school in one of the villages deep in the heart of the scheme – or miles from anywhere. On the visit to the Navy, trained by the Yugoslavs, we took a fast patrol boat trip out into the Red Sea from Port Sudan. That morning in my hotel room chest of drawers I had found an old pre-war laundry list which included such items as 'chemise' and 'cotton gloves'. At the Air Force centre we had encountered blue overalled Chinese supervising the maintenance of Fighter 5s (the Chinese version of the MIG 15) in one hangar and white-overalled Russians in the next doing likewise to some MIG 23s. It appeared that neither ever spoke to the other – language problems or otherwise. The course finally terminated on 10th May. It had been a long haul six days a

week from 7.00 am to 1.00 pm and in the ever increasing heat. As it began
to 'stoke up' towards the really hot season, and during the TEWT phase,
we were out on the Karrari Training Area (scene of the Battle of
Omdurman) by 5.00 am and away by 11.00 am. The end of course party
took place in the grounds of the National Folklore Society and was a
splendidly uninhibited occasion. Organised by our tame Head Musician,
the National Dance Troupe were produced *en masse*. They included the
delectable 'Nightingales' (Sudan's then answer to the Beverley Sisters). It
all made for a happy, dancing and laughing evening. During the party
presents were generously showered upon the team and their wives. You
simply cannot beat the Sudanese for generosity and hospitality. It was a
fitting close to what had been a memorable, enjoyable and thoroughly
satisfying course.

Early on I had contracted that we should close the College over July and
August – the very hot season and punctuated by a mix of 'haboubs' (sand
storms) and violent electrical storms. The Staff College very kindly provided me with sanctuary during my UK leave, for Everest Road now
belonged to another and my furniture was all in store (at my expense,
unlike the 'pads' on the team). I had a few days with the Hattons, a very
restful month in my Cornish retreat and used the remainder of the time to
sort out the way ahead. In between times I played a good deal of tennis
with Peter Dell, Derek Boorman and John Stibbon (later General Sir John
Stibbon, KCB). I learned that I was next headed for BAOR at the turn of
the year to be Colonel AQ to the 4th Division. John Oborne, then the
Deputy Commandant at the Junior Division of the Staff College (JDSC) at
Warminster, had been earmarked to replace me. In fairness to the Sudanese I felt that I should see through the first term of the SCSC Course due
to begin in August, especially as at that point the two students to attend
the Camberley Course in 1973 were to be selected. Suffice it to say that
we all returned in good heart in late July. The hot dry heat had been
replaced by a level of humidity akin to what I had experienced in Bahrain.
There was also still the odd 'Haboub' to contend with – sand everywhere.
We soon settled back into the Khartoum routine. Though life in the city
was a bit limited, and especially after the expatriate community had
shrunk following the 1969 ructions, we made the most of it. A Nuffield
Trust motor boat, the swimming pool at the Sudan Club, the yacht club
based on the *Melik* (one of Kitchener's surviving gunboats), and the golf
club (all oil and sand) served to help to keep us reasonably content.
Perhaps our greatest asset was, however, membership of the Sudan LTA.
Most afternoons we went down there and made up a four from whomever

was waiting to play. You might finish up playing with the Bulgarian Economic Attaché, a Sudanese Colonel and another member of the team. I partnered the Hungarian Ambassador (a one time Honved footballer) in the Veterans' Handicap doubles. Afterwards the British Ambassador said to me, 'Do you think that was wise, Colonel?' My reply was simply, 'Have no fear, Sir, I am not about to join Philby and the others.' Having said all that, time, distance and the desert did limit the extent of our travels. We did, though, get most on visits to the Dinder Game Park (the best I have viewed). Some also made the historic old port of Suakin (where the famous cats are enormous), the coral reefs at Port Sudan, the Fifth Cataract in the Sabuloga Hills and the pyramids at Shendi. Closer to home, we viewed or visited the Liger in the Khartoum Zoo, the reconstructed Nubian Temples in the National Museum, the Presidential Palace, the Mahdi's Tomb, the Khalifa's House and the 21st Lancers Memorial on the field of Omdurman. Whilst he was with us Angus Fairrie, a keen military historian, actually produced an Omdurman mini-battlefield tour. He had laid especial emphasis on the part played by Macdonald and his Sudanese infantry and presented the script to the College before he departed. Another who derived particular joy from his time with us was David Goodman. A dedicated birdwatcher (or twitcher) he was in near paradise as he went about the place clutching a borrowed volume of *Birds of the Sudan*.

We did have our moments of excitement too. One evening during the 'haboub' season we were returning from our Friday evening 'run ashore' to the Oasis Hotel when we were stopped by the police. Across the square from 'Knightsbridge' 'Black September' terrorists had got into the Saudi Arabian Embassy. They had killed the American Ambassador and the Belgian Chargé d'Affaires. The Saudi Ambassador and some of his staff were still being held hostage. A cordon had been thrown round the area and so everybody came back to 'Tangier House' as I had christened it. Next morning I was taken forward to view the scene, between 'haboubs', and one could see the terrorists, in their balaclavas and touting Kalashnikovs, positioned about the roof. My advice was to tighten the cordon and to bring in some Saladin armoured cars to make a show of force and then to begin some loud-hailer negotiation. Within twenty-four hours the siege ended peacefully. Thereafter we were all given a rather sleepy sort of police 'watchman' (Bulgarian trained) for house protection. We were also well into the SCSC First Term when the Egyptians struck across the Suez canal to begin the 'Yom Kippur' war. The Sudanese had long maintained a brigade in defensive positions along the southern sector. The initial success of the Egyptians prompted much joy about the syndicate rooms. It soon turned into deep gloom as the Israelis got the upper hand. It was interesting that several Egyptian Antonov bombers were, during the period, to be seen in heavily protected sangar-style shelter bays on the fringes of Khartoum airport. In another field there was great excitement, particularly from the wives, during a week-long visit to the city by HRH Princess Anne. Much to the irritation of the Embassy staff she gave the team a great deal of time and attention during a garden party laid on by the Ambassador. Ma'am and I kept meeting since the Sudanese, never too hot on protocol, had seemingly only circulated one invitation list. An unforgettable experience was the drive to work on the first morning that traffic was required to switch from left to the right of the road. It was even more hair-raising than usual.

Whilst we had been preparing for the Reorientation Briefing, there had been visits to Omdurman by both the Ethiopian and Somali Staff Colleges. The former had included in their party a naval Captain whom I had taught at Camberley the previous year. It had been intended that he should go to Greenwich but, due to some mix-up, he had appeared at Camberley instead. After these visits Peter Dell had laughingly said one evening, as we sipped martinis at sunset on the vast terrace of the Grand Hotel overlooking the junction of the Blue and White Niles, 'Why don't we go into business as 'African Staff Colleges Ltd'? He was fairly 'warm' since the Sudan Staff College model we had pioneered was shortly to be taken up by Ghana, Nigeria, Bangladesh and Zimbabwe, in that order. Likewise British military assistance began to sprout in the form of British Army Training Teams (BATT) world wide and from Namibia to Mozambique. The challenge had been met. A total of 74 précis, 57 exercises and 9 presentations had been produced to match the syllabus. This had required a great deal of both teams. We would, however, never have been able to meet this bill, especially reproduction-wise, without the splendid backing of both the Staff College at Camberley and its Junior Division at Warminster. In the case of the TEWTs we had had to blend Soviet equipments into our range tables and the like. We became experts, for example, in the characteristics and capabilities of the T52 tank. The real lesson learned from this venture was don't let the Foreign Office commit the Services to anything without prior and proper consultation. We were thrown in at the deep end through the sheer naivety of those on the ground in Khartoum. One wonders how they really thought we were going to achieve the aim with no typewriters, no clerical staff nor office back-up. Having got us there, they likewise did very little to help us. They had been

prepared, for example, to let us (families and all) be covered medically by
the Sudanese Military Hospital. Having viewed the set-up, had we gone in
with earache we would no doubt have come out with something much
worse. The MOD finally paid for cover from the private Khartoum Clinic.
In comparsion with the Gulf and that high grade team I had experienced
there, led by Sir Stewart Crawford, it was a distinct diplomatic eye
opener. Before I departed I selected the two Students who would become
the next DS after the 1973 Camberley Course. At the mid-way point in the
SCSC they were way ahead of the remainder. Their English comprehension was excellent, as was that of their wives. They would clearly give a
great deal to the Camberley course and get much benefit from it. One was,
however, a sailor and the other a 'trucker'. This caused some initial upset.
However, I stuck by my decision and I was supported by the President. It
was, in fact, the sailor who, a few mornings later, told me that he had
heard on the news the previous evening that I had been awarded the
Gadara (or Order of Merit). It was presented to me next day by the
President. A farewell party followed in the Officers' Club (the old Sudan
Club) when presents were again showered on me. Two mornings later I
arrived at the airport to depart by Sudan Airways for home. Everybody
was there to say goodbye, including the President and the Staff Band.
Having said my farewells and seen the famed tin trunk aboard, the Boeing
707's starboard engine went unserviceable. This had happened too when
the Vice Adjutant General (later Lieutenant General Sir James Wilson,
KBE, MC) was about to depart after his visit to us. We switched him
down to Entebbe and thence on to London in time to make his regular
Saturday afternoon football correspondents match report. In my case the
Al Italia representative (and *Melik* sailing chum) slipped me a First Class
Boarding Ticket for a plane leaving that evening for Rome. I eventually
got away in great style and, as I sipped champagne in the 1st Class Cabin,
chuckled at such memories as the night Mahmoud, my cook, served up a
much prized delicacy as 'Avocado with Custard'; or when, discussing the
especial Senior Command Course reports, the President had queried the
symbol 'D' against the name of the officer listed bottom in the 'Order of
Merit'. 'That cannot mean 'Distinguished' in this case,' he said. 'What
does it mean? Demote? Deport? Do to death? or what?' 'No, Your Excel-
lency,' I had replied. 'It means "Derived much benefit from the course".'
'You actually mean he "failed",' he had tartly responded. You can't fool
some even part of the time.
    I changed at Rome for London and only had some twenty minutes in
which to catch the connection. I did not think my tin trunk would make it

in the time. I was met at Heathrow by Tony Ward, then on his last student term, who had been sent with a staff car to collect me. As we waited by the baggage claim the famous trunk emerged and before my small hand grip. Next day I had a long debriefing session with the Commandant. He had once more kindly agreed that I could use the College as a sanctuary before moving on to BAOR. It was now early December and Ex BLUE LAMP was on again. I joined Johnny Watts's syndicate for the day. Rightfully we were now at Intermediate Course level. I was also invited to join Ronnie Laughton's party for the Pantomime – no channel crossings this time. It was good to be back amongst so many friends. It had all been an experience and sometimes a very lonely one. At last I felt I was getting back into the mainstream and I was looking forward to going to Herford after Christmas. Before the week was out I had bought that MGB sports car I had always wanted but could never afford. There is after all perhaps something to be said for Seconded Service. I was still, however, to be haunted by my 'old colonial' image, as subsequent events would show.

Chapter 12

The 'Compleat' Logistician

Just prior to Christmas 1973 Intake I (or the 'Guinea Pigs') had held a Twenty-Fifth Anniversary Dinner in Old College at Sandhurst. It had been a great reunion and the organisers had really gone out far and wide to produce a majority turnout. On the whole, one gathered the impression that those who had gone early had done rather better than those who had left it to their mid-thirties. Amongst those present had been Ted Burgess. Then a Brigadier, he was currently Commander Royal Artillery (CRA) to the 4th Division. I hadn't seen him since our Sandhurst days but he assured me that I would enjoy the HQ and the very happy atmosphere that stemmed from the top. I spent Christmas with the Hattons and New Year with the Trants. David Goodman was a guest too on New Year's Eve and so we swapped a few Khartoum stories. During the second week of January I headed for Harwich in the new 'racer'. I wasn't too sorry to be on my way since a spate of industrial troubles had led to the introduction of the three-day working week and petrol rationing was threatened. I took the very comfortable Prins Line Ferry from Harwich to Hamburg and then went by autobahn via Hannover to Herford, the home of the 4th Division. A town of some 60,000 people, it lies in the heart of North Rhine Westphalia and was then a recognised centre for such diverse products as high grade furniture and cigars. It had been a sizable garrison town prior to the war, though never too popular with the Wehrmacht. It was said that they had reckoned it to be too low lying to be healthy. Certainly during the hot summer of 1976 it was so breathless that I could have been back in Khartoum. For those unfamiliar with the area, I would simply say that the scenery did not fascinate nor the average Westphalian engage. That afternoon I took over a pleasant flat above a flower shop in the Mindener Strasse. A garage went with it and it was within easy walking distance of

British Army of the Rhine
(4th Division)

BALTIC SEA

N

NORTH SEA

Hamburg

Bremen

River
Ems

River
Elbe

Hohne
O

River
Weser

River Aller

XX
4

Hannover

Brunswick

Hameln
O

Herford

Detmold
O

Munster O

Bielefeld

Paderborn
O

River Lippe

Dortmund O

Soest
O

O Iserlohn

O Dusseldorf

Rheindahlen
O

Cologne

50 miles

VIII. British Army of the Rhine (and especially 4th Division Area), 1974–1976.

the HQ. There was a staff car and driver, an orderly provided by the 2nd Battalion from Werl and a cleaning lady for what appeared umpteen hours a week. It seemed that the 'quality of life' had a good deal to commend it in Herford.

On my first morning I had an introductory session with the GOC. Major General Mike Gow (later General Sir Michael Gow, GCB). A Scots Guardsman and very proud of it, he had seen service with the Guards Armoured Division in NW Europe. Later he had commanded 4th Guards Brigade. A distinguished Wykehamist he was a very big man in every respect. He possessed a delightful turn of phase and a lovely sense of humour. Above all he was a natural communicator with soldiers and they loved him. I always suspected, however, that beneath it all he did not suffer fools too gladly. From day one we hit it off and established a relationship that I believe we have valued – then and since. Certainly he was a great supporter over the remainder of my service. Clearly he was a little concerned as to my lack of BAOR experience. I could understand this. However, as an ex-Camberley DS himself, he took my point that, with my logistic and administrative background, I just needed time to acquaint myself with the BAOR 'cries'. Thereafter we both felt that I should be able to see the wood for the trees. I left his office feeling that I had gained his trust. It was now up to me to break down that BAOR 'mystique'. I sensed it would help that within the HQ, besides knowing Ted Burgess, I had also been acquainted with the Colonel GS, Mike Palmer (later Major General Sir Michael Palmer, KCVO) since Sandhurst days. The Divisional HQ controlled operationally the 6th and 20th Armoured Brigades. The former had its HQ at Soest near the Mohne See (of 'Dambuster' fame) and was commanded by that great personality Harry Dalzell Payne (later Major General). Harry had appeared on the same 'Blue List' as me and we had first met when he attended my revamped version of Ex BLUE LAMP as an MOD observer. 20th Armoured Brigade was centred on Detmold and had Maurice Johnston, last seen in Borneo on the Simmangang convoy escort run, as its commander. Both were cavalrymen – very much the armoured brigade command vogue at the time. Administratively in peace time we housed some 46,000 soldiers, UK based civilians and dependants within the divisional area. Many of the units belonged operationally to HQ 1st (BR) Corps. We ran this sizable show through five Garrison HQs – Detmold, Herford, Hameln, Paderborn and Soest. The first and last were administered by our Brigade HQs. The others were managed, at our behest, by HQ RA 4th Division (Herford), HQ RAC 1st (BR) Corps (Paderborn) and the HQ RE 1st (BR) Corps (Hameln).

My role within the HQ, as Colonel AQ, was that of chief logistician and chief administrator. Operationally I and my AQ team were required to ensure that the division was properly maintained in war. In short, it was our task to make sure that rations, fuel and ammunition never ran out, as much equipment and as many vehicles as possible were retained in a battleworthy state and that casualties were treated and evacuated speedily. We operated from a Rear HQ, some fifteen to twenty kilometres behind Main HQ, and there controlled a Divisional Administrative Area (DAA) in which were based the various divisional logistic units. We went into the field regularly both on divisional and corps exercises. Once we had got a grip of it I believe we had the most alert and the sharpest Rear HQ in BAOR. Working on the principle that any fool can be uncomfortable, we also prided ourselves on being the most well found. To support me in this task I had a head 'trucker' (Commander RCT), a head 'witch doctor' (Assistant Director of Medical Services), a stores and spares 'king' (Commander RAOC) and a master 'fitter' (Commander REME). They in their turn controlled the transport regiment and the other specialised divisional units that provided medical, stores and workshops cover in the field. I was particularly fortunate to inherit a largely new and very bright team at Heads of Service level. I think I came to know them well enough that the rather lighthearted job descriptions above (especially framed for the uninitiated) would have not caused offence. Though they had more recent BAOR experience than myself, they were new to both their rank and appointments. In Bob Blewett (later Major General) I sensed that we had a future Director General of Medical Services in our midst. Sadly he died suddenly, just when that goal appeared in sight. Jerrie Hulme (later Major General) had been a DS at Camberley towards the end of my time there. A great humourist as well as a very able guy, he subsequently made Director General of his Corps. The other Hume in the team, Bob, was an electronics 'wizard' and had recently been a DS at RMCS Shrivenham. He possessed a wonderfully dry wit and loved his field soldiering. His Corps lost a potential Director when he left the Army early. David Fairs, a very steady number, made up the team but was somewhat out on a limb as he was based at Duisburg with his regiment. The 'scrum half' behind this pretty strong 'pack' was the Deputy Assistant Quartermaster General (Operations) (DAQMG (Ops)). The post had, in recent years, been filled by a Canadian exchange officer. It all had something to do with the Division having at one time been commanded by a Canadian. In my time this very 'hot seat' was filled, in turn, by three very able young 'truckers' – Bob Little, John Guthrie and Bill

Leach. Dressed in his unified green uniform, we knew the incumbent as the 'Woodsman'.

With the backing of this very capable team we set about the logistic 'education' of the 'G' (or Operations) 'snobs' who worked on the floor above us. Some years later I was to overhear a new member of my MOD staff say, 'The nearest I have ever been before to the 'Q' world is the Colour Sergeant's stores.' We encountered just such another very early on at the Divisional Study Period. This 'toffee-nosed' young man managed to dismiss the logistic implications of the divisional deployment in war in a five-minute spiel. I was so angry, and happily the GOC had sensed it, that when I went to see Mike Palmer the 'foul' had clearly been registered. It never happened again and next year we really did go, in some detail, into the problems associated with outloading, reinforcements and the like. Our next little brush with the 'G' world arose when we came to conduct the first exercise of the training season. This was a divisional CPX known as Ex KEEL HAUL. It was customary to run such exercises in 'cleared' or '443' areas as they were known. New to the game, we went along with the system. It wasn't until we got to our first Rear HQ deployment area, that we, the new boys, realised that it was exactly the same village as had been used the previous year (and I suspect the one before) since everybody knew precisely where to go. In short, nobody had been put to any test at all. When this happened a second time at the next location, I determined it should not occur again. We were in a cleared '443' area and so as long as we stuck within it we could always select another village. I chose one off the map, told the team and then got Bob Little to conduct a 'recce'. When the next move came, and to the surprise of many, we went to 'X' rather than 'Y'. It was chaos as near pandemonium set in at the other end. This time we really did have to think and go where we were directed by the advance party rather than memory. Needless to say, we got our message across and next year the exercise was held over different ground. By the conclusion of Ex SUMMER SALES, the annual Corps CPX, we reckoned that as a team we had cracked it. We had mastered the BAOR 'cries' and had fully matched the logistic exercise play. That evening we had a small impromptu party at Rear HQ to celebrate. Thereafter we never really looked back and when it later came to the Ex WIDE HORIZON trials we were the HQ entrusted to conduct them – logistics and all. To cap it that autumn, we ran a series of demonstrations to highlight the field functions of the logistic units and a notice appeared on the floor above us at Herford that read, 'Have you consulted Q?', 'Chiefie and his Indians', as we became known, had seemingly achieved their initial aim. Having said all that, I believe we could be accused of having simply fooled the system that then pertained in BAOR; for, whilst during three training seasons we had become adept at moving Rear HQ, and its associated logistic units, from one hide location to the next, we had only ever 'played' at the more likely problems to be confronted on the nuclear battlefield. It is one thing to offer up a sound 'notional' solution for transmission over the radio on a CPX, quite another in our case, I suggest, to conduct such as an outloading or dumping programme for real in a nuclear setting. I know that at the time we had enforced restrictions on fuel consumption and track mileage. We were also attempting to conserve on spares. Our reputation had, however, been made on CPX 'make believe' – as were many others, I suspect. Some of those went on to stardom: good luck to them – we all need a share of it to succeed.

Whereas we only practised our logistic functions during the training season, we were taxed administratively all the year round. For in my other hat, and like my logistic team in theirs, we had a major part to play in maintaining the 'quality of life' from day to day across the length and breadth of the divisional area. There were, for example, rations to be delivered, children to be taken to school, medical centres to be run and a welfare transport fleet to be kept as serviceable as possible. In this we were, of course, assisted by those Heads of Service who had largely an administrative function only. By this I mean the head 'schoolie', the senior chaplain, the chief paymaster, the catering 'king' and the provost representative. In this respect we were particularly lucky padre-wise. First we had Duggie Dennis, who introduced that excellent annual field outing for the vicars – Ex PARSON'S PLEASURE; then Jim Harkness, who later, and deservedly, made it to Chaplain General. As I have told him many times since, he owed it all to his 4th Division upbringing. The main problems at that time were the continued need for more married quarters, the ageing state of our welfare transport fleet, the maintenance of and improvements to ancient barrack accommodation (everything we occupied had been built by either the Kaiser, Hitler or the Canadians), lack of spare parts for all and sundry and the enforced family separation occasioned by Op BANNER (Ulster tours). The latter had been aggravated by a quarters' purchase and building programme that had mistakenly gone for too many high-rise flats. We now had, for example, young Mavis aged eighteen years, and who had never before been 'beyond the end of Margate pier', 'stranded' in a flat on the sixth floor of the Hackedal Estate in Detmold. Husband John, aged twenty-one, had just begun a four-month tour with his unit in Ulster. She had no car, couldn't speak a word of

German and had no real friends. She was utterly dependent on the garrison bus service to the nearest NAAFI shop for survival. The British Forces Broadcasting Services (BFBS) helped radio-wise but at that time only German TV was available. (I used to watch *Kojak* but, like Mavis, couldn't have told you what it was all about unless I had seen the episode in UK before). The unit families' officers and the various wives' clubs did their best. They hoped that John had put her in touch with both before he left. He seldom had. There could, however, never be a true substitute for 'mum round the corner' and in time we got it agreed that the Mavises of this world could go home to mum if they so wished when hubby was in Ulster. It didn't solve the issue but it certainly eased it. We also bent over backwards to meet the youth problem. Youth clubs were established with proper youth leaders in all the main garrisons and stations and transport to and from was provided. During the summer holidays, when we always had the UK based school kids with us too, we laid on an extensive programme of camps and other venture style events. To back these we brought over further accredited youth organisers to assist. You can, though, only please some part of the time however hard you try. For I recall an incident at Paderborn where the youth leader, having assembled his stores to build a mini-obstacle course, collected his party together and then explained to them what was to happen. Whereupon a 'charming' young lad (of *Just William* ilk) shouted, 'You build it, mate, and then we'll play on it' and screaming with laughter ran off with his chums in close pursuit.

As the headman of the 'quality of life' team you tended to be regarded by some as a super 'Mr Fix-it' or a cross between a sort of Yellow Pages plumber or DIY expert. It was one thing to be summoned by the General to see if you could sort out his excessive water bill (a leak in the pond at Taurus House was found to be responsible). It was quite another, at a cocktail party in the Mess, to be cornered by one of the senior BFES lady teachers (known as the 'Grimmies' by the young officers) and be told that the plumbing in her Mess needed urgent attention. The noise made by the central heating pipes was keeping her awake at night. I referred her to the 'Q' rep at HQ Herford Garrison. On another occasion a Brigade Commander's wife gripped me during a dinner party over a patch on the ceiling where water had recently come through from a bath overflow. The ceiling needed repainting as soon as possible, she said. I directed her concern to her husband's DAA & QMG across the table. A CO invited me to Sunday lunch. We had been DS together at Camberley. He then spent the afternoon walking me around his barracks questioning the phase one barrack modernisation programme. I got my Works 'King' to ring him next morning. I don't think he ever knew it but we only kept General Mike's big Ford Granada Staff car on the road until he left (and long after all the others had been withdrawn) through Bob Hume's enterprise in obtaining spares through our embassy in Paris. Tall as he was, it was the only car he could sit in with his hat on and sadly there were no 'Rollers' for issue to divisional commanders. I did, however, rally to the cause when the need arose for a weekly paper columnist. *Sixth Sense*, or the divisional newspaper, produced in Soest under the auspices of 6th Brigade was in danger of going under. Above all it needed better marketing, more advertising and a wider circulation. We reckoned it should be pushed as, at least, the 1st Corps weekly, if not that of BAOR. Happily we eventually got it accepted as the latter. In the interim we had some fun. The General wrote regularly as 'Mabel Crump'. She represented 'the women behind the men behind the guns'. Topics varied from 'better cookbook menus' to how to enjoy that R & R break with hubby home from Ulster. For a long period nobody knew 'Mabel Crump's' identity. One day, however, the new ADC blew it by posting the copy in an envelope stamped 'Office of the GOC 4th Division'. It did not, however, daunt our master. Caroline Dowdall, the Commander Royal Engineers wife, came up with a column entitled 'The Distaff Side' and covered such as fashion, flower arranging and the like. I chose the pen name 'Max Comfort' and produced some 100 articles designed to stir the community conscience on such diverse matters as vandalism, litter, drinking and driving and those pet German hates – cleaning cars and hanging washing out on Sundays. I also did a regular monthly book review which amazingly prompted one GOC's wife to ask me if I had actually read the books in question. In lighter moments, and in this case after a spell in hospital at BMH Rinteln, I came up with such as, 'Why not put your daughter on the wards, Mrs Worthington?' To this day, and whenever I bump into such as the then Corps Commander, General Sir Richard, Worsley, I am greeted with, 'How's Max today?'

We ran our first Ex ICE BREAKER for the logistic units in January 1975. It was the only time we could obtain a block booking space on a major training area – Haltern. It was planned on the lines of what we had done in HQ 39th Brigade with our signal squadron at Otterburn back in 1965. In short, all the logisticians, who were incidentally responsible for their own defence in the field, were given the chance to field fire, throw grenades, fire the rocket launcher and so on. The instructors were borrowed from 1st Queen's, then based in Werl. The ten-day training period concluded with a march and shoot type competition which included some practical first aid and watermanship. It was adjudged a real success by all

The 'Drum Major, Logistic Staff Band' – Herford 1975 (a Bramshill 'Trophy' is aloft!).

concerned and became an annual event. 'Chiefie and his Indians' also used the occasion to discuss amongst themselves, and to iron out their first thoughts, on how they might tackle the Ex WIDE HORIZON trials later in the year. Before we, however, come to those, I believe one might just mention the visit of Major General Cushman then the Commandant of the US Command and Staff College at Fort Leavenworth, Kansas. He had appeared at Herford not long after we had returned from Haltern. We had given him one of our 'plush' divisional briefings. As he left he said to the GOC, 'General, you and your Colonel AQ must come to Leavenworth to lecture to my faculty on your divisional organisation and functions.' I recall, after he had gone, saying to General Mike, 'I expect that's the last we will hear of that.' How wrong I was, since within three weeks an official request had been made to HQ BAOR. Despite an offer to fly us from Frankfurt, we were required to make the long and tedious journey from Herford to RAF Brize Norton in deepest Gloucestershire, there to join the weekly RAF Support Command scheduled VC10 Service (known affectionately as 'Crab Air' to most Pongos) to Washington – on this occasion via Ottawa. The plane was also carrying the Commandant of the RAF Staff College on his way to lecture at the USAF Academy at Colorado Springs. Whereas we had been limited to a single 'bearer' for the GOC, our airman's party included three 'hewers and carriers'. Once airborne the GOC, by then in need of some stiff refreshment after the long journey, leaned across to me and said, 'When do we get a drink, Charles?' I replied, 'The plain answer, General, is that we don't. The ADC should have warned you that the RAF are still living in the age of Prohibition.' Some six hours later and very 'dry' indeed, the General snatched a quick 'snifter' (or two) in the VIP lounge at Ottawa airport. Thereafter all was 'dry' again until we reached Andrews Air Force Base. On the return journey . . . but then that's quite another story.

On arrival we were put into the Arlington Marriott Hotel and over the weekend Andy Watson (later Major General) and his British Defence Liaison Staff (BDLS) team very kindly took us under their wing. We flew down to Kansas City on the Monday morning and left one sweet little air hostess musing, 'He's lovely and he really is a real British General.' We spent the Tuesday rehearsing our 'Morecambe and Wise' type act. This by now included the changes to the divisional organisation and functions proposed under Ex WIDE HORIZON. We were at it for five hours on the Wednesday and that evening were taken in to Kansas City to watch Ice Hockey and to dine. I could have done without the former and certainly didn't do justice to the biggest steak I have ever seen. We left after lunch on the Thursday, at which the Commander of the 4th US Infantry Division, down from Fort Carson, had presented us with a model of their divisional emblem – the 'Iron Horse'. In the form of a horse's head, it was in fact made of iron and not plastic. The single 'bearer' in our party made sure the BDLS team took over its onward despatch to Herford once he had got it as far as Washington. That evening General Mike and I had a 'private' prawn feast in a restaurant specially recommended to us. Next day I made a rather special pilgrimage to Miffie's grave in the Arlington Cemetery and that evening Betsy and George Soltan threw a splendid party for their best man. At it appeared many I had not seen since those far

off Berlin days. It had been a good week and I had offered to 'swap' with
our liaison officer at Leavenworth. He was not happy with his lot. The fact
that he was living at the point where the great Oregon Trail had begun did
not inspire him. He did not, however, inspire Mike Gow enough even if a
'swap' had been possible.

General Mike left us just before the Ex WIDE HORIZON trials began.
He went off to the Ministry to be Director of Army Training (DAT). Our
new master was Major General Nigel Bagnall (later Field Marshal Sir
Nigel Bagnall, GCB, CVO, MC). He had won an MC and bar with the
Green Howards during the Malayan emergency. He had subsequently
transferred to the 4th/7th Dragoon Guards. He had a reputation as a
'hatchet man' and certainly John Ballenden, the new Colonel GS, and I
both gave ourselves short terms of survival. As it turned out, our new boss
proved a good friend to both of us. He was very sharp and incisive with an
excellent brain. He tended to disguise a good sense of humour. He was
also never too big as to not heed advice, especially in the logistic field in
which he professed scant knowledge. It is not my intention here to discuss
the merits or otherwise of the Ex WIDE HORIZON trials. We conducted
them continuously over a period of six weeks. Suffice it to say that the
prime aim and object had been to dispense with one level of command.
This was to be the brigade level and the implications in the logistic field
suggested a more flexible forward replenishment approach to compensate
for the loss of the brigade administrative area. For the purposes of the
exercise the division comprised five battle groups of which a couple were
actually 'live' on the ground. The remainder were manned at CPX level
only. The 'live' battle groups had been made up to full strength and were
based about The Queen's Royal Irish Hussars (QRIH) and the 2nd Light
Infantry. Both were supported logistically by 'live' Immediate Replenishment Groups (IRG) formed from within my logistic units. In all my three
training seasons in BAOR this was the first (and last) time I saw units
actually exercised for real. It makes for a difference from CPX play, I
assure you. Very early on it became only too apparent that the span of
command was too great for effective control at divisional level. The
compromise was to introduce an intermediate Task Force HQ – a Brigade
HQ under any other name. It fooled nobody and in due course Task Force
HQs reverted to Brigade HQs. In our case the trials began with the
outloading of the new and purpose built ammunition depot at Pombsen.
For real and at night it took a great deal longer than on any CPX. It didn't
help that the access road permitted only single passage in parts. IRGs and
unit echelons sometimes failed to meet up. Grid references had got cor-

rupted over radio nets, maps were misread or vehicles broke down. There was also the hazard of sabotage action. In short, for the very first time in my experience we were all, and that included the logisticians, playing it as near as real could be. The plain fact was that, confronted with both the realities and imponderables of war, we were not as clever as we thought we were. It was a salutary lesson for us all.

Due largely to the language barrier, we lived generally like a race apart in our military cantonments. There were, of course, notable exceptions such as Mike Palmer and the other now senior cavalry brotherhood who had spent most of the last fifteen years (or more) on the BAOR armoured regiment 'treadmill' – Detmold, Hohne, Munster and Paderborn. They could communicate and understandably had established relationships in the local social pecking order. The majority, like me, and who had nobly got the chief 'schoolie' to organise some language classes for the AQ staff, were never really likely even to be able 'to offer Helga that cigarette on the local Bahnhof platform': lesson 3, if I recall correctly. We accordingly made our own fun wherever and whenever we could. To overcome the rather 'claustrophobic' garrison atmosphere I tended to get away to UK for a welcome break every six or so weeks. At Bank Holidays I sought sanctuary generally on the Belgian coast. Maurice Breda still ran the Le Carlton at Le Zoute and remained an excellent 'mine host'. On a couple of occasions I made it to Naples where Bruce Thomas was then on the NATO staff there and where we revived a few Borneo and Latimer memories. The 'black-tie' dinner party was then very much a feature of the garrison social scene and especially at Lieutenant Colonel and above level. This was despite the fact that, come the evening, most households only supported a 'self-help' domestic service scene. In short, a long-dressed and flustered hostess divided her attention between the kitchen and dining room; and where the key to culinary success or otherwise hinged on a deft partnership with hubby at the serving hatch. On such occasions the AQ team tended to finish the evening with a 'Vera Lynn Sings' session around Jerrie Hulme at the piano. All the old wartime favourites were featured. Thereafter the 'Logistic Staff Band', led by its 'Drum Major' (yours truly), would 'Beat Retreat' through the officers' married patch. A combination of a couple of tin whistles, a mouth organ, a number of combs and loo paper and a toy tin drum enabled us to render 'Colonel Bogey' and a fair Sousa selection. We only ever received one complaint and that came from the head 'schoolie'. On the basis that 'if you cannot beat them then join them' he paraded with us next time round. Sometime after I and others had departed, Bob Blewett let on to General

Nigel. I gather he too subsequently dined out on the story. It also helped across divisional boundaries that the senior management of the 1st and 4th Divisions were very well known to each other. Mike Gow and Major General John Stanier (later Field Marshal Sir John Stanier, GCB, MBE, DL) were old chums and Mike Gray was the latter's Colonel GS. The Colonel AQ, Richard Jerram (later Major General), was an old friend from both my Indian Army Cadet and Sandhurst days. A fairly well built couple, we were designated by the Corps Commander at a Study Period as his logistic 'second row'. As is so often the case, 'two is company and three is a crowd'. We both tended to refer to the 2nd Division, very much the odd man out, as 'Monty Mangham's Flying Circus'. Most unfair, I'm sure, and somewhat embarrassing when, at a later date, I came to work under the very charming gentleman concerned in the Ministry. But the infantry and cavalry have always tended to take a shy at the gunners when the opportunity presents itself – or the '9 Mile Snipers' as my father knew them!

Sport-wise I played a lot of tennis. I was even the nominated reserve for the HQ & Divisional Signal Regiment team in the BAOR Cup. We also attempted to foster Anglo-German relations with a so called mixed-doubles 'friendly' match with the Herford Tennis Club. My partner was the wife of the 2ic of the Signal Regiment. No mean player in any company. Our opponents were a couple of the 'herrenvolk' in their early twenties. 'Helmut's' first service removed the racquet from my partner's hand. This was certainly not social (or goodwill) tennis and thereafter we played (and lost) for the honour of St George. We never repeated the exercise. Chance permitted me a great opportunity to foster boxing – always a great love of mine. Early on Mike Palmer had invited me to take over divisional boxing, then at low ebb. At that time only an Army Open Team Competition was run and in recent years this had been dominated by 1st Queen's, the King's, the Parachute Regiment and 10th Regiment RCT. These 'gladiators' had virtually so monopolised the event between them that everybody else had shied off. Army boxing was clearly going to die unless we could break this stranglehold. I had an idea and discussed it with Bob Marshall, the divisional PT 'King'. We took the seven weights units were most likely to be able to fill (later increased to nine) and framed a Divisional Novices Boxing Competition about them. A truly 'beginners please' event in which an individual could only compete in up to a total of eight bouts. That first year, 1974, we had seven entries. The year after we had fifteen teams enter. The year after that it became a BAOR event and later still an Army one. More later when I became Vice Chairman of Army Boxing.

Suffice it to say here that the chap who really deserved the credit, Bob Marshall, never got it. I believe those in the 'striped PT jerseys' in Aldershot, and who controlled Army Boxing at the time, resented the fact that they had been truly shown up by one of their own at the sharp end. Not everybody is boxing mad. However, one cannot but fail to be lifted by one of these inter-regimental occasions, both Messes in their 'glad rags', each team well supported and a Band to hand to add tone in the interval. It is also a great test for the RSM or Master of Ceremonies. The noise is unbelievable and the strong unit pride is there for all to register. The atmosphere can become electric when all is dependent on the result of the final bout of the evening. Enough said, other than to repeat that such occasions typify what the much maligned and misunderstood regimental system is all about. For if you are a Queensman it's more than life is worth to be 'thumped' by a Green Jacket – and vice versa.

During the summer of 1975, and not long before the Ex WIDE HORIZON trials began, the then Military Secretary, Lieutenant General Sir Patrick Howard-Dobson, had visited Herford. He had suggested to me that I was likely to make the 1976 'Green List' (yes – another!) for promotion to Brigadier. In almost the same breath he had invited me to think about a Defence Fellowship in the academic year 1976-1977. I heeded the 'message' and was encouraged in this by General Nigel since he had done one a few years back. The cry was that 'there was a need to encourage suitable candidates'. So I got down to it and produced a thesis topic – the 'Rationalisation of the Support Services'. It had long concerned me that with the Defence Budget under continuous review we required, for example, three separate medical services, differing catering training schools and the like. I was, however, only too aware that too many single-service interests were then at stake to make this a popular choice. Indeed, this proved precisely the case when I attended the high level final selection board at the Ministry in early 1976. The Naval Secretary was at great pains to explain to me that quite a different being, and associated training programme, was required to man the galley in HMS *Tartar* than the cookhouse in 1st Queen's. He was, likewise, adamant that the Naval chaplain, apart from his sea legs, was quite a different soul to the Army padre. I was not too surprised, therefore, when my terms of reference were amended to read 'Support in British Forces Germany – the Options for Rationalisation in the Longer-Term'. I was, however, granted the concession whereby, in the final chapter of my thesis, I would be permitted to consider 'The Wider Implications of the Study'. The next step was to determine the most appropriate Defence Lecturer to sponsor my thesis. Since it had a distinct budgetary flavour, this was suggested by the Director of Army Education as David Greenwood at Aberdeen University. He ran the Centre for Defence Studies there and had previously had Eddie Fursdon (later Major General) under his wing for a short time. I flew up to Aberdeen to meet Greenwood and view the setting. It was early in the year and it was a beautifully sunny spring-like day in the Granite City. I was 'fooled' by both the weather and first impressions. Suffice it to say that after Ex SUMMER SALES that July I began my handover to my successor. He was David Ramsbotham who had just given up command of a Green Jacket battalion. We had last met in Borneo. I don't believe he was initially too excited to be joining the AQ Team. I did, however, point out to him a board in the office that indicated that all previous incumbents had gone on. I was to be no exception since two weeks earlier I had been selected for promotion to Brigadier in the next financial year. After David Ramsbotham (later General Sir David Ramsbotham, KCB, CBE) the post went to a 'true' logistician and the myth was finally buried that the Colonel AQ needed to have a teeth-arm background. Around this time Paul Travers took over as Quartermaster General, the first to hold the post from the logistic corps.

Before I left for home, and a quiet sojourn in Cornwall, I did some essential first hand research at both Rheindahlen and Lahr. In the first instance I discussed some thoughts and ideas with the Heads of Services there, both Army and RAF. Not surprisingly I ran into a good deal of vested interest 'stonewalling' and especially if I even murmured such possible 'heresy' as the creation of a Logistic Corps. Down at Lahr, near the Swiss border, I took a first hand look at what unification seemed to have done to the Canadians. It was clearly not a happy experience, though still in its early days. A Logistic Corps did seem, however, to have got successfully off the launching pad. I also called into the MOD, and the Staff College Retrieval Cell, to collect some Defence Training Committee Reports, relevant White Papers and some Defence Estimates I had earmarked for study. I was already aware that David Greenwood held much of the NATO publications material I was after. Whilst in Camberley I just checked in at Messrs Overs to ensure that those items I had taken out of store to brighten the flat in Herford had been returned to their repository. It was all still costing me a lot in storage charges. I made Aberdeen a fortnight before the Michaelmas Term was due to start. This was at the especial request of Greenwood. It was a hell of a drive from Cornwall so I broke the journey with the Humes, then at Malvern, and again at the Percy Arms at Otterburn. Unsure as to what the accommodation stakes would be,

I had booked myself in initially at the Station Hotel. Clearly my allowances would not cope with this in the long term. During my 'recce' it had
been suggested that I might be able to rent one of the cottages the University owned in Old Aberdeen. To cut a long story short, I finally finished up
in Crombie Hall, a students' hall of residence, and shared a postgraduate
floor (including bathroom and kitchen) with a couple from the West Bank
of the Jordan, an American from the deep South, a Turk, an Irishman from
Cork and a rather spotty Danish young lady. I was known generally as the
'War Lord'. I took breakfast in the Mess at the Bridge of Don Depot (they
couldn't, however, accommodate full Colonels!), lunch in the Senior Common Room (no more than a canteen) and dinner at the Station Hotel. I
survived but no real thanks to my sponsor, for it was a lecturer on the
Economics Faculty that found me the accommodation and Professor Reg
Jones, CB, CBE, of World War II 'Enigma' fame (he wrote his *Secret War*
book the year I was up), who took me under his wing thereon.

    I had let it be known to David Greenwood during my 'recce' that I had,
since the grant of my defence fellowship, been selected for promotion to
Brigadier. Once in Aberdeen I added the rider that it was more than likely,
therefore, that I would be unable to complete the full academic year. The
point did not seem to register with either he or the King's College Principal. It didn't help, therefore, when just before the end of my first term MS
rang me to say that they wanted me, together with my thesis, in the
Ministry by mid-May 1977. I think they felt that, in my case at least, the
fellowship was merely being used as a time filler. I had some sympathy
with their feelings but against this background, and a distinct personality
clash, life became difficult. Greenwood was no logistician and his background was that of an ex-RAF 'schoolie'. We had, therefore, little in
common. He was, however, a budgetary expert and well versed in the
literary arts. I learned a great deal from him in how to express my findings
on paper to their best advantage. Time clearly was not on my side if we
were to produce a study that would register. There was no scope for
lengthy debate, prolonged musing nor academic pontification. We had to
get on with the thesis and fast. That is why I had done the most basic and
essential research before my arrival. This was a different genre to the
style preferred by my sponsor and, thereafter, we had to agree to differ.
Needless to say the clerical and production back-up provided by David
Greenwood's Centre for Defence Studies was nigh outstanding and the
finished product most professional. In sticking to my guns, and really
getting something worthwhile down on paper, I had been greatly encouraged by the backing of Professor Reg Jones. The thesis was fed into the

MOD system just about the time I arrived to take up my new appointment as Director of Administrative Planning (Army) or DAP (A). It caused something of a stir in the QMG's world and opinions were sharply divided. The 'vested interests brigade' saw it as a somewhat savage attack on the administrative and logistic establishment. There was a clear reluctance to concede any hallowed ground. 'Too futuristic' was the cry that echoed through the corridors of AQ power. Suffice it to say that some fifteen years on the recently formed Adjutant General's and Royal Logistic Corps both bear a very strong resemblance, in title and composition, to the Administrative and Logistic Corps I had recommended. I was clearly just a little ahead of my time.

I had enjoyed putting the thesis together. I had, however, not really had much fun in Aberdeen. I was very much 'cut off' from my chums and whilst I sought to explore the Grampian Region the weather that year defeated me, for by early November the first snow had fallen and, whilst I did make Balmoral and Braemar, I didn't get much further afield. Professor Reg introduced me to the Royal Northern Club and I generally dined there each Monday evening. There I met a Senior and distinguished Scottish legal figure who had spent most of the war as a Jap POW in Changi and elsewhere. He showed me some wonderful pen and ink sketches he had made at the time, buried and later recovered after the war. We generally lunched at the Club each Friday after the Professor had taken me to the Gordons RHQ for a 'wee dram' or two. I was administered by the University Officer Training Corps and they were very kind to me. They asked me to all their social events and I responded by giving talks on 'Borneo' and 'Northern Ireland'. I did get down to London a couple of times on liaison visits to the Ministry and recall taking Mary Ames to the Regimental Cocktail Party – that year in the House of Commons. I also joined an RAF Nimrod sortie out of Lossiemouth in order that I could get a first hand view of the Brent and other offshore oilfields, for at that time Aberdeen was experiencing the early North Sea oil boom. I have been back since and I shall always recall the many miles I walked along that lengthy esplanade – often in pretty miserable conditions. I finally drove away in mid-April and sought temporary sanctuary with Jill and Ted Maslen-Jones at Liss before moving up to London and the Millbank HQ RAMC Mess. They were the daughter and son-in-law of the Hattons, who had both sadly died during my time in BAOR. After having held senior AQ staff appointments at both brigade and divisional level and, with one now scheduled in the Ministry, I had begun to feel like the truly 'compleat' logistician. But I remained an infantryman at heart.

Chapter 13

'One Star' Ceiling

I moved into the Millbank Mess in mid-May in Jubilee Year. It was, however, to be only a temporary arrangement, for during my latter weeks in Aberdeen Richard Vickers, last seen handling all that baggage in Kuching, had very kindly offered to let me rent his charming flat in Cornwall Gardens. I had gratefully accepted but necessarily had to 'wait out' for a few weeks until he moved across to BAOR to take command of the 4th Division in Herford. It was, however, from Millbank Mess that I stepped out along the Embankment on my first morning, soberly clad in dark suit and clutching my despatch case in my tiny hand (both then sure symbols of MOD employment). As I approached the Main Building, I was 'ambushed' by Mary Ames (then in the Navy Department) on behalf of King George's Fund for Sailors. She was so well positioned in Horse-guards Avenue that you could only but 'stand and deliver'. (A lesson that registered when I later became involved with the great annual ABF char-ity 'ambush' on the approaches to the Chelsea Flower Show.) I found my way to the Seventh Floor and the office of the Director of Administrative Planning (Army) or DAP (A). There I met up with Tom Jackson, whom I was to relieve. A Green Jacket, he had, like Paul Travers his predecessor, also been Colonel AQ, of a BAOR Division. It seemed then almost a prerequisite for the job. Prior to coming to MOD he had done the course at the Royal College of Defence Studies (RCDS). He was now going to Winchester to be Divisional Brigadier of The Light Division. I sensed that like me, a logistician by direction rather than desire, he was happy to be returning early to his more natural habitat. By a strange coincidence a similar 'wind of change' was to blow my way later in the year.

The Ministry of Defence (MOD) had been created in 1964 or a couple of years after I had left the old War Office. In essence it now comprised a joint Central Staff supported by separate single Service Departments. In the 'Q' or logistic ministry scene, into which I had now been cast, the Chief of Personnel and Logistics (CPL) was responsible for initiating and co-ordinating logistic studies and policies affecting all three Services on behalf of the Defence Council. This function was discharged through a pair of high level Committees – the Principal Administrative Officers' (PAO) and the Principal Personnel Officers' (PPO). My master, General Sir Patrick Howard-Dobson, then Quartermaster General (QMG) was a member of the PAOs Committee. He was assisted by VQMG – then Major General Desmond Maugham, with a very astute financial acumen. When dealing in the Central Staff 'market' I answered, like my naval and air force equivalents, on behalf of our Departments to the Assistant Chief of Defence Staff (Personnel and Logistics) or ACPL, then Major General Peter Blunt. A very wise and distinguished logistician, he also maintained a healthy sense of proportion at all times. My primary function within this framework was to oversee 'Q' operations and plans in meeting both operational emergencies and civil contingencies. Additionally my staff controlled the level within, and the distribution from, the 'QMG's Cup-board' – or what equipment and spares were available for issue at any one time and this included the proper maintenance of the War Reserve. As if this was not enough to keep us fully occupied DAP(A) and his staff were regarded as some sort of logistical 'Ombudsman's' Office. Files were floated at us from all directions seeking our 'blessing' for this or that and largely irrelevant to our main purposes in life. I soon learned to initial such files, add a new addressee or so, and continue the motion. I am sure some such files are still circulating today or have long since been 'mis-laid' in transit. They were generally the product of 'beavers' trying to justify their being and there were plenty of them about the Ministry in those now far off days. As was listed as almost a footnote in the MOD Directory, I had one other prime function. As Chairman of the Joint Services NAAFI Coordinating Committee, I answered to the Chairman of the NAAFI Council on behalf of the three Services. At that time the Chief of Fleet Support (CFS) (later Admiral Sir James Eberle, GCB) was filling the appointment. Described as the 'fittest Admiral in the Navy', and frequently to be seen 'at the double' in Dolphin Square, he and his fellow service councillors – QMG and the Air Member for Personnel – required to be briefed in detail before each Council Meeting. As I found out in a very short time, this could become a rather time consuming process, especially if it conflicted with something rather more urgent in the 'Q' operational field. Having said all that, I have, elsewhere within these pages, described variety as the spice of the soldier's life. I shall hereon, therefore, seek to highlight by function some of the more memorable events or incidents that punctuated my eighteen-month tour as DAP(A). I arrived to find that we had recently mounted a sizable reinforcement of the Belize (once British Honduras) garrison. This had been in response to some more than usually noisy sabre rattling by the Guatemalans in respect of a long-standing territorial dispute. We now had virtually a brigade group in the colony and with it a small number of a wide range of vehicles and equipments. These included such as Stalwart, Scorpion, Scimitar, LAA guns and the 105 mm pack howitzer. It was, however, always questionable to my mind whether the Guatemalans possessed either the real will or ability to mount anything more than a propaganda border foray. Despite the numerous rivers I could not see them penetrating either the Maya Mountains or the deep central jungle in any strength. Be that as it may, we were now committed and that great personality, Major General Peter Leng, then Major General Operations (MGO), had a firm grasp of the nettle. The immediate need, as I saw it, was to introduce a true sense of logistic reality to the situation. Or in the first instance to ensure, as soon as possible, the deployment of the logistic manpower, equipment and spares so as to provide proper maintenance for the variety of equipments now on the ground. In short, we required to establish a true AQ staff and something equivalent to a brigade administrative area (BAA) – and soonest. From my previous experience in Cyprus and the Far East, I also felt we needed to be sure that we did not unnecessarily stockpile ammunition and stores we would be unlikely to require in the long term. I had in mind especially such as defence stores (e.g. barbed wire and sandbags) which readily deteriorate in tropical climes. There was also a need to hold closer to hand some highly technical spares that might, or might not, be called for by the additional Hunters and helicopters now in the colony. To this end I went to see my old chum Reynell Taylor (later Major General), then Peter Leng's right-hand man as Brigadier General Staff Military Operations or BGS(MO). He was 'team leader' of the Army Departments operational 'triumvirate' at 'One Star' level. DAP(A) was another and the third was the Deputy Director of Army Staff Duties or DDASD. After some discussion we agreed on a somewhat original proposal – a floating stockpile. Or a Royal Fleet Auxiliary (RFA), positioned some way off shore, where emergency spares or stores could be collected by helicopter if the need arose and which could be withdrawn once the immediate crisis was over. After one RFA relief the second was quietly removed never to be replaced. With the 'threat' now seemingly less imminent, our task switched to improving the lot and 'quality of life' for those remaining in the enlarged garrison. The focus turned towards bettering the camp accommodation, improving the NAAFI and other canteen and welfare facilities and obtaining some of those Nuffield Grant boats. We even found some 'hirings' to accommodate the families of those on two-year staff tours. Just before I handed over I paid a brief visit to Belize. It reminded me very much of my 'look in' on Guyana all those years before. I, however, rated Belize City (the biggest town though not the capital) rather less exciting than Georgetown – and that had nothing to do with the cricket ground in the latter. I did, however, get considerable satisfaction in seeing a proper 'Q' system now fully functional in the theatre. I also recall eating the biggest avocado pears I have ever seen and this time without custard.

At the time I took over my desk on the Seventh Floor I found that MGO had recently initiated the RARS Study. This was in effect a study relating to the rates of ammunition expended by the Israelis during the Yom Kippur War, first in containing the Egyptian assault across the Canal and next in the delivery of the counter stroke; the aim being to relate the findings to the short war (five to seven days) scenario on the North German Plain. Whilst it was all great stuff, I was frankly delighted when, very early on, Desmond Mangham, with his feet very firmly on the ground, registered the 'Q' concerns (or 'spanners') as regards such basics as cost, carriage and storage. One did not need to be a 'Senior Wrangler' to recognise that the bill for extra transport and new ammunition storage bunkers would take some 'selling' in Treasury circles and could only probably be achieved by some very substantial cuts somewhere else in the overall defence budget. It was also very unlikely that the West Germans would take too kindly to a fresh rash of ammunition bunkers being studded across the North German Plain. In short, the aim of the study, whilst sound, failed to properly assess the difference between what might be desirable and what is actually practicable in peace. It also tended to highlight the variation in thinking on the likely duration of any conflict with the Soviets. For whilst one section of my staff were assessing the ramifications of the RARS Study against a short war scenario, others, involved in the US/UK Logisticians' talks, were concerned with the development of Bramley as a major US Ammunition Depot and the reception of US convoys in Southampton Water as late as D + 40. These latter talks were conducted under the aegis of ACPL and all were held in the same building. At a 'No 11 Board' Meeting (an informal weekly gathering of 'One Star' Directors) I hosted before I left MOD, I made a point that I hoped that by the time I returned, somebody who have decided which war we were preparing to fight and for how long.

Since the General Strike of 1926 the Ministry has maintained (and regularly updated) a series of contingency plans designed to cope with strikes and other industrial unrest within the major public utilities and services. For example, in the mid-fifties troops had frequently been deployed in the London Docks during periods of industrial troubles there. In November 1977, after the breakdown of lengthy pay negotiations, the Fireman's Union suddenly called a major strike throughout the country. The Services were immediately called in to maintain fire cover with the assistance of the police. DDASD, Lord Guy Alvingham (later Major General and a fellow Camberley Student many years back) was at the Army Department helm and was, in fact, the co-ordinator for all three Services. The 'triumvirate' was soon assembled in his office as he unravelled the relevant contingency plan. Since no attempt was to be made to cross picket lines at fire stations, to release regular equipment for use, the plan hinged essentially on the serviceability, distribution and manning of a number of 'cocooned' ex-wartime Auxiliary Fire Service (AFS) fire engines. Known as 'Green Goddesses' (the AFS colour was green), they had last been issued to the Mobile Defence Columns (MDC) in the mid-fifties and had since been stored in depots about the country. There remained some question as to how many there actually were and where they all were. We were still discovering them some weeks into the strike. In addition to hoses and basic fire fighting equipment, such as axes, the vehicles were also purported to carry helmets, wellingtons, and oilskins for the crew. We, in fact, discovered that the latter were generally of standard middle size issue. This not unnaturally presented some problems. The Gurkhas were, for example, literally standing on the bottoms of their oilskins; the Grenadiers had them up to their knees. In short, in the 'Q' world our first priority was to get the crews properly fitted out. Through the good offices of the Logistic Executive at Andover, contacts with naval stores depots and local purchase we soon had a well-clad fire fighting team. Suffice it to say that some people in the waterproof manufacturing trade made a 'penny or two' in providing overtrousers. Others did well in producing blue flashing lights to affix to support vehicles and big woollen 'oversox' to go with the wellington boots. It is always easy to be wise in hindsight and, looking back, there can be no doubt that we would have got off to a better start had we known, before the strike, the actual numbers of 'Green Goddesses' available and where they all were. Likewise it would have helped to have known what was on each vehicle. Above all I believe we on the Seventh Floor should have been brought in on the act much earlier. Once there was a first smell of a possible strike we should have been fully acquainted with the contingency plan. Perhaps we should have reacted earlier and certainly thereafter, when such as a tanker drivers dispute began to threaten, we were down on the Fifth Floor reading up the relevant plan. It was, however, my first experience in the civil contingency field and we all learn by our mistakes.

Once the troops and 'Green Goddesses' had been deployed throughout the length and breadth of the country the next 'Q' priority was to ensure that they were as well found as possible. Where crews were based on barracks and air stations this presented no real problems. Many others were, however, lodged in TA Centres and Police Stations. Others, like in my early Ulster days, were housed in vacant warehouse-type premises. In these circumstances we had to provide beds and bedding plus cooking and catering facilities. However, the British Serviceman remains highly adaptable to both challenge and circumstances. I recall visiting a Green Jacket unit in the Mile End Road. They were enjoying the temporary task, saw the need for it and had recently performed well at the scene of a local fire. They had also made themselves as comfortable as possible in a pretty aged TA Drill Hall. In fact, having ironed out the wrinkles and got the system working, we reckoned that the third need was to keep the crews aware that senior management had not forgotten them. This was especially important morale-wise once the strike ran on into its second month. It actually lasted nine weeks and during that time we persuaded our masters that they would do us best service by getting out and about. QMG, always a great 'chatter-up', revelled in this role and it was certainly much appreciated by the lads on the ground. The strike ended almost as quickly as it had begun. The Services and the Police had maintained an adequate if not strictly professional service. There had been no major disasters even though the only specialised breathing apparatus available had been held by a few RAF teams. It would have been wrong to draw any false conclusions from this strike. We had possessed the ability to cope – or just. Later when it came to the threat of a power strike it was evident that we no longer had sufficient expertise to even maintain the national grid at minimum level. Likewise, whereas we could provide a number of drivers capable of coping with any tanker fleet dispute, we could not deploy them without crossing picket lines and so aggravating the situation. In short, there was now a strict limit on what the Services could do to assist in the face of most civil contingencies arising from industrial action. Since the cuts imposed by 'Options for Change' this capability has been even more

reduced. It is also perhaps of interest that the bulk of the 'Green Goddesses' have since been sold overseas.

Some rather 'wild' decisions could be made, and 'throw away' lines be
uttered, late on any Friday afternoon in the MOD and just before the
weekend rush to the country began. Certainly this was my experience on
more than one occasion. In this instance it was Maundy Thursday, 1978,
and the Easter Break was virtually upon us. In the past twenty-four hours
it had been announced that, as soon as possible, the UN were to deploy a
small peacekeeping contingent along the Litang River in the Lebanon. It
was to be known as UNIFIL. Dr Owen (later Lord Owen), then Foreign
Secretary, had agreed that the UK would provide the force with 2nd Line
logistic support from our bases in Cyprus. I had meanwhile been in touch
with the Colonel AQ at HQ British Forces Cyprus and he had indicated
that he foresaw no real problems. He merely requested that once the
UNIFIL Chief Logistician had finished his 'recce' (due the following
week) he be directed to Cyprus carrying his likely requirements bill in his
back pocket. Around 4.00 pm that fateful afternoon I was summoned to a
senior presence some floors below and told that I was to fly to New York
soonest and to establish from the UN the probable logistic support bill
they envisaged. I would hasten to add here that it was not a Senior
Logistician addressing me. In fact, my masters were unaware of these
goings on until a good deal later – Easter had begun. I pointed out to the
General that by the time I reached New York it would be Easter there too.
An 'unknown soldier' wandering around an empty UN building seemed
unlikely to achieve anything very constructive. I then proposed the 'get-
together' suggested by the Colonel AQ in Cyprus and added that either I
or my AA & QMG (Ops), a Lieutenant Colonel, would represent the MOD
at the discussions. At that point the penny seemed to drop and it was
recognised that I was probably talking good sound commonsense. About a
fortnight later a session took place in Cyprus with the French Colonel and
his logistic team. We were represented by my AA & QMG (Ops) and he
came back with only one bid that couldn't be met from within the Cyprus
base – a quantity of 'Portakabins'. These were later purchased on behalf
of the UN and shipped out to Cyprus.

The UNIFIL saga did not, however, end there. Dr Owen was very
keen that we should do something rather special to support the Fijian
contingent. A Fijian battalion had done us proud during the Malayan
Emergency and he was anxious that we should reciprocate in some
small way. He chose the provision of equipment as the means. His main
bid was for a sizeable fleet of Land-Rovers. A supplementary request was

made for a number of General Purpose Machine Guns (GPMG). He was clearly not best pleased when we advised him that all the new Land-Rovers due off the production line were already bespoke, and that only a single GPMG remained uncommitted in the 'QMG's Cupboard' at that time. All we could, therefore, offer up were reconditioned Land-Rovers from the BAOR Reserve Pool held in the Antwerp Forward Base. These vehicles were earmarked for issue to TA units reinforcing BAOR in an emergency. I had viewed them recently, when visiting the Antwerp Base with Paul Travers then Brigadier AQ, HQ BAOR. Though they were perfectly serviceable, one could not guarantee their roadworthy life thereon. It could have been as much as another 40,000 miles – it might have been less than 400. They were really not the ideal gift to offer in the circumstances. Nor were reconditioned Light Machine Guns (LMG). All this did not make Dr Owen a very happy Minister but if he did feel he had 'some gravy down his front' then the fault lay with his staff, not we on the Seventh Floor – for had they thought to ask before their master 'lept' no false expectations would have been aroused. I still wonder whether those concerned really understood, and which we were at pains to explain, the husbandry associated with the proper care of the 'QMG's Cupboard'. For we did try to show how the new equipments purchased were directly related to the specific bids contained in the Defence Estimates and the associated re-equipment programme forecast in the Defence White Paper. In short, everything that came out of the factories generally had an immediate home to go to. The remainder was earmarked for the War Reserve and this was said to be inviolate in peace. This brings me to a somewhat startling sideline, almost unwittingly unearthed by my staff, in a review we had initiated in respect of major equipments in the War Reserve and notably the aged Centurion tanks listed. These were supposed to roll towards Dover in the lead up to mobilisation. In recent years, and during my travels between one major training establishment and another, I had noted the increasing habit to have some major piece of equipment on display at the camp entrance. In several instances I had recognised them to be tanks and mostly Centurions. Just lately I had visited the Humes at Arborfield and had spotted one there too. To cut a long story short, most of these display tanks, often filled with concrete and minus guns and radio fittings, were still very much part of the listed War Reserve. Few could have ever have made Dover even on a tank transporter. Suffice it to say that they were discreetly replaced by a new Chieftain buy. So in the end the War Reserve tank element went by chance from 'rags to riches'.

Earlier I mentioned that when dealing in the Central Staff 'market' I answered, like my naval and air force equivalents, on behalf of our Departments to ACPL. In this context, and with Major General Peter Blunt at the helm, we attended the regular NATO Logisticians Meetings in Brussels and the annual US/UK Logisticians' session in either London or Washington. There was always a lot of high level 'jaw-jaw' on these occasions and at 'one star' level one felt almost an appendage. However, I much enjoyed the Brussels visits and especially the comfort and cuisine of the excellent Belgian Officers' Club there. Elsewhere I have described the war we were discussing in the US/UK logisticians' forum and the only visit that produced in my time was to the proposed ammunition depot site at Bramley. It did not excite me as did not the then 'youngest General in the US Army', or so the story went. In his late thirties and heading the US team, he was a Major General in the US Chemical Corps. He was then holding the head logistician's appointment at HQ USAREUR – the equivalent to HQ BAOR. It was my misfortune to be seated on one side of him at the dinner we hosted. All I can remember of a very boring evening was a frightening rundown he gave me on his outline daily schedule. 'I rise, Charles, at 5.00 am and jog till 5.45. A shower and a light fruit breakfast and I am in the office by 6.15. A quick read of the overnight signals and the daily staff briefing begins at 6.30. I never leave the office before 7.00 pm in the evening and I work six days a week. Sunday is my day of rest and I always include a round of golf.' I just felt for his family and even more for his staff. Having said that, I had noticed that in Whitehall the early morning 'fever' had begun to catch on there too. I was now at my desk by 8.15 am at the latest and, as I entered the building, I generally ran into the MGO and the Vice Chief of the Defence Staff (VCDS) (then Admiral Sir Anthony Morton from HMS *Sea Eagle* days). Some years later my old chum Paul Travers was to admit to me, that as QMG, he was often in his office by 7.30 am. One did sometimes wonder whether all this earnest endeavour was really necessary when our commitments, and especially overseas, were less than they had ever been and were still on the decrease. I have always been one who believed that too many telephones and typewriters about encourage the 'underemployed', in any HQ or Government Department, to create work to justify their very existence. I am sure this is true where overmanning exists.

An entertaining little chore was the half-yearly attendance at meetings of the FINABEL Logisticians' Committee. Sponsored by France, and outside the realms of any strict NATO tie-up, it included representatives from Italy, UK and the Benelux countries. Gatherings were held under the chairmanship of a Colonel Prieur from the Logistics Division of the French Defence Ministry. The official language was French and all delegates were accompanied by an interpreter. One can appreciate that this tended to slow down the discussion of papers and the proceedings could become tedious in the extreme. Each nation hosted the meetings in turn over a three-day period. The last day was always devoted to a service interest outing and hosts tended to vie with each other to produce the most hospitable and memorable occasion. I inherited a meeting which somebody had rather 'mistakenly' scheduled for the Jubilee Bank Holiday weekend. We found ourselves, for instance, as the only people in the Ministry on the Friday morning. I will simply say that a viewing of the Massed Bands on Horse Guards, a trip to the RAOC computer at Bicester and a conducted tour round the Oxford Colleges followed by dinner under the MOD in King Henry VIIs wine cellar went down quite well, even if not really quite my choice. It certainly, however, did not match, for example, a subsequent French-hosted meeting in Bordeaux. There we visited the Saint Emillion vineyards in the morning, lunched in a superb restaurant in the delightful resort of Arcachon (with the biggest sandhill in the world) and in the afternoon toured the Landes rocket test site further down the coast. It was there that I first heard mention of the Exocet missile and witnessed a trial firing. I floated a paper on casualty evacuation in the field. It had always worried me in BAOR, since in war, we relied so heavily on reservists and TA units to bridge the gaping holes in peace. It was still being discussed when I left and, at that rate of progress, could still be. For without simultaneous translation, in the style of the NATO Logisticians meetings, the pace of business was truly painful. It is perhaps just of interest here to mention that whilst at Oxford I got the current Defence Fellow there to show me his accommodation and outline his lot. He was living in College in the traditional fellow style lodgings. He also dined regularly at high table. In short, he was enjoying what I had always supposed senior academic life to be all about.

As 'Max Comfort' I had fiercely attacked the 'League of NAAFI Knockers' in the pages of *'Sixth Sense'* during my time in BAOR. I was aware that a number of the more senior wives, with some colloquial German to hand, could 'shop around' on the local economy. They could as such, often get a cheaper and better deal than at the NAAFI Shop nearby. But, as Harry Dalzell Payne once said, I believed that without NAAFI the majority of the families, and especially the junior ones, would have starved. I was then perhaps a good choice to carry the NAAFI banner at MOD level and especially as Chairman of the Joint Services NAAFI Coordinating Committee. My first move was to take the Committee, which included the Service representatives attached to NAAFI HQ, to the main warehouse at Bulford, there to view the range of goods on offer and to discuss and recommend possible new lines. It was an eye opener to all concerned. The second move was to arrange for CFS to have a NAAFI tour of BAOR and Berlin. I didn't really believe a sailor could head the NAAFI Council if he had no real feel for the main problem area. Being the really big man he was, the Admiral fell in with the idea and actually enjoyed a very good trip hosted by NAAFI. My third and final venture in this field was to take on the Treasury in 'close combat' over their proposal to raise rental charges against NAAFI for the use of their premises in barracks, on airfields and the like. This would have been a fair one had they been competing on the same terms as Tesco's and so on. However, NAAFI had to operate where the need arose and not necessarily where there was a vast profit to be made. This was particularly true as regards isolated barracks and air stations. Likewise NAAFI profits were generally

Conducting the City of London School CCF Annual Inspection – London 1979.

Time for a 'drag' at a 2nd Royal Anglian Company base – Londonderry 1980.

'ploughed back' into the Services through the rebates made to units (in more recent years rebates accruing from tours in Ulster had provided units with rich pickings to support welfare and sports grants). So I arranged a day out with my Treasury 'beaver' and we visited a mix of NAAFI shops at Barton Stacey, Bulford, Tidworth and Upavon. I offered the following week to do a similar tour about East Anglia. It seemed that these 'stone-walling' tactics saw 'the new ball off', for during the rest of my tour the matter did not raise its ugly head again.

During the summer of Jubilee Year I had lunched at the RCDS at the invitation of Patrick Palmer and others from those Camberley DS days. Whilst there, Mike Reynolds told me that at the end of the course he was to go to Bassingbourn as Divisional Brigadier, The Queen's Division. He and Anne had already been up to see the house that went with the job. I thought nothing more of this until one evening in November when Mike rang me and said that, due to some chain reaction, he was now to be Deputy Adjutant General (DAG), HQ BAOR. He suggested, there and then, that I should now go for the Bassingbourn post. His words were, 'If I am not now to do it you should.' I have to say that it is one I had always had my eye on and for which General Mike Gow, in particular, had recommended me. I was equally aware that I was holding a good appointment, one which had seen such as Paul Travers proceed to high places. My prospects were clearly not so great and I saw myself being firmly and finally classified as a 'Q' man. My real fear being that I might eventually end up as Chief of Staff (COS) to the Logistic Executive or, worse still, as Director of Army Quartering. Both Major Generals' posts, indeed, and sporting the appropriate pension. I had, however, been a little riled during the fire strike when a very senior civil servant had made the very false assumption that I must have had a logistic corps upbringing. He expressed very considerable dismay when I pointed out that I was an infantryman through and through. Not too surprising really, I suppose, since my opposite numbers had begun, one as a purser, the other in the RAF Secretarial Branch. Like Tom Jackson before me, I had seen a couple of our contemporaries, Peter Sibbald and Lennox Napier (later of some renown as the Chairman, Central Transport Consultative Committee), make it to Major General from the Divisional Brigadier's chair. Peter Welsh was to do likewise later. I, therefore, decided to take a calculated risk and change 'One Star' horses in midstream. I went to see QMG (by then affectionately known as 'Marco Polo' as he seemed in permanent 'Q' orbit about the world) and he reluctantly agreed that my name should go forward to MS. I have always had the suspicion, then and since, that with my old mentor, General Tim Creasey, as then Colonel Commandant of the Division I might have been 'pushed' had I not volunteered. I had a very flattering send off when the time came and, as QMG put it in his own words, 'The Fifth and Sixth Floors now 'think "Q" almost without being reminded and it has been the greatest help to have a proper soldier, who is also a logistician, in your chair.' Kind words indeed, and whilst I had again been classified as a logistician I was still a proper soldier at heart – whatever that may mean.

In fairness to the Vickers it behoved me to find another tenant to replace me in the flat. General Mike Gow came to the early rescue here, saying that he knew that VCGS (then General John Stanier) was looking for a 'pad' in Central London. Early contact was made and, thereafter, I handled the takeover through his MA, Jeremy Blacker (later Lieutenant General Sir Jeremy Blacker, KCB) who had been a student during my DS days at Camberley. I had enjoyed my eighteen months in London and especially Jubilee Year. There had, however, been ups and downs. The flat was burgled one October Friday afternoon and it was an unpleasant sight that greeted me as I returned home with my weekly shopping order from the Chelsea Barracks NAAFI Shop. I lost a lovely antique clock and some sentimental silver pieces that I had taken out of store whilst in London. They were never seen again. I also had the roof of my new MGB sports 'slashed' one evening. However, on the plus side I got away most weekends to friends and saw a good deal of Mary Ames, Tonia Bern-Campbell (from the Le Zoute connection) and Sue Kavanagh. The latter, a delightful young WRAC lady, had been at Corps HQ whilst I had been at 4th Division and had 'saved me' when I needed a partner to attend the Herford 'Grimmies' annual Christmas Party. I wasn't going to go to that one unescorted! She had, in fact, first caught my eye as she threw up a salute with one hand and paraded her dog in the other. After Aberdeen it was good to have some social life again and there were some memorable evenings in the company of Reynell Taylor and Johnny Watts (then Commander SAS Group) at the Special Forces Club. I was, however, not too sorry to be on the move again.

At the start of World War II, RAF Bassingbourn had been a Fighter Command Station. In 1942 it had become the home of a USAF Bombardment Group and remained as such until the end of the war. It had then become a Training Command Station and had been particularly associated with the Canberra conversion programme. During the war the only damage had been self-inflicted when a Bomber Command Whitley, due to a major magnetic compass error, had picked up the Thames estuary in place of the Rhine and dropped a stick of bombs across the runway. The station had been rechristened Bassingbourn Barracks in 1970 when the HQ and Depot, The Queen's Division had taken up occupation. That is not to say that the Divisional System had not given birth back in 1968 and my first contact with it had been by letter and signal during the Bahrain tour. By the time I arrived the set-up was well established and the HQ functioned from a very suitably converted section of the very sizeable Lutyens-designed Officers' Mess. There was also a very large house, once the property of the Station Commander, that went with the job. My predecessor had not lived in it, preferring to occupy a flat in the Mess during the week. It had been made clear to me by the Director of Infantry (later Lieutenant General Sir David Young, KBE, CB, DFC), my immediate master, that he wanted no further 'absentee landlords'. My AAG or right-hand man, was initially John Pollard. We had known each other many years and he had been a staunch supporter during the absorption of those 4th Battalion personnel at Lingfield some years back. He had recently commanded in the Oman. Sadly he never completed his tour as cancer tragically claimed him. The vista was by no means scenic since the Cambridgeshire 'prairie' was on our doorstep. The city of Cambridge was some twelve miles to the East and Royston some three miles South. London was a good one and a half hours' drive (in good traffic conditions) and so I found it best to persuade my friends to come and enjoy a Sunday Curry Lunch at Canberra House and many did.

My task under the Divisional System was essentially to supervise the recruiting, basic training and manning of the three Large Regiments that made up The Queen's Division – The Queen's Regiment, The Royal Regiment of Fusiliers and The Royal Anglian Regiment. This covered nine Regular battalions, seven TA battalions and two Ulster Defence Regiment or UDR battalions (the 5th (County of Londonderry) and 10th (City of Belfast)) which were then affiliated to the Division. Let us expand on this somewhat bland statement, in turn, by function. Recruiting involved both officers and soldiers and, in the latter category, included both junior leaders and plain junior soldiers. Basically the Divisional recruiting area covered Greater London, the Home Counties, East Anglia, the East Midlands and the special Fusilier enclaves in Lancashire, Northumberland and Warwickshire. Each Regiment deployed a number of special recruiters within the Army recruiting organisation plus a Regimental Information Team (RIT) and a Regimental Careers Officer (RCO). Most of these folk were 'borrowed' from battalions and were shown against their strength. The RIT were primarily concerned with 'shewing the cap badge'

about the regimental recruiting areas at major events and shows in their
Counties. Where possible they sported a display and were supported by
regimental bands or corps of drums. They also had a major part to play in
assisting with training at the annual camps of their affiliated Combined
Cadet Force (CCF) and Army Cadet Force (ACF) units; for it was this
'partially committed' group of youngsters we rather naturally viewed as
potential 'seed corn' for the future. It was also a fact that between Selsey
Bill and King's Lynn, and about those Fusilier 'pockets', there were
plenty of little lads, with berets resting on their ears, who merely needed a
little 'nudge' our way. The RCO, on the other hand, concentrated his
efforts on what we termed the regimental 'favoured' schools; all had
about a dozen each and where the RCO kept his foot firmly in the Common Room door. To press our case one stage further, we even hosted a
Headmasters' Conference at Bassingbourn in my time. Each Regiment
went for their 'favoured' schools and actually persuaded the majority to
attend at Headmaster level. Once Regiments had made their Potential
Officer (PO) selections, they attended a Pre-RCB session at Bassingbourn.
Modelled on the real thing at Westbury, we attempted to sort the 'wheat
from the chaff'. Whilst we could not deny any a chance to try their hand at
Westbury, the advice to either 'Come back again in a year's time when
you have hitch-hiked across Canada' or 'Stick to Lloyds Bank or Tesco's,
this is really not your scene' usually dissuaded the obvious 'no-hoper'.

Basic training at Bassingbourn then covered the adult intake, the junior
soldier element and the TA recruit cadres. The Junior Leaders were
trained separately at Shorncliffe. The facilities at Bassingbourn were
generally adequate, though we did have to run a small Battle Camp up at
Warcop to cope with the more advanced phases of the recruit syllabus and
notably the field firing. It was a bit of a 'sausage machine' and the wastage
was higher than we would have liked. Much of this was linked to either
medical or motivation weakness. It was amazing how many 'ills' came to
light once earnest training began and which had not been unearthed by the
initial medical examination at the recruiting office. Likewise, once it
became a little tough, those with their hearts not really in it began to
steadily surface. They were simply not the material one could risk on a
dicey patrol on a dark night in the bandit country of South Armagh.
Having said that, it was always a pleasure to mix with the mums, dads,
grannies and all who came from far and wide to view the Passing-Out
parades. Over tea in the NAAFI, they would extol our virtues in how we
had really made something of little 'Willie'. As I recall one grandma
saying to me, and who had been in the ATS during the war, 'He was a

little weed was young Jimmy when he left us. Just look at him now – a
real soldier.' In the case of the TA we ran a concentrated fourteen-day
recruit cadre that guaranteed an acceptable if fairly basic standard. It was,
however, a good deal better than any TA unit could do under self-help
arrangements and they learned to accept that fact.

Manning was, however, the major problem area for recruiting and
wastage (or run out) never quite tallied. Recruiting was likewise uneven
between Regiments. You don't find too many young recruits on the 'Costa
Gereatrica' 'twixt Folkestone and Eastbourne. There are rather more to be
had in the East Midlands and Northwest. Likewise there had to be priorities related to current tasks and roles. A battalion on operational duty in
West Belfast had clearly a greater need than one in the third echelon
Home Defence role in Connaught Barracks, Dover. Likewise when it
came to the half yearly postings meetings (or 'markets' as some termed
them) and the placing of WOs/SNCOs for appointment, the TA Home
Defence battalions inevitably finished up at the bottom of the pile quality-
wise. Everybody wanted the best and there had to be priorities here too.
Especially, as in this connection, we also had a recognised responsibility
for the career planning of both Officers and WOs/SNCOs. It was up to me,
based on the findings of the CR reporting system, to pick out the 'fliers'
early on and thereafter to 'stream' them towards in one case command;
the other to a quartermaster's commission. It was mainly in this manning
and careers hat that my unit visits were conducted. Firstly to get any
armoured 'whizz kid' BAOR Brigade Commander off the back of a CO
whose battalion was somewhat understrength. Most of such young gentry
had never done a tour on the streets of Ulster and so found it difficult to
comprehend that, in infantry manning priorities, the operational requirements 'across the water' took pride of place over the training needs of
BAOR. In one case I had to make the point that, if I couldn't provide that
extra company to fill that blue chinagraph oblong on his GDP map, he
would have to rub it off. In any event it was not the CO's fault but mine.
As it happened during my Bassingbourn tour many of the Brigadiers like
Patrick Palmer, Guy Watkins and Mike Swindells had been DS with me.
This made for understanding. The secondary aspect of the visit, besides
getting the Brigade Commanders view on the unit and the CO (and form-
ing one's own – they generally tallied), was to interview all officers and
WOs/SNCOs who had some career concern or whom the CO wanted me to
'gently insert the boot'. In this sort of 'honest broker' guise I was the
agent of Stanmore for the Officers and the Exeter Record Office for the
WOs/SNCOs. In short, I never committed myself to promises which

couldn't be fulfilled or to prophesies that were unlikely to stand up in time. In this field I soon became acutely aware as to exactly how career conscious the modern generation were. I found it almost unhealthy, especially amongst the junior officers. I felt they were just not enjoying life as much as we had. Most knew all about 'Pink', 'Blue' and 'Green' Lists long before I had ever heard of any of them. I found it equally trying that some who were clearly never going to make it above Major, and now had a guaranteed career to age fifty-five years, couldn't see the benefit of stepping out of what had now become something of a 'rat race' for the pleasures of the 'Paradise Trail'. A seconded and well paid accompanied tour in the tropical surrounds of Brunei was just one such opening. Colonels of Regiment were kept in the picture on all these issues through their RHQs and once a year, generally at HM Tower of London where the Fusiliers retained their RHQ, the Colonel Commandant had a session with them to keep the party sweet. As outstations of the Directorate of Infantry we batted an agreed infantry line in all matters of major policy. We just differed a bit in our styles of dress and headgear.

My remit from the Colonel Commandant was to visit all Regular battalions, wherever they might be stationed, at least twice a year. Sadly in my time I was restricted overseas to Berlin, BAOR and Gibraltar. I was also a near season ticket holder on the shuttle to Belfast (with such as the BBC's, Kate Adie) to see units across the province including our affiliated UDR battalions. As regards the TA, and our associated CCF and ACF contingents, the priority was to attend the annual camps. In so doing I became familiar with training areas as far apart as Gairloch Head in the North of Scotland and Penhale deep in West Cornwall. Being a conservative by nature, my favourites remained Otterburn and Stanford (where much of *Dad's Army* was filmed). On my first return to Berlin (after some twenty-nine years) I behaved like a true tourist and the CO of 2nd Royal Anglian kindly lent me his car and a guide. I discovered that the Rodes House at Wannsee was now a Convent (how Miffie would have smiled), the NAAFI Officers' Club to still be fully functional and the Wall to be an obscenity. I took the opportunity to go through Check Point 'Charlie' into East Berlin and did some Dresden china window shopping in the Unter den Linden. Whilst the surrounds and the people were drab, to my mind the City that side of the Wall had been more tastefully restored to its former glory than the glitz and garishness that now dominated West Berlin and especially the Kurfurstendam. But then perhaps I am old fashioned. It was a truly nostalgic visit and I never ceased to enjoy the subsequent ones that followed including, on one occasion, attendance at the truly remarkable Berlin Tattoo. Expense seemed no object under the terms of the Berlin Budget and I can recall watching the Royal Anglians re-enacting a scene from the Sikh Wars which included four elephants pulling heavy cannon. The elephants had been brought over from a zoo in the East Midlands and the cannon manufactured in the local REME workshops. All the Sikh and old military costumes had been hired from a costumiers in London. All rather far removed from Les Wilson's 'self-help' Tattoo at Hamala Camp. I had never before been to Gibraltar and at the time the frontier was closed. We toured the Rock in the CO's car and some twelve minutes later we were back where we had started. It was that claustrophobic and I was not too surprised that the battalion concerned, well into their second year, had gone somewhat limp. To fire their annual range course they had, for example, to be flown home to Salisbury Plain. After a surfeit of ceremonial, such as the Keys Ceremony, the sight of millions of stalagmites and stalactites in the many caves and the impressions formed during my initial tour I came to describe Gibraltar as 'Royston by the Mediterranean'. It certainly seemed about as exciting and when I had my interview with the then Governor, General Sir William Jackson, GBE, KCB, MC, and who I had last known as QMG, I made the point that I would do my very best to ensure that no Divisional battalion caught 'Gibraltar Fever' again if I could possibly help it. None did, I am happy to say, though I was to return some years later in my Colonelcy hat and after the frontier had been opened. I still rated it a 'dud' posting for such as an infantry battalion and I am delighted that it has now lapsed forever.

A range of 'extra-mural' type activities tended to ensure that one was never at a loose end. In my home defence capacity as military adviser to the Sub-Regional Controller administering Bedfordshire, Hertfordshire and Essex, I played my part in a pair of major civil defence CPX and notably the last big one, Ex SQUARE DEAL, held in the autumn of 1980. I and my team, a combination from my HQ and RAF Henlow, occupied a splendid 'funk hole' (or underground command bunker) in the centre of Hertford town. I was able to maintain my BAOR records of never donning an NBC (or 'noddy') suit. I just wondered for real how many would have actually joined me before the nuclear exchange had begun in earnest. It would have been asking much of those concerned to abandon their families whilst they went safely (or reasonably) underground. I believe we would have been beset by some demand for shared family shelter and it would have been difficult to have denied this. Thankfully it never came to that nor to the horrors outlined in that excellent TV film – *The War Game*.

Presenting the Junior Team Boxing Trophy to Depot, The Queen's Division –
Shorncliffe 1981.

I have to admit, however, that I was greatly impressed by the state of the bunker and its communication outlets. Clearly the Home Office had not been idle in this field and the well-run course I attended at the Civil Defence Staff College at Easingwold had been an eye-opener in several respects. Emergency planning had clearly gone ahead apace, despite lack of funds and a rather 'Cinderella' status. I believe I first met Major General Mike Walsh, then DAT, during my Guyana 'swan'. He had been doing a unit 'recce' at the time. Aware of my keen interest in boxing, he invited me to be his Vice Chairman and the Chairman of Junior Army Boxing. I'm not sure that this was too popular a move among those in the 'striped PT jerseys' in Aldershot. They still had it in for me. Be that as it may, with the help of Nigel Lewis, one of my staff and a former Sandhurst Boxing Blue, we revamped and revitalised the Junior events. We also persuaded the management to introduce a new competition at adult level, the Intermediate, between the Open and the Novices to cater for those young boxers who had by now more than eight bouts on their card. Additionally we promoted an Annual Junior Army fixture versus the Welsh Schoolboys ABA, at which event we awarded Junior Army Colours. They became much prized. We had previously approached the young naval entry, the RAF apprentices and the Metropolitan Police cadets but none were keen to take up our challenge. A pity, we felt, since properly controlled the noble art is still, in my belief, a character-building sport. It takes some guts to even step into the ring. It all, however, gave me great pleasure even though I'm sure we 'ruffled a few feathers' in the process. Andy Watson, then GOC, Eastern District, and last seen in Washington during the Leavenworth visit, next approached me and asked whether I would be prepared to take on the Chairmanship of TA Rugby Football. It was said to need a 'shot in the arm' and that the annual fixture with the Regular Army was in jeopardy. Knowing that John Pollard, my AAG, was a player of some repute, I agreed and we began a systematic talent trawl of all TA units, University OTCs, School CCFs and County ACF associations. This unearthed a welter of experienced individual talent, including a couple of former internationals. We then arranged a trial match at the Postal Depot at Mill Hill and subsequently a fixture versus a Public School Wanderers XV, both through the good offices of Rolph James, the head 'postie'. We beat the Regulars in both 1979 and 1980. They then began to take the TA seriously and won the key Fiftieth Anniversary Match which we staged at 'Twickers' in 1981 and where BP produced a special trophy for subsequent annual competition. We felt then that we had just done something to get TA Rugby back on its feet.

Following the successful Lancaster House Conference in the Autumn of 1979, a some 1,500 strong Commonwealth Monitoring Force, under Major General John Acland (later Major General Sir John Acland, KCB, CBE) was deployed to supervise the ceasefire between the Rhodesian Army and the ZANU and ZAPU guerrillas. The force included a number of young officers and NCOs from all Regiments in The Queens Division and was withdrawn after the general election at the end of February 1980. A few days later I attended the annual Army versus Navy Rugby match at Twickenham with Bruce Thomas. During the interval I took a 'leak' in the Gents and exchanged pleasantries with Charles Huxtable (later General Sir Charles Huxtable KCB CBE) beside me. Nothing more was said. I was, therefore, somewhat surprised when he rang me the following Monday morning from MS at Stanmore to say that, on the Friday prior to the match, I had been specially selected to command the training team that was to replace the monitoring force, the aim being to help build and train the new Zimbabwe Army by amalgamating elements from both the former Rhodesian Army and the guerrillas. No mention was made as to when I would be required to move nor the rank of the appointment. I didn't think to ask about either, since I assumed I would be given time to conduct a proper handover at Bassingbourn (and to restore my furniture, etc.) and, that as I was replacing John Acland, it would naturally be a 'Two-Star' appointment. How wrong I was, for within twenty minutes I received a call from one of my least favourite Colonels GS on the MOD Sixth Floor saying that I was required for briefing the next day, was to depart on the Friday and that the team leader would only be a Brigadier. That's when I began to get really angry and this developed into near 'mutiny' when I discovered that neither the Colonel Commandant nor the Director of Infantry, my masters, had been consulted. It was all news to them too. To cut a long story short I had no doubt that a combination of my 'old colonial' image and bachelor status had dictated my 'special' selection for the post. I finished up virtually 'bouncing on the knee' of the Military Secretary himself and, despite his plea that I was the CGS's personal choice (then General Dwin Bramall), I declined the appointment on the grounds that, in this instance, I was not a volunteer for seconded service and that, if only 'One Star' was on offer, I already held the best infantry Brigadier's post in the Service. I also made the point that, like most 'singleton's these days, I possessed more than a kitbag and small pack and couldn't possibly get packed up and stored by the Friday or in two days' time. Especially as one of the Army's most senior 'walking welfare cases' I had no family nor relations to conduct the exercise for me. Somebody may have been trying to do me a long-term favour for subsequently the appointment was upgraded to 'Two Stars'. At the time I believe things were insensitively handled and that the affair smacked of one of those typical late Friday afternoon 'off the top of the head' MOD decisions to which I have previously referred. Suffice it to say that I had clearly 'burnt my boats' at this point future career-wise. Shortly after I received my 'consolation prize' when I was appointed an Aide-de-Camp to Her Majesty. I can recall some years earlier commenting on such an appointment when in the office of the Staff Captain to VQMG. A wise old bird, he had simply said, 'Get that, Sir, and it's the 'kiss of death' career-wise.' The day of my appointment I rang him and the score was 'fifteen-all'.

Tim Creasey had been a firm ally during these troubles and I know he felt that I had deserved better and had been somewhat shabbily treated at a key point in my career. It was he who arranged that I should see my time out at Bassingbourn. It had been a very popular decision across the Division so he told me. From there on I decided to indulge my prime time in fostering the cause of The Queen's Division, my aim being to really put the Division on the map. During those final years we won every boxing competition in the Army, were runners-up in the Methuen Cup at Bisley

With the prize-winners following a Juniors Passing-Out Parade – Bassingbourn 1982.

and ran a highly successful Massed Bands event on Horse Guards. We had some 500 drummers and musicians on parade and our affiliated UDR pipers made their first appearance at such an occasion. Next morning the Commandant General Royal Marines (then Lieutenant General Sir Steuart Pringle, KCB) is said to have sent a message across to CGS on the lines. 'I didn't appreciate that we were anticipating so many casualties in the Queen's Division.' The significance being that during my time as DAP(A) and to save further cuts, we had given bands a field medical role in war. Some years later some twenty or more bands were deployed in the Gulf. Only one cloud darkened those final Bassingbourn days and that was during the Falklands War in 1982. To my mind, and most other dedicated and proud Line infantrymen, it will always remain a deep hurt that not one single such battalion was deployed during the campaign. Insult was added to injury when my 'old push', 1st Queen's, then Canterbury based, were sent to 'pick up the empties' at Bisley in place of the Gurkha battalion despatched with the Task Force. A battalion which only recently had received some 300 reinforcements from their training centre. Enough said, other than that it will be the first (and hopefully the last) campaign in which the Line regiments are not represented. The story doesn't end here since in 1979 I had been appointed Deputy Colonel, The Queen's Regiment. I was later to become 'Tribal Chief' and so I remained closely linked to the Service for another six years. I left Bassingbourn with the thought that I had given some service to the Division and that they knew it. All were very generous in their parting plaudits, none more so than the great man himself and who had been my mentor over so many years – General Sir Timothy Creasey KCB.

Chapter 14

A 'Charitable Chieftain'

I had re-established the Hythe connection during the summer of 1977. In the July I had been invited to attend the laying-up of The Queen's Own Buffs Colours in the Warriors' Chapel in Canterbury Cathedral. For the visit I had got my PA to book me into the Imperial Hotel at Hythe and, thereafter, began an association that continues to this day and which undoubtedly influenced my retirement choice. For each month, whilst in the Ministry and at Bassingbourn, I spent a weekend at the hotel. I accordingly became deeply attached to the area and I had always fancied a retirement by the sea and not too buried in the depths. If I was to be Colonel of The Regiment, as seemed likely, I needed also to be within easy reach of RHQ at Canterbury. All this presupposed that I could get a job which would enable me to live and work from Hythe. The days had long since passed when retired senior Army Officers withdrew to their family estates or, as in Agatha Christie's novels, became the Chief Constable of Borsetshire. Few had family estates in the new post-war generation of Army Officers, promoted by the Intake I (or 'Guinea Pig') breed and even less could not afford to supplement their retired pay with a 'second career' as it became known. I didn't even possess a home. So during my latter months at Bassingbourn I began to give both serious thought, bearing in mind that there was to be only one mouth to feed and I did want to settle on the 'Costa Gereatrica', as it is affectionately known. I made my view clear when I was summoned to attend a resettlement interview at HQ London District. For after a rather turgid spiel from some young 'basketweaver' (or resettlement 'schoolie) in which it was made clear to me that, as a Brigadier, I was 'neither fish nor fowl' in resettlement parlance, he noticeably lost his interest when I said that, 'Had I wanted to make the Board of ICI I would have left the Army at twenty-

206

five years and not at the age of fifty-five.' He nearly yawned when I added the rider that, 'My criteria was thereon simply to keep mind and body active at reasonable recompense in congenial company and surrounds.' Having been in what had become (sadly in recent years) one 'rat race', I certainly had no desire to enter another. For, whilst I appreciated that I would probably have to commute to London (a ghastly thought), I did not fancy becoming the administrative minion to some young thrusting commercial management team – whatever the salary. Likewise, as the likely next Colonel, I needed to be in a position to conduct those biannual visits to the regular battalions and camp sessions with the TA and cadets. I didn't imagine that too many employers would be too happy if I said I needed to take three days off next week to visit 1st Queen's in Gibraltar.

Suffice it to say that my very old friend Rowley Mans, whose Deputy Colonel I was, suddenly came up with what, in time, became the ideal solution and one which I much enjoyed. It transpired that the Army Benevolent Fund (ABF) were seeking, from November 1982, a new Eastern Regional Organiser based then on the Duke of York's HQ, in Chelsea. The Region covered Greater London, the Home Counties and East Anglia – or virtually The Queen's Divisional area. It was a three-day working week in London and, as it was put to me, 'The way in which you make up your working time is up to you. I can only say that I think you would find it very satisfying, in that one feels one is at least doing something which is worthwhile and it also keeps you in touch with your friends. You also have the great advantage that you are entirely your own master.' I have to say that the remuneration was nothing startling. It, however, improved greatly over the years and produced a small second pension. It seemed that luck had come my way. I was accepted at an interview with the then Chairman (General Sir Robert Ford, GCB, CBE) and Controller (Major General Peter Bush, OBE) and then applied to retire three months early as from 1st November 1982. The next step was to find somewhere to live in Hythe. Mike Vincent, a very helpful local estate agent, produced me a list of some dozen places to view within my price range and preferred parameters and I took a couple of days off to conduct the search. It was a lovely sunny July morning when I stood on the patio outside the cottage at 62 North Road and admired the fabulous view right round from Folkestone Harbour to Dungeness. I then cast an eye over the premises within. It was, in effect, precisely what Mother and I had had at Marlow but on two floors rather than one. I could also see in my mind's eye just where the furniture would fit in. It had, though, only a shower and no central heating and the whole place badly needed redecoration. However, I made my bid later that day and it was accepted. I moved in on 28th October and christened the place 'Nile Cottage' to mark the Tenth Anniversary of the Khartoum adventure. I began commuting to London by Network SE the following week. But more of the ABF later since, by the time I began in the charity market, I had already been Deputy Colonel some four years and was about to become 'Tribal Chief'. I also went on in the ABF employ for some three years after I had given up the Colonelcy.

The history of the Regular Army dates from the restoration of the monarchy in 1660. Before the Civil War there had been no standing army, apart from a small force of Yeoman of the Guard. Previously armies had consisted of men recruited specially to deal with a national crisis or an overseas expedition. The great majority of the soldiers had been raised by feudal lords and landowners, who formed units from their retainers and usually commanded them in person. These troops fought under the banners of their masters and, in most cases, wore their livery or uniform. The continuance of this tradition can be traced up to the middle of the eighteenth century, when regiments were still known as Colonel Oglethorpe's (now The Black Watch) and so on, and the Colonel's coat of arms or crest was emblazoned on the colours and on the Grenadier caps of the men. These days Colonels of Regiments are appointed by Her Majesty and the tenure is normally for five years. Whilst the post is now essentially an honorarium, carrying the title and no pay, allowances for travel, etc., are payable at a Major General's entitlement. The Colonel is generally a senior serving or retired officer of the regiment concerned. Sometimes, however, he may be invited to fill a vacancy outside his own regiment. Having said all that, they still carry some considerable sway within the regimental system. They select and chose their young officers, determine regimental policy in such matters as dress, finance and ceremonial and above all largely dictate who should command their battalions. It is likewise they who recommend those for appointments as Honorary Colonels to TA battalions within the regiment. In times of 'stress', such as was most recently occasioned by the cuts proposed by 'Options for Change', they have a right of access to the CGS for a personal hearing. They can always resign over a matter of principle. Equally they can also be sacked, as a couple were when they declined to accept the amalgamation of their regiments.

Having said all that, Rowley Mans was in his final and extended sixth year when I retired. As his single deputy I had been able to combine much of my (and his) regimental responsibilities with those of Divisional Brigadier and especially in the visits field. If I went to see 1st Queen's in Werl, or 5th Queen's (V) at annual camp in Otterburn I did so 'double-hatted'. In so doing I was able to take a good deal of the travel load off my master. Once I had, however, duly retired life became a great deal more difficult despite the licence afforded me by my ABF job. It is, though, one thing to go to Colchester for the day by staff car, quite another on a self-drive basis in your MG Metro (to which we were now reduced) – especially if, with no orderly, you have to do all the pre-pressing and polishing yourself the evening before. I did, however, manage to keep the visits ball-rolling that year but my primary task became to examine the possible establishment of a new regimental museum within the Inner Bailey at Dover Castle. The offer had been made by Lord Montagu, then Chairman of English Heritage, and who was about to develop the site as a major tourist attraction. At that time the forbear regiments all maintained their own museums and, following the recent MOD Billington Report, had been persuaded generally to seek local civic patronage and shared museum accommodation. The Queen's Regiment Museum was housed behind the guardroom in Howe Barracks, Canterbury, and adjacent to RHQ. However, in the ever increasing security climate, few could gain barrack entry to visit it and even less knew it was there. The Dover Castle offer would permit us a display on a site that even then drew some 250,000 tourists annually. Les Wilson, then filling a Retired Officers (RO) appointment on the RHQ staff, joined me in conducting a feasibility study on the lines of the new style National Army and Guards Museums. That is to say, the diorama type presentation in historical sequence and supported by associated and period artifacts. We knew this would be costly if we were to move truly into the modern museum presentation mode. We, however, felt that we could probably raise the necessary money with a well ordered appeal. We first, to our surprise, had to overcome some rather petty 'filibustering' from within RHQ itself. Mostly Canterbury settled, they were concerned that once the museum was established in Dover Castle they might be required to move there too. Once we had disabused this 'red herring' the Regimental Committee backed the project and early in my term as Colonel I initiated a Dover Castle museum appeal. I invited Colonel Sir Colin Cole, KCVO, TD, Garter Principal King of Arms and then Honorary Colonel 6th/7th Queen's (V), to chair the appeal committee. With his widespread City contacts we were not to be disappointed. For within six months he and his team had raised the £75,000 we required as our initial share in our deal with English Heritage. With our cheque on the table they were spurred into action. Amongst the early and most generous donors was Her Majesty The Queen Mother, Lord Warden of the

Cinque Ports and Constable of Dover Castle. She has retained a keen interest in its development ever since. The new museum was officially opened by the Lord Lieutenant of Kent (Colonel The Rt Hon Robin Leigh-Pemberton, PC, Governor of The Bank of England and Honorary Colonel 5th Queen's (V)) on 16th May 1987 or Albuhera Day (the Regimental Day). Designated as 'All The Queen's Men' the museum is now one of the major tourist attractions within the Castle. Needless to say, the seemingly tireless Les Wilson is for ever improving the display. Perhaps, however, my time as the single Deputy Colonel will best be remembered in my guise as the then Chairman of The Regimental Association. For it was wearing that hat that I was largely instrumental in introducing both the Annual Grand Reunion and WOs & Sgts Past & Present Dinner events at Bassingbourn. Both went from strength to strength and I have no hesitation in publicly admitting that I 'cribbed' the latter idea directly from the Royal Anglians. Once again, however, I almost had to drag RHQ along with me.

My predecessor had been instrumental in finally putting the finances of the Large Regiment on an even keel. He had also done a great deal to promote closer ties 'twixt the old comrade associations (OCA) of the forbear regiments and the new regimental association. They all now paraded at the annual reunion with their banners and standards and recognised the link in some revision of their titles. It had all been progress in a somewhat delicate and touchy field. Against this background, and my five years as 'No 2 on the gun', I decided to make the following the goals of my Colonelcy – the development of a greater feeling of self-esteem within the Regiment, a big improvement in the quality of our Officer recruiting and the upping of our manning by better adult and junior recruiting and cutting wastage. I believed they were the most pressing needs at that time. As regards self-esteem I just felt that, though we were recognised as good, we just did not do enough to make the point. In this respect I will simply highlight a prime example of what then bugged me. One of the battalions was leaving BAOR at the end of their tour. They had a good record and had maintained their high mechanised standards despite the interruption of a couple of short Ulster tours. They decided to finish with a 'Trooping the Colour' Parade. I had invited Her Grace Lavinia, Duchess of Norfolk, KG, CBE, to take the salute and I accompanied her to BAOR. It never occurred to me to query the guest list. I merely expected the C-in-C, Corps Commander and both the Divisional and Brigade Commanders to be present; as clearly did Her Grace, as she commented on their absence. Instead we conducted the most splendid parade as if 'in camera' or behind closed doors. A parade which exemplified, in full, just how adaptable the good infantry battalion can be. For the unit had had only three weeks in which to produce a show that would have done credit to Horse Guards and had been preceeded by four weeks on the Soltan training area. It had been something for all BAOR to witness not just the regimental family. I had subsequently to write to all the 'Chiefs' concerned to apologise. Fortunately all were chums from those Camberley or MOD days. We had simply, once again, missed a big trick when we really had something to show off about. 'Think big and act big' was my continued message thereafter.

Following an RMAS Passing-Out parade, not long before I retired, I sat at lunch (with my aiguillette nearly in the soup) next to a young 'gentleman' who had just received a short service commission (SSC) in the Regiment. I was not impressed and afterwards I recall saying to Rowley Mans, 'My mother would turn in her grave if she knew that boy was to be commissioned in The Queen's.' During my Bassingbourn days I had equally been pretty depressed by some I had witnessed at the Pre-RCB sessions and who professed a wish to be commissioned in the Regiment. I was also aware that a number of COs were none too happy with some of the young officers (YOs) they were receiving. We were also having a problem at Sandhurst where our best material was steadily being 'poached' by others. Some of this wastage was self-inflicted as the 'wheat' were put off by the 'chaff' they had not expected to be accepted as candidates for the Regiment. One such example lived just below me in Hythe. The stepson of a retired Lieutenant Colonel in the Regiment, he was sponsored to Sandhurst and accepted by us. He was later 'poached' by the Guards. Another Colonel's son became a cavalryman. All very sad but indicative that all was not well in the regimental officer recruiting camp at that time. The key posts in the system were that of Regimental Careers Officer (RCO) and our Regimental Representative at Sandhurst. In the first instance one needed character and continuity and in the latter brains and polish. We had had too much upheaval in the first instance and had not always had a young 'flier' with charm at RMAS duty. I resolved to sort this out as a start. My next thought was to invite all Schools Liaison (SLO) and University Liaison (ULO) Officers to a session at the Duke of York's HQ at Chelsea, followed by lunch. It subsequently became an annual event. At this gathering I indicated that to meet my Officer manning bill annually I required some fifteen Officers to be commissioned from all sources in any one year, most of them to come from Sandhurst. I then said that I would look at anyone they sent me provided he matched the following criteria. That is to say, he appeared to have some spark behind the eyeballs, something between the ears, seemed healthy and was deemed couth. We played it from there and happily they responded. We began to look at improved quality over a wider spectrum. We perhaps realised that we had broken through when young Mallon won the Sword of Honour at Sandhurst in April 1987, the first time the Regiment had gained this distinction in nineteen years. We could not afford to be complacent but certainly both the quality and flow were vastly more encouraging. This was also reflected in the views of COs. They seemed very much happier with the YOs they were now receiving. At no time was I, however, prepared to drop my selection standards to meet the purely manning need, not even at SSC level and sometimes this rather niggled a decidedly inflexible and typically RO dominated RHQ. I was less concerned with figures than I was in ensuring that our Queensmen were best officered and especially where they were at risk in Ulster. Like Tim Creasey I still preferred to see a good Colour Sergeant leading a patrol in the Falls or Shankill Roads than an indifferent YO. I still hold to this view.

On the manning question I felt that we needed to put more effort into backing that potential 'seed corn' pool – our affiliated ACF detachments across the Home Counties. We already ran an annual competition, known as the Cumberland Sword, for the best individual cadet badged Queen's. I introduced another for the best junior cadet – Kirke's Cane. We also laid on an annual session, at either Shorncliffe or Crowborough, for all the cadet instructors. Usually held in September, it was a sort of yearly 'State of the Regiment' briefing and included interest talks by YOs from battalions. It seemed, however, to me that after the RIT had done its stuff at the various county annual camps they appeared to go into 'winter quarters'. Likewise I also thought that the regular battalions, both at home and overseas, could assist by sponsoring some school holiday visits. We did get the RIT out and about at ACF centres on winter evenings and weekends and the battalions came up with some good visits both at home and in BAOR. We also did a great deal more to improve the regimental image about the overall recruiting area in support of such as the County Shows and major charitable events. We eventually ran to a highly successful Freefall Parachute Display Team, the 'Flying Dragons', kindly sponsored first by the Prudential and later Danepak. We still, however, suffered from an identity problem and I can recall attending an excellent 'Beating Retreat' by the Albuhera Band at Eastbourne and, as they marched off, the announcer saying, 'Our thanks to the Band of The Royal Sussex, our

County Regiment, for that excellent display.' I could have wept with frustration. I regularly put my foot in the door of recruiting offices about our area. I was, however, forever conscious that, as hard as we tried along the 'Costa Gereatrica' and elsewhere, we were never going to be able to man three regular battalions without the backing of the Divisional system. In short, we would inevitably have to rely on moulding to our regimental ways a proportion of uncommitted recruits entering Bassingbourn (now our Depot) from the Midlands, NW and elsewhere. We have done just that over the years and one day one hopes we shall be able to establish regimental association branches in these areas which have supported us manpower-wise so well. I certainly never solved the manning issue in my time. I believe I, however, got the messages across that the junior entry was best fostered from within our affiliated ACF detachments, and that adult-wise we needed those uncommitted lads and that, it was up to us, to ensure that we looked after them like our own and encouraged them to extend their service as true Queensmen. The same message was, of course, equally applicable where our own kith and kin were concerned. It had, however, to be put across firmly to the junior management that every man needlessly lost, by runout or discharge by purchase, had to be re-placed the hard way and there was no automatic replenishment 'pipeline' manned by the Colonel of The Regiment or anybody else. In short, the old-style platoon roll book of yesteryear was not sheer 'bullshit'. We really had known our soldiers and what made them tick. I recommended to several COs that they try the tip that great old master of man-manage-ment, General Sir John Mogg, GCB, CBE, DSO, had given me during a visit to Lingfield some years before. 'Charles,' he said, 'Before you interview Cpl Bloggs concerning his application for discharge, call in the platoon commander and ask him why this excellent NCO wants to leave the Army. He'll probably bluster or have no idea but the message will spread like wildfire amongst the subalterns.' It certainly did and whilst we didn't solve the problem we all thereafter did something to contain it.

At the time we became a Large Regiment we had inherited a couple of very distinguished foreign royals as Allied Colonels-in-Chief. I am, of course, referring to those Honorary Knights of the Garter HRH Princess Juliana of The Netherlands and Her Majesty Queen Margrethe II of Den-mark. After the sudden death of the first appointed Colonel-in-Chief, HRH Princess Marina, Duchess of Kent, these charming ladies held joint communion over the Regiment. As Colonel I visited Amersfoot and Co-penhagen at least once a year, generally twice. During these audiences I gave the royal ladies a run-down on regimental events since my last visit.

They always showed genuine interest. Royal visitations this side were more difficult to arrange but during my time as both Deputy and Colonel Her Majesty visited 1st Queen's twice and 5th Queen's (V) the once. When in Copenhagen I usually renewed my acquaintance with our affiliated Royal Danish Life Guards and, when visiting Holland, always looked forward to that excellent lunch in the 'Auberge La Provence' restaurant at Laren. During my time as Colonel I became a holder of both the Orders of Orange and the Dannebrog. Elsewhere in the visits field I returned to Gibraltar and BAOR and, of course, Ulster. I, in fact, conducted my first visit as Colonel to Northern Ireland over what later became known as the 'Great Weekend'. At the time all the regular battalions were on duty in the Province. The 1st and 2nd Battalions were on two-year resident battalion tours in Omagh and Londonderry respectively. The 3rd Battalion was on a four-month emergency tour in West Belfast. I stayed the first night with the 3rd Battalion in the Springfield Road police station. Next morning at around midday, detachments from all the battalions, together with their Regimental Colours, paraded before the City Hall for inspection by the Lord Mayor of Belfast. We had inherited the Freedom of the City from the Royal Sussex, who had been raised as the Earl of Donegal's Regiment and had been nicknamed 'The Orange Lillies'; so we were determined to exercise that privilege, as a complete regiment as best we could, whatever the troubled times. Despite the obvious need for a lack of publicity there was a good crowd to witness this truly unique occasion. An excellent civic luncheon followed in the City Hall. That afternoon I moved on to Londonderry and my first task there was to take the parade at which the Albuhera Band was created. In brief, we had been presented with the option of maintaining three small battalion (or 'village') bands of a bandmaster and twenty-one musicians or merging them into two decent-sized, and musically balanced, regimental bands of a bandmaster and thirty-six bandsmen. I had chosen the latter course, as had other Large Regiments like the Fusiliers, Light Infantry, Green Jackets, and The Parachute Regiment. Time and engagements were to prove that we had made the right decision in the circumstances. Finally we moved across to Omagh to see the 1st Battalion. It had been a long and tiring weekend but it had achieved the aim – for all to meet the new 'tribal chief'.

Against my better judgement I had been persuaded to visit 3rd Queen's in Fallingbostel in early February 1985. The weather was even more chill than usual at that time of year and especially on the North German Plain, not really the best weather in which to chat up soldiers doing maintenance tasks on a vehicle park. It was also bitterly cold along the Channel coast.

'Chatting up' the 1st Queens wives Gibraltar 1986.

Suffice it to say that during my three-day absence the tank burst in my
attic and the cottage was flooded. In the following August, after six
months in the Shorncliffe Mess and at great expense to the Insurance
Company, I got back into Nile Cottage. I never made any 'peak' winter
visits again. They simply were not necessary nor desirable. In due course I
returned to Gibraltar to visit 1st Queen's. They were in the capable hands
of a CO who had previously done duty on the Rock – he knew and foresaw
the pitfalls. He was, however, assisted in his task by the fact that the
frontier was now open and field training was now possible in Portugal.
There was, however, still no classification range to hand. A recent visit by
CGS had also shaken up the security on the Rock. This had led to a major
exercise in which the battalion had run rings round some marines (or
'bootnecks' as we knew them) who had been landed surreptitiously by
night. Morale was high and in very sharp contrast to my previous trip
some years back. I didn't, however, change my view on this as a battalion
duty station. During this visit, and to highlight the extent to which Ulster
had begun to feature in the infantryman's pattern of service, I presented a
Long Service & Good Conduct Medal (LS & GCM) to a Colour Sergeant
who had already done some thirteen tours in the Province, of variable
length, over the then past eighteen years. Nearer to home, I was always
invited to have a day on the Hythe ranges, or the adjacent North Downs
training area, when UK based battalions were conducting what has become known as their 'Northern Ireland Package'. Based generally on
Lydd Camp, they were given a very testing time by the Northern Ireland
Training Team (NITAT). This included a very live 'riot', with petrol
bombs and all, and a similarly realistic patrol field-firing exercise in a
typical Ulster Estate street type setting. The last visit I made there was to
1st Queen's and they had just been issued with the new SA80 rifle.
Despite the criticisms that have since been aired in the Press, and elsewhere, following that eventual 'advanced field-firing exercise' in the Gulf
I was highly impressed with its accuracy.

   During my tour there were some memorable occasions to recall. The
Divisional Massed Bands event on Horse Guards was repeated in June
1985. The first evening was our regimental night and I had invited the
Prime Minister, accompanied by her husband, to take the salute. He had
served in one of our forbear regiments during the war. She couldn't have
been more charming and the 'Iron Lady' accepted the instructions given
her as to the form to be followed once on the dais without a murmur.
Those in attendance that evening included 'Charlie's Angels' (as they
were known) and many other friends. The occasion was marked by a

Regimental reception in the Banqueting Hall in Whitehall. I next got John Fieldhouse, my old Latimer chum, to do me a favour on Putney Heath. On 14th October 1961 the old Queen's had marked their 300th Anniversary by positioning an obelisk on the site where Percy Kirke was purported to have stationed his standard whilst raising The Tangier Regiment of Foot. Over the years it had been desecrated by a combination of dogs muck, graffiti and sheer vandalism. At considerable expense it had been tastefully refurbished. There was to be a ceremony to mark its restoration. The year previous, 1985, there had been much 'blarney' connected with a clutch of Regiments celebrating their 300th Anniversary. It occurred to me that we could suitably mark our 325th Anniversary about the unveiling of the restored obelisk. With our strong naval ties it seemed appropriate to invite a senior sailor to do the honours and who better than CDS. Rather aptly we followed the ceremony with a formal lunch at a nearby hostelry which had once been a telegraph relay station between the Admiralty and Portsmouth. There then followed, in mid-1987, what became known as the 'Royal' fortnight. It began on the Isle of Man where HRH Princess Margaret was to officiate at the annual Tynwald Ceremony in the presence of HE Vigdis Finnbogadóttir, the President of Iceland. The Guard of Honour was to be provided by 6th/7th Queen's (V) then doing their annual camp on the island at the old RAF base at Jurby. To bolster their presence I had thrown in, in full dress, a Regimental Band and a couple of Corps of Drums. It was a memorable occasion and, besides being presented to HRH, I was required to join the procession to St John's Chapel. The battalion put on a first class guard that would have done any regular unit credit and the Guard Commander certainly scored a 'bullseye' when he greeted the Icelandic President in her own tongue (thanks to the personal assistance of none other than Magnus Magnusson). I did have time out to do a tour of the island – quite beautiful in places. My hotel was, however, largely full of motor cycle enthusiasts, and mostly American, who were dying to try their hand on the TT circuit. Every man (or woman) to their own pleasure, I say. The next event in this notable fourteen days was when Her Majesty The Queen Mother, on her annual Lord Warden duty round from Walmer Castle, indicated that she would like to view the new museum to which she had so generously subscribed and which had not long been open. Les Wilson and I duly did the honours and that marvellous lady was full of praise for all the work Les and his team had done. Finally one evening in London HRH The Duke of Kent, the Fusiliers Colonel-in-Chief, opened the rebuilt TA Centre at Clapham which was to become the HQ of the newly formed 8th Battalion, The Queen's

A briefing in the 3rd Queens Operation Room – Aldergrove 1988.

Fusiliers (V) and which had become part of the Regiment. The battalion was a joint venture between ourselves and the Fusiliers when the proposed London Regiment (V) had foundered in early 1984. The 'Celtic fringe', the London Scottish and London Irish, had opted out after invoking the backing of their very distinguished Colonels-in-Chief. 'Options for Change' resurrected the issue and the Londons are shortly to become a fact of life in the TA ORBAT. The new Large Regiment, the Princess of Wales's will, however, retain a rifle company at Edgware and a large hold over HQ Company at Camberwell.

My tour ended with the rather special and royal occasion described in the preface. Everybody was very generous in rewarding my stewardship and I was deeply touched. It had not all been smooth sailing for at Christmas 1985, and fairly early into my Colonelcy, I had suffered a heart attack. I was 'picked up off the floor' by an excellent cardiology team, then headed by Brigadier Ian Crawford (later Major General) at the Queen Elizabeth's Military Hospital (QEMH) at Woolwich. I shall always be extremely grateful to them. At the time I became Colonel I had had John Holman appointed as my single Deputy. He had been a student of mine at Camberley, had been an excellent CO, was widely respected within the Large Regiment and was a great communicator with soldiers and cadets. He had just been appointed a Colonel GS at HQ SE District at Aldershot. It seemed an ideal choice in every respect. We had, however, both got other jobs to hold down and unlike my 'double hatted' stance at Bassingbourn, he could simply not make the same contribution as I had done to 'shield' Rowley Mans. We both did our very best but it was not helped when staffing problems arose in my London ABF team. Equally the RHQ staff were, and no doubt understandably, not quite up to the standard I had come to expect in the Ministry and at Bassingbourn. They also seemed to sometimes fail to appreciate that, whilst I was prepared to give a great deal of time to the task, I had another job to do and needed to have some time to myself even if only to housekeep, as a bachelor, for survival. In short, I had clearly overdone it and had suffered accordingly. I convalesced at Osborne House, then recently taken over by the Civil Service Benevolent Fund, and not quite the place legend had had it to be. To save a million quid from the Defence Budget the story has it that the MOD broke the trust. It remains a mystery, however, that in so doing they did not invite the Service Charities to share in its future running. Enough said, other than that whilst walking in the lovely grounds I thought over the future management of the Regiment. A day or so later I sat down in my room overlooking a wintry Solent and produced what I entitled 'The

Osborne Diktat'. In summary, this resulted in the early appointment of
three more Deputy Colonels (to which we were entitled as a Large Regiment). The division of responsibility was such that three took over the
interests of a regular and TA battalion each and the other was solely
concerned with the cadets – or that 'seed-corn' of which I have written. It
worked and we should have done it ages before. We had been blinded by
the contribution I could make from Bassingbourn. When I gave up on 31st
December 1988, I had been ten years wearing one Colonel's hat or another and forty-three years sporting the same cap badge (or variations of
it). I had over that decade seen Captains rise to command and Lance
Corporals reach WOI. I knew the Regiment and they knew me. It was a
signal honour to have been their Colonel and nobody could take the pride
and pleasure I had felt away from me. If anybody was now to ask me
which I would rather have been, Director of Army Quartering or Colonel
of The Queen's Regiment, I would have to say, and truthfully, the latter.
Equally, had I ever made the former appointment, it is as 'Tribal Chief'
that I would rather be remembered. It would be wrong here not just to
mention the Honorary Freemanship the Worshipful Company of Haberdashers' bestowed upon me just before my tenure expired. With my City
background I had long wondered how a Regiment with the Freedom of
The City of London (through the Queen's Own Buffs connection) had no
affiliation within the 'square mile' amongst the livery companies and
especially 'The Great Twelve'. We worked on it and, in February 1984,
the affiliation was formally recognised. For the steps I took to foster and
develop this happy association I was most generously rewarded. On 1st
January 1989, Mike Reynolds succeeded me and became the last in a line
of five Colonels of The Queen's Regiment.

I had not really become conscious of the Army Benevolent Fund (ABF)
until the summer of 1980. After a charity cricket match between a Divisional XI and a Middlesex XI, a member of my staff approached me as to
the disposal of the proceeds. He said, 'Sir, why not the ABF, or charity
begins at home in this instance.' No doubt the fault was mine but one
perhaps felt that the fund was remiss in not putting itself across more
positively within the Service. It may be that, since we all purportedly gave
a proportion of a day's pay to the fund annually, it was thought the
emphasis should be rather more on increasing public awareness. Whatever the case, I arrived to take over Eastern Region willing and ready to
give back to the Service something positive in return for the many years
of pleasure it had given me. I found that the office was run by a couple of
very charming and industrious ladies who were essentially concerned

with what can only be described as the 'mail shot' business. That is to say, they despatched appeal material to potential new donors and followed up annually those who had subscribed before. There was always the hope that this mail approach might produce a number of covenants. At this time the Regional appeal stood at about £80,000 annually and the bulk of that total emanated from this direct mailing assault. There were some eleven County Committees said to be functional within the Region and most had been in being since the Fund established a regional organisation back in the mid-1960s. They covered the Home Counties (including Middlesex) and East Anglia. There was, though, no Committee in Central London. However, once I began to examine the structure in some detail I discovered that the Committees in Cambridgeshire, East Sussex, Hertfordshire and Suffolk had either withered or were in limbo. The others thrived but lacked any clear regional direction as to their annual goals. In short, the spirit was willing but they needed some concrete ideas as to what was, or was not, a possible fund-raising venture in their particular area. For what might be possible in and around Chichester, for example, might not, for a number of good reasons, be a starter in Lowestoft. They also needed to know exactly what resources could be mustered to assist them with regional backing.

I, therefore, resolved that my first aim should be basically to restructure the Regional County Committee organisation, to establish some annual committee targets and to increase the 'mail shot' business by the steady infusion of lists of new names for approach. All very obvious, one might say, but quite time consuming with such a small staff. We began with the committees, and I am happy to say that a combination of good friends and willing contacts came to the rescue. The biggest struggle was strangely in East Sussex. An Inner London Committee was started with Andy Watson, then Lieutenant Governor of The Royal Hospital, as Chairman. Old chums like Lady Scotter, Lady Travers, Brigadier Anne Field and Major General Robert Staveley (another Intake I 'Guinea Pig') soon rallied to the London banner. Besides resurrecting these committees we also had to find 'homes' for some of them and others, in which to conduct their quarterly meetings. In this respect the TA were most helpful in granting access to their Drill Hall messes. The next task was to lay down some clear guidelines as to what it was reasonable to invite the committees to organise in any one year. We came here to the very acceptable conclusion that each should try and run one major committee sponsored event in either half of the financial year. That is to say, something in the autumn/winter period and another event over the spring/summer months. Initially we came up with a simple formula, say, a curry lunch and supporting raffle during the former and a 'Beating Retreat' and reception in the latter. As time went by we became altogether more enterprising and expansive and, you name it, and somebody tried it, and generally led by our Inner London team or our 'flagship' committee. Events ranged from antique roadshows, clay shoots, wine tastings, greyhound racing sponsored evenings, major band concerts, gourmet dinners, video race evenings, Tattoos, sponsored walks and rides and major raffles to Xmas 'Fayre' type stalls and the like. Quite apart from the funds these events helped to raise, they steadily increased the awareness of the overall appeal in the public eye – most important with ever more seeking to 'cast their net into the charity lake'. In producing the military support to back many of these occasions, and especially where messes and bands were needed, the Queen's Divisional contact base was invaluable. I also very quickly learned that if you hadn't got the neck to ask you might never get what you were after. Such as Gloria Hunniford, Lord Tonypandy, Lord Chalfont, Lord Oaksey and Max Hastings, plus all the major London antique dealers, all responded to our approaches most nobly. Later, when my old Director of Music, Peter Hannam, became Senior Director of Music to the Household Division, then I had a marvellous lien on the 'Big Bands'. For I have to say here that if you want to fill the Albert, Festival or Fairfield Halls then it has to be a big Guards or Marine Band. Where the Line Regiment really comes into its own is in presenting a combined Band and Drums 'Beating Retreat' display on a major showground in support of a County Show. Equally, their drummers are unbeatable when it comes to including the 'Beatings' at a major Band Concert – and it's something the public love to be in the programme.

In pushing the 'mail shot' business I made up lists of 'potential donors' from selected names in Regimental, Sports Club, Old Boys and other directories and from the social columns of such as *The Times* and *Telegraph* and the letters pages of *Country Life* and so on. I even delved into *Who's Who*. Whilst we could be said to be 'stabbing in the dark' we did have success and, on occasions, very large sums were donated or, better still, covenants made. Initially our strike rate averaged about four positive responses in every ten appeal letters mailed. Later, as money became tighter and the charity market expanded considerably, this fell to between two to three per dozen. It was clearly a very worthwhile, if somewhat tedious exercise, since each favourable reply had to be responded to. In the first year it, however, did much to raise the Regional take to over £140,000. This had all been achieved over the hiatus of an enforced move from the Duke of York's HQ. For some reason or another, relations with our landlords, the Greater London TAVRA, had always seemed a trifle brittle. It was not too surprising, therefore, when the TA Directorate were required to quit the Old War Office Building during renovation work, that it was the ABF who were requested to 'surrender' their accommodation. Unlike the RAF Benevolent Fund, who had purchased their own premises some years back, we had always looked to loaned Service accommodation. There was rumour that we might have to move to Aldershot; hardly the ideal solution, since we really needed a Central London HQ if we were to remain in the public eye. Shared premises were eventually rented in the Royal Entomological Society's building in Queen's Gate and Peter Bush offered us the 'Crow's Nest' (as it became known) right up in the old servants quarters. However, whilst not really ideal, we remained at the hub and this had its advantages. My old chum at Mill Hill, Rolph James, had offered me an office in the Postal Depot. It was, however, just that too far out and I should have had to recruit new staff. As it was, Mrs Pam Hobson, who had been such a stalwart at Regional HQ over the years, retired within a year of the move. Mrs Sullivan (Hazel I) thankfully stayed and made it three times a week up all those stairs. A retired high grade MOD/PA, she continued right up to the day I left London, and has had a big hand in the proof typing of both this book and the *General Salute* paperback – a wonderfully loyal aide through thick and thin. We had added Mrs Lucas (Hazel II) shortly after our Queen's Gate move (on a part-time basis too) and very good she was. We were less successful in replacing Mrs Hobson and we didn't get it right until around the time I returned to duty after my heart attack. Then Mrs Suzanne Archer was recruited and we had a team that could cope with the ever increasing business on all fronts. By this time we had even persuaded the management to go into the gifts market. Once we got a range of quality items, at reasonable prices, committees were encouraged to run stalls at selected events. The monies were coming in fast and by the five-year point we were about to break the £200,000 mark for the annual take. In the financial year I left London (1990-1991) the total topped £225,000; so perhaps we had done something to help to put the Army's National Charity back on the map and despite a nasty health shock in the process.

The Chelsea Flower Show collection was the principal Regional money spinner. It had been going some seven years when we took it over and it was sponsored by the Middlesex Committee. In the collection conducted at the time of the height of the Falklands War they had taken some £14,000. This was way above any previous takings. Whilst there was

The Army Benevolent Fund Chelsea Flower Show Collection – London 1990. (A Chelsea Pensioner alongside Janet Hester (née Rodes) – a positive illustration of that 'Special relationship'!).

something on the files concerning the event, and I had sought the advice of the Middlesex Committee, I went into my first collection in the 'semi-dark'. Especially as regards the arrangements to count and bank the take. This concerned me since I had recruited a considerably increased number of collectors both civilian and service. The 'counting house' was adjacent to the Museum Curator's Office, and within an hour, it was quite clear that the few volunteer helpers provided by the Committee were never going to be able to cope. I hastily rang Peter Tower, a very old chum from Camberley days and then COS, HQ London District, with a cry for help. Within an hour the entire pay team of 1st Irish Guards, from across the road at Chelsea Barracks, appeared to restore order. They remained with us for the rest of the week, conducted all the bank paying-in runs and at 'close of play' took the unbanked takings across to a safe in the barracks. From then on a pay team from London District became a regular feature of our annual service back up. Despite all the hassle we took over £17,000 that first year. Thereafter we went from strength to strength and at my last collection the total reached over £38,000. Our team of collectors ranged from In-Pensioners from the Royal Hospital to a mix of servicemen and women and an army of 'Friends of the ABF' as we termed them. Many initially were friends who brought their friends and over the years we fielded wives' clubs from units about the Southeast. We were there from the moment the gates opened at 7.00 am till around 6.30 pm and it was indeed only the truly brazen who made it from the London Gate to the Show entrance without 'submission'. They were about, however, and I can recall watching one very distinguished parliamentarian do precisely that. We offered our helpers a 'gratis' chance to view the show and provided light refreshments and drinks over the luncheon period. The Divisional Depot furnished an administrative team to keep the show daily on the road and the RIT handled the 'feeding of the 5,000'. RQMS John Willis, a Lance Corporal in the Band when I commanded, was my right-hand man each and every year. It was a great partnership and I shall always be very grateful to him. We indeed shared some good laughs across the years – plus a beer or more in the Pensioners' Canteen with my first Platoon Sergeant.

There were, of course, other money-spinning, fund-raising highlights across the Region and over the years. The inter unit clay shoots at the Northwood Shooting Ground of Holland & Holland were a great success and very popular. Teams were sponsored to the tune of £400 each and entries came from as varied a field as The Honourable Corps of Gentle-man at Arms, through HQ Household Cavalry and The King's Troop to

The Royal Military School of Music and the Ordnance Board. Over £9,000 was raised in an evening at a much enjoyed greyhound racing event at Wimbledon Stadium. All the races and dogs were sponsored by big business or individuals and a major collection was taken during the event. The Band Concert I would have loved to have run in Central London (this was the territory of our National Enterprises Section and in which I was not permitted to 'play') was, in fact, held at the Fairfield Hall in Croydon. A packed audience enjoyed a rather special military band mix – the Bands of the Scots Guards and WRAC supported by the Corps of Drums of the Royal Regiment of Fusiliers. In the same vein, every other year, Peter Hannam and Bill Powers (a very enterprising member of the Bedfordshire Committee) ran the Luton Musical Pageant with a take bordering on five figures. This is but a sample of the bigger and more profitable events. There were many smaller ones about the region which were equally as successful in their way in both raising funds for the charity and increasing the awareness of the appeal amongst the public. We did, however, have our disasters too, since not everything we laid on was a winner. A great deal depended on the choice of venue and the weather. Whilst Committees could influence the former they couldn't the latter – even with prayer. On one occasion a Committee chose to run a major Bands display at an outlying though very popular racecourse. On a lovely summer's Saturday evening, however, the public did not trek out from the neighbouring county town. It was not on a bus route for a start. Next time they ran the event at a barracks within the town and it was a huge success. In support of a major charitable event at Mickleham, near Leatherhead, we really produced the martial goods: Display Teams, Bands, Parachutists, Helicopters, Tanks and all. We set it all out on the Saturday. It rained steadily from dawn on the Sunday and was a complete wash-out. All we took was £120 on the ABF Stall. The organisers were uninsured and so we gave much goodwill for no reward. All part of the hazards that confront any charity organiser.

I had originally intended to give the ABF five years of my life. During the autumn of 1989 (some seven years in) I was having dinner with Roly Guy (then ABF Chairman and Governor of The Royal Hospital) when I told him that, whilst I was happy to do my eighth Chelsea Flower Show, I would not be doing one again thereafter. To cut a long story short, it was finally agreed that I should hand over in London in October 1990 and then set myself up in Shorncliffe to produce '*General Salute – or a laugh with Senior Army Brass*' for the 1991 Christmas Stocking 'filler' market. John Holman very kindly produced an office in Napier Barracks and loaned

Penny, his delightful wife, as my secretary. 'Hazel I' assisted with the typing. Les Wilson put me in touch with George Harris, an excellent printer at Sandwich, and Mrs Archer maintained the accounts. In addition, I enlisted the aid of Charles Stadden with the cover and Mrs Jill Green (a daughter of Peter Hannam) and Lieutenant Colonel Desmond Freeland (a one time ABF Grants Secretary) for the cartoons. 'Max Comfort' also helped with both the editing and the drawings. All the production and printing costs, and more, were met by generous sponsorship and the 'great men' of the past twenty years or more, and some distinguished service ladies, came up with the tales – some better laughs than others. We were, however, just grateful for the superb response. The book was generally well received and had a very good write up in *Soldier* Magazine and elsewhere. I was particularly pleased to receive the following kindly comments from a couple of my former masters, namely Generals Sir Michael Gow and Sir Patrick Howard-Dobson. The former wrote, 'How much we enjoyed the book which you master-minded for the ABF. It will give pleasure and amusement to many', and the latter, 'Many congratulations on the brilliant job you have done as Editor; it really is a splendid collection of stories'. By the time I came to hand over the sales to London some 3,000 copies had been sold. Designed also as a good travel, beach, bedside or hospital bed read, the paperback clearly still has a market. I had satisfied a desire I had had for some years and I believe usefully. I was happy then to take my small ABF pension, as from 1st March 1992, and become what I described locally as a 'self-employed author'. This then quelled any further discussion as to what I was now going to do next.

I had enjoyed my time with the ABF and it had given me much pleasure and satisfaction. I had also appreciated being my own master. It also helped in one's 'second career' that you actually knew what you were about and were proficient at it. I know it assisted, in my case, that I had the friends, contacts and those key Divisional and Regimental connections to develop and embellish my approach to the task. For example, it was Henry Blosse-Lynch, an old mess mate from my Lisburn tour, who steered the Northwood shoots to such success. Through the Haberdashers' link and our Honorary Colonels, some good City contacts were to hand. Without some very true friends it would have been much more difficult than it was to get some of the ailing committees back on to their feet. Lady Howard-Dobson, for example, stepped smartly into the breach in Hertfordshire. I enjoyed the Committee contacts and I believe the feeling was mutual once we had got over a few early 'hiccups'. I may not always have enjoyed the drive back on a dark wintry evening. I was, however, being paid to do the job. They were just willing volunteers. It is here perhaps that most charities I know, and certainly the one I worked for, tend to miss a trick and fail to properly respond to this 'grassroots' enthusiasm. By this I mean that every now and then they would like to see one of the top management attend their meeting or event without having to be asked. Or, perhaps, the Grants Secretary could appear one evening, of his own volition, to highlight where all the money received was being spent. I know my view, in this respect, is shared by a couple of 'Charlie's Angels' who have both held key Regional appointments in two major National Charities. In short, every now and then the Head Office need to be reminded that no charity can succeed without good 'grassroots' volunteers and that these good folk need encouragement from the top by personal contact from time to time. Enough said, but I know that many of my helpers in Eastern region slightly resented the 'aloofness' of those in 41, Queen's Gate. I am sure there is a clear message here somewhere, if only 'keep in touch with your workers'.

We are not quite at the end of the story since, fifty-one years on from donning my first uniform with the City of London School JTC in 1941, I still have a tunic hanging in the wardrobe; for on the 14th February 1992 I was appointed a Deputy Lieutenant of Kent. Likewise after a lifetime of Service to Her Majesty there is a case to reflect on what might have been, where different policies could have changed things and the possible way ahead for the twenty-first century Serviceman. These thoughts will be elaborated upon in the final chapter. Meanwhile, as I muse on the likely topics for discussion, I shall look back without anger. As I hear the regular 'crack and thump' from the nearby ranges and spot the tracer as I close the curtains in the evening I will naturally recall that the infantry remain the redoubtable 'Thin Red Line' despite 'Options for Change' and all. I was just very proud to have been part of it through several a vicissitude.

Chapter 15

Reflections

Had 'Peace in our time' prevailed, as Mr Chamberlain had promised on his return from Munich in 1938, then this book would never have been written; for my future was determined by World War II that began a year later. Otherwise the nearest I would probably have got to the Services would have been as a member of the TA. Having said that, and had I gone in 1946 to OCS Bangalore, I would probably still have ended up in civil life. For only a handful of 20B Platoon were offered Regular Commissions back in the British Army and then mainly in the Corps and Services. The key to the actual future lay in the chance notification of the decision to reopen Sandhurst in January 1947 just a few weeks before I was due to embark for India. By sheer good fortune, and perhaps not too much thought, I seized on the opportunity of Sandhurst entry and its long term prospects. It could, however, as I have indicated, all been so very different. Fate in the form of chance continued to play a big part in determining my subsequent career, none more so than in 'being in the right place at the right time' or vice versa. My Service was no exception in this respect and, to begin the musings in this final chapter, I propose to highlight some key 'what might have beens' had chance not dictated differing sets of actual circumstances.

As one of the original new Sandhurst Intake I 'Guinea Pigs', I clearly, on paper at least, had a flying start. It is, however, I suggest significant that despite the fact that some 300 and more like me crossed the Start Line ahead of the pack, we only produced between us, a couple of full Generals and eight Major Generals (and some of these could be listed as 'late declarations'). Not one of us made the Army Board. I don't really regard this as a very high strike rate, especially from a group that had undergone such a stringent selection process in the muster of that first post-war

Intake. This prompts me to wonder, in retrospect, what might have been the case had the key promotion to Lieutenant Colonel 'goal posts' not been moved to our significant disadvantage in the late 1960s. On the face of it we initially received some benefit since I, for example, took command at age forty years – two years before the norm at that time. However, once 'the pitch became even shorter', and one could be promoted to Lieutenant Colonel at age thirty-seven years, then we surely, as a group, had been career 'fouled' by the system; for we had clearly been required to 'sacrifice' some service and valued experience to those 'breathing down our necks' in the 'Career Stakes'. From hereon it was to be something of a 'Handicap Hurdle' event rather than an 'Open' race. I first appreciated the extent of the 'handicap' I was carrying when, as a DS at Camberley, the batch of ex-COs posted in to join me were all my junior in age by three to four years. No excuses are being offered up but I just have a feeling that Intake I might have done better as a whole without this weighty 'handicap'. Most of us, as the statistics I quoted suggest, never quite recovered.

I sometimes now wonder what might have been had career planning been, post Staff College at least, what it is in, say, The Queen's Division today. The Green Jackets have for long been renowned for their significant and recognised lead in this field. It is not surprising, therefore, that in most recent times they have largely dominated the senior appointments in the Army. However, I don't believe many others paid much attention to any 'streaming' process until a great deal later. Certainly they did not look above command or consider the higher promotion prospects beyond. Like many others of my generation I had little confidence in, or contact with, the career planning process until the Divisional system got into its stride. As we have seen in these pages, the 'singleton' label played, rightly or wrongly, a significant part in my career. It didn't deny me command and by sheer chance it got me that splendid Borneo break. Looking back, and now knowing that I had been listed in my Staff College report as a potential DS, I am not too surprised that its expediency earmarked me for the Aden Protectorate Levies (APL) rather than BAOR. Likewise, and as we have seen, it certainly combined with my 'old colonial' image to make me a front runner for those BATTs in both the Sudan and Zimbabwe. I can't help but reflect on how things might have panned out had I been married to 'Miss Right'; or the attractive and really 'switched on' young lady who thought the 'sun shone out of my backside' and was prepared to follow the drum wherever that might take her. Come the 'swinging sixties' and I could frankly not find a starter who felt either that way about Millman or his chosen career. As it turned out, I don't think I lost out on the deal and I am sure that my marital status would not have denied me elevation to the appointment of Director of Army Quartering! It did, however, ensure that I was kept well clear (possible security risk and all that) of the Defence Attachés (or 'Cocktail Cavalry') List. In hindsight it is always easy to be full of wisdom and I, therefore, doubt if the current career management approach would have permitted that rather wasted and fruitless 'mark time' period 'twixt my enforced Borneo departure and my return to BAOR two years later. One here is also bound to ask oneself, in retrospect, what might have been the case had I been allowed to complete my Brigade Major (BM) tour and then return to BAOR; first as a company commander and later as 2ic of a mechanised battalion. I could then have had time to earn those vital mechanised 'spurs'. Fate dictated otherwise but I am now pretty sure that I should probably have gone back to BAOR from Lisburn instead of to Latimer. For I have now no doubt that, lacking any mechanised experience, I never actually stood any likelihood of even 'smelling' a BAOR Brigade Command – that's quite apart from the 'old colonial' image and combined 'singleton' label then beginning to stick a trifle too firmly.

I had a very varied and challenging command tour, certainly rather more fulfilling personally than might have been the case in BAOR. Career-wise I was, however, operating outside the 'European League' and the Ulster troubles were only just beginning. Generally speaking I was, therefore, in the wrong places at the wrong time. We were about to leave the Gulf for example. Likewise it didn't help that during my two and a half years at the helm I was reported on by four different Brigade Commanders at one time or another. One of these covered the Gulf, another Londonderry and the remaining two the interim periods 'in limbo' at Lingfield. The first got me to Camberley as a DS, a second made it an OBE and one of the others did me no favours! Or, put another way, I believe he lost me a vital year in the race towards the 'Blue List'. If I had come up in 1971, and not a year later, I would have missed the Sudan and might have assumed my senior logistician's mantle in BAOR much earlier. It was, however, not to be and I suspect that I would not really, in retrospect again, have wished to miss that Khartoum experience. I was, after all, virtually my own boss and have always rather enjoyed playing it my way. We will never be quite sure either what would have actually been the future had I gone to Zimbabwe to run the BATT there. The post was subsequently upgraded to 'Two Stars' when Patrick Palmer was eventually brought in from the 7th Brigade in BAOR to run things. From there he went on to command 2nd Division. I don't think this would have been my luck. Finally, of course, the decision to change Brigadiers' appointments in midstream was mine and mine alone. That it did not work out quite as I had gambled was fate. Perhaps I would have made it to Director of Army Quartering or COS Logistic Executive. Both those who followed me into DAP(A)'s chair did succeed to 'Two Stars' in the Ministry. So I really only have myself to blame if I didn't make it into *Who's Who* or reach that extra pension scale. As I said in the last chapter, I look not, however, back in anger. The chances was there and I took most of them. That the dice did not always roll my way is what life is all about – chance and how one reacts to it. For as Anita Loos once put it, 'Fate keeps on happening' and I can certainly vouch for that during my service experiences. In short, you won't go through life without some ups and downs and, hopefully, mostly the former.

Next I offer up some thoughts on where I consider different policies might just have changed things to possible advantage. Once again this is necessarily a hindsight viewpoint and I have tackled them in the order in which they have been touched on in the preceding chapters. Early on I hit out at the present Sandhurst course and suggested it was neither one thing nor the other. In brief, it produced no better trained martial product than the former Mons OCS and academically it left a great deal to be desired. My feel remains that, in this age of ever more higher education and an increasingly competitive careers market, we should use the opportunity presented by the 'Peace Dividend' to take a further and truly comprehensive look at Sandhurst and what it should now be about. Above all I believe we need to conduct a detailed study of what we should be seeking to produce from RMAS to meet the requirements of the career officer of the next century. In this context it is my humble view that we should now seek to introduce a complementary degree course on the lines of both West Point and RMC Kingston. I was first impressed by the West Point slant during my visit back in 1951 when, listening to Clarke Baldwin, then an instructor at the academy, I rather felt that I, too, would have liked to have left Sandhurst with a degree under my belt. A more recent visit to that lovely setting on the Hudson River, some forty-one years on, has only gone to endorse my original viewpoint. In addition to Military Studies my suggested degree course would include such as International Studies and Business Management. Termed a General Studies (or something akin) degree it would also provide for a long term CV asset to meet the inevitable second career need in an ever tightening job market. I and my generation had only our service experience to offer up and even the

Charity business is beginning to demand academic labels these days. In this age the potential bursar also needs rather more than a good 'prize day' manner to meet the job specification. Moreover, this concept would obviate the current trend to 'snatch' selected YOs from their units in their early development years to attend 'In-Service' degrees at RMCS. Shrivenham, Oxbridge and elsewhere. One such subaltern of mine had yet to mature as a platoon commander before he was selected for a degree course at Shrivenham. Whilst he got a good science degree, he never made it beyond Major thereafter. I also suspect that the Sandhurst degree product would prove a rather more valuable asset than the imported graduate with a fairly indifferent degree in, say, twelfth century History. I had one of these too, and to quote my late grandfather Millman, 'he could not have sold iced water on a hot day at Margate.' Eventually I had to suggest that he transfer to the 'Basketweavers' or leave. He chose the latter course. In summary, I trust I have done enough here to just suggest that we would be doing an injustice to the next officer cadet generation if we did not get our heads 'out of the sand' where the Sandhurst issue is concerned.

Not long ago I read an article in *The Times* by Sir Michael Howard, now the Lovett Professor of Military and Naval History at Yale University. In it he suggested that the modern YO was probably tougher and more classless than in my day. If by tough he meant 'macho' then I would almost certainly agree with him. However, this 'macho' image can sometimes, I suggest, seriously 'backfire', as has been the case in Ulster and elsewhere on several occasions in recent memory. It wasn't our style in my day, when we aimed to gain respect by leading from the front, doing things best, really knowing our men, enjoying their company and behaving, at all times, as they expected of their officer. We were also very fit and healthy and played every game under the sun regularly. We even boxed. Today's young man has few sporting attributes to offer up or that was certainly my experience both as a Divisional Brigadier and Regimental Colonel. We didn't seek to ape the 'Les Paras' of Linda La Plante's opening sequence in the TV *Civvies* series and it would not have been an image we would have sought to foster. We could take the very rough with the none too smooth and still smile. They had to be tough to survive the bitter cold of the Korean winter, the searing heat of the Radfan and the height of the monsoon in the Malayan jungle. They were no slouches neither during those 'Claret' cross-border operations in Borneo. So perhaps before we become mesmerised by those Falklands 'yomping' memories we need to look a little further back to keep a true sense of proportion in this matter. As regards class I would suggest that, in fact, little has changed other than that the spectrum of schools from which the Officer Corps is now drawn has widened very considerably. The soldier still, however, expects his officer to be something different from himself. Provided that criteria is met then it matters not, to my mind at least, that these days there are fewer Etonians and Carthusians than there used to be coming out of Sandhurst and that the current CDS was at Aldenham and not Winchester. To sum it up, and as I put it on a Jimmy Young show fairly succinctly back in 1984, 'We can still be professional and smile a bit.' *Soldier* magazine had latched on to something I had written in the Regimental Journal.

Some years ago I was invited to watch an inter-unit military skills challenge on TV. A team from 1st Queen's were to compete. In one test their tank-hunting party got themselves into an excellent fire position from which one would have bet they couldn't have missed. They did with both missiles. Afterwards somebody said to me, 'Their approach work was near perfect so what a pity they missed.' I merely winced since against a skilled enemy you only get one chance, for whatever the weapon the aim must be to obtain a 'kill' first time. I cite this instance to highlight a current and serious deficiency in our battlefield skills – the low standard of musketry in the modern army. A trend that developed during World War II has now become a fact well exemplified by the low success rate in Ulster, and especially on operations in the 'bandit country' of South Armagh. One result of the trench warfare in Flanders had been the high level of marksmanship that pertained generally. In many cases it matched sniper standards. The subsequent slaughter on the Somme and elsewhere understandably influenced the approach to casualties in World War II. Vast quantities of ammunition, of all natures, were expended to 'keep their heads down' or to 'blanket the enemy'. Such cries took the place of that Israel Putnam made famous at the Battle of Bunker Hill, 'Men, you are all marksmen – don't one of you fire until you see the whites of their eyes.' In Vietnam the Americans went one stage further when they re-sorted to prophylactic fire, or 'knocking the hell out' of the next strip of jungle, before they 'swept' it. I still recall that day on Hythe ranges, back in early 1949, when Mr Hale had given that brilliant demonstration of true marksmanship with the old bolt action rifle. He and his breed had sought to restore shooting standards in the post-war Army. The National Service training 'sausage machine' had, however, proved counter-productive. By the early sixties the self loading rifle (SLR) was on issue and another skill in the art of musketry was to be lost forever. There had then, however, still been the chance to go back to first principles and ensure that no one progressed to classification shooting (and certainly not field firing) until they could consistently obtain at least a two-inch group in the centre of the then standard four-foot target. Certainly, when I first joined the old Queen's, I went on shooting until I became a marksman. Nothing less was expected of a subaltern and positively not the Weapon Training Officer (WTO). By the time I joined the Queen's Own Buffs at Colchester in the early sixties such standards were no longer demanded and musketry was seemingly regarded as just another skill required of the modern infantry-man. From then on the emphasis appeared to switch to field firing and we lost sight of the basic fact that, if the soldier couldn't group satisfactorily at 100 yards, then we might as well issue him, like David, with a catapult. I am no 'gravel belly' and do not consider that theirs is the style we are after. I believe, however, that we must get back to basics and ensure that the 'Shoot to Kill' doctrine means precisely that. This may seem all a bit tedious and old fashioned. However, at Lucknow, during the Indian Mutiny, it was the effective retaliatory fire of the Officers besieged in the Mess Bungalow that finally silenced the mutineer snipers. Such effective retaliatory fire is the skill we need to develop in self-defence situations as arise in Ulster and, in the future, under the UN banner in Bosnia and elsewhere. Let's heed a very clear message whilst we can.

A few years back I was required to write the Foreword to the History of our TA Battalions. An extract read as under:

'As one whose parents were both "Terriers", and served in World Wars I and II, this fascinating booklet provides a forcible re-minder of just how much the nation owed to two generations of Territorials in two World Wars. A sacrifice not forgotten to this day and a tribute to the valour and determination of the part-timer at war. I have no doubt that if called upon again tomorrow this well tried reserve would prove itself once more.'

Genuine sentiments I assure you since, though I have long queried the true value of the TA in its BAOR reinforcement role (now hopefully never to be tested), I have always backed the need for a part-time reserve. Its existing composition is what I would challenge. For if the role of the TA remains 'to provide a highly trained and well equipped force which will complete the Regular Army ORBAT in a time of national emergency', then we almost certainly require to take another close look at it in the light of recent events, particularly since the end of the Cold War. For I would argue that 'Options for Change', in this field at least, did not go far enough. There have indeed been major attempts in the past to rationalise things in both relation to cost and role. In the mid-sixties a review by Dennis Healey greatly reduced the size of the then unwieldy TA and, in particular, the divisions which could never have been mobilised in time to take part in a nuclear war in Europe were disbanded. A much smaller field force was retained with a primarily BAOR rapid reinforcement role. However, there remained the sceptics, such as myself, who still could not see, say, 5th Royal Anglian (V) reporting to their various drill halls about East Anglia in strength, and at the 'drop of a hat', and then being in a position to dig slit trenches along the River Weser some forty-eight hours later; not against the short warning scenario for sure. Recent events in the Gulf highlighted the gaping holes in the Regular Army ORBAT. The extreme shortage of medical personnel and other key specialists, like HGV drivers, in the support services were there for all to see. As I wrote all those years ago in that winning George Knight Clowes Essay after Suez, it remains, I am sure, this area into which we need to concentrate our future efforts. It may not be as exciting as being a Scimitar driver in the Royal Yeomanry or a bombardier in the HAC. 'Hard cheese' but we do now need to ensure value for money and especially against an ever diminishing Defence Budget. Likewise I am sure we could usefully adopt the US National Guard profile in that, in addition to Home Defence, the Reserves could also become practised in such skills as rescue and first aid, whereby they could be usefully deployed to assist in a variety of regional or national emergencies ranging from flood disaster to major rail and motorway 'pile-ups'. Earlier this year it took over twenty-four hours to clear one of the latter in the Midlands. Finally, if it is a combination of cost saving and rationalisation that we are after, then I am sure there is a need to obviate the duplication of administrative effort that presently exists between the UK Static Chain of Command and the various TAVRAs around the country. We only need one organisation to administer the much larger Regular Army.

The Battle of the Bogside in August 1969 destroyed the credibility of the RUC in the eyes of the predominantly Catholic community in Londonderry. During those long drawn out barricade removal negotiations with the DCDA even the moderates on the committee reckoned that hostility to the force was both deep and widespread. The Hunt Committee no doubt registered this fact and seemed keen, during our discussions with them, to return to an unarmed force, as elsewhere then, in the UK. As you have read earlier, they almost bought our idea to replace the 'hated green' with the standard blue police uniform. Once it was, however, agreed that we should open a 'Bogside Police Post' at St Cecelia's School, I believe we missed an even bigger trick by not manning it with men and women volunteers from forces elsewhere about UK. A detachment of some 100 such personnel, and described as the nucleus of the new 'City of Londonderry Borough Police' could, I am sure, have taken much heat from the fire. We had done something very similar in Cyprus years back and only recently a volunteer 'Bobbies' detachment had replaced the 2nd Parachute Battalion in Anguilla. It might have been going backwards in police organisation, and especially if we had done something similar in Belfast, but it could have removed a root cause of what then was no more than civil disorder. The RUC could have been retained as the provincial force elsewhere. Some time later when I discussed this idea, with both staff and students, at Bramshill I formed the distinct impression that there would have been no shortage of volunteers. Once again it is always easy to be wise in hindsight and it could only have been a short-term solution. It would, however, probably have afforded time for proper consideration of the long-term issue, for the sight of those big blue helmets might just have helped to ease the tension at a critical time. Now we shall never know.

As history will illustrate, the military have at oft times been deployed in some strength in aid of the civil power within the UK. A century ago there was, for example, the Peterloo 'massacre' (as it was later termed) and in more recent times the wide deployment to maintain law and order during the General Strike of 1926. Not until the late sixties, however, did it become truly evident that the police alone would be unlikely to be able to cope with mass civil disturbance in the future and especially by traditional methods. The Grosvenor Square anti-Vietnam War mass demonstrations in late 1968 were barely contained by the longstanding linked arm police crowd control tactic. This might have been able to cater with crowd control problems at a Wembley Cup Final. It certainly could not cope, even backed by mounted police, with determined riot. Elsewhere in Europe at that time, and notably during the student riots in both Paris and Berlin, much more stringent dispersal methods had to be used by the French CRS and their West German equivalent, the Border Police. As has been described elsewhere in these pages, we first came to really confront the problem in Ulster in mid-1969 when the RUC were driven off the streets of Londonderry. Our initial and traditional answer was to deploy the Army to restore law and order. At that point in time control was exercised by the military with the aim of restoring civil, and this included police, authority as soon as possible. Some twenty-three years and more later the military are still deployed in very considerable strength about the

Province in aid to the civil power. Times have, however, changed and the key difference between now and then lies in the current policy of the 'primacy of the police'. In short, the Police, rather than the Army, are now in the front line. Many of them are now armed, equipped, deployed and tasked as if they were gendarmerie or a 'third force'. In the light of these changed circumstances one could now, in my view, argue quite reasonably that the military are no longer being properly employed as soldiers but rather as if they were akin to French CRS type units – or more bluntly put as a 'third force'. Or apart from their field deployment in the border areas, and in the 'bandit country of South Armagh', they are being used as a form of gendarmerie rather than in their true military role. Nobody will deny that much valuable combat and command experience is being gained daily by the junior ranks and junior leaders in Northern Ireland. The strain on the Infantry, who have borne the brunt of the load over the years, has, however, been heavy indeed and has recently been exacerbated by the cuts dictated by 'Options for Change'. There is now, therefore, a very serious degree of overstretch within the Corps and any partial relief of the Ulster commitment would be welcomed greatly.

The Ulster Defence Regiment (UDR), despite its sectarian limitations, to some extent met the 'third force' requirement. This especially pertained within the Permanent Cadre elements which were primarily recruited from ex-British Army soldiers who had married local girls during a tour in the Province. It was, however, never really deployed as such for largely political reasons. It has since been absorbed into the new Royal Irish Regiment within the Regular Army. It did though, to my mind, establish the principle that there was now a need for some form of force 'twixt the Regular Army and the Police in tackling the ever increasing problems associated with civil disorder and plain terrorism. This now applies across the country as a whole where, as the fear of both violent affray and terrorist activity have manifested themselves, individual police forces have tended increasingly to train, equip and deploy their own armed specialist squads or mini 'third force' sub-units. I believe the time has now come for us to recognise these plain facts of life and to accept that we are doing the nation, and certainly neither the Army nor the Police, any favours by continuing to turn a Nelsonian 'blind eye' to an issue that will simply not go away. The Army, and notably the Infantry, would be happy to stick to their primary and preferred role and I know many good 'coppers', both men and women, who would rather return to their truly 'community policing' task. In outline I am thus advocating a study into the early formation of a national 'third force', or Royal Gendarmerie, for use within the UK as a whole; battalions to be deployed on a Regional basis with company strength sub-units on 'back-up' call to the various Police Authorities. As in the case of the UDR Permanent Cadre, I do not believe there would be any real problem in recruiting. For a start I would go for the fit and healthy leaving the Services at the eight or twelve year points. Perhaps this is really something we should take a serious look at before too long.

Camp followers have for long been a feature of our armies. For example, when the King's Baggage Train was overrun at the Battle of Naseby the wagons were found to be largely manned by Irish females. Wellington's Army during the Peninsular Campaign contained a sizeable camp follower contingent. In more modern times, and notably during the 'bonanza years' in BAOR, the 'camp follower' element rose out of all proportions. In my time with the 4th Division the divisional area alone supported roughly three dependants, or UK based civilians, for every soldier on the ground. The administrative infrastructure designed to cope with this load had become almost too comprehensive and mighty cumbersome. As one youth leader from Liverpool commented during the 'wash-up' that followed the 1975 Divisional Schools Holiday Programme, 'The kids and wives are really spoiled here. They don't seem to have to think for themselves and if they sneeze it seems somebody will even rush up with a paper handkerchief. It must all be costing the taxpayer a bomb and what happens if the balloon goes up?' The lad had actually hit the bull with both barrels. It was all taking too great a share of the Defence Budget and we could only effectively evacuate the families in the early warning scenario – not one many truly believed in. In short, by the mid-1970s we had hung a great families' administrative load about the neck of the authorities in BAOR and one which they could well have done without. When I first joined 1st Queen's, and during these far off Iserlohn days, the battalion contained around some thirty per cent married personnel (or 'pads'). These were mainly in the Officers' and Sergeants' Messes. By the time I returned to the same battalion in Munster in 1967 this ratio had almost directly been reversed. The 'singletons' were now very much in the minority. When I arrived in Herford nearly a decade later the single element generally ran out about the twenty five per cent mark. Some would say that this was all a reflection of the times and that in modern society folk were marrying much younger. Whilst I would not dispute this fact, I still believe we could have stuck out for the unmarried recruit and, having enlisted him, put rather more time and effort into catering for his special needs. As it was, we sadly went the other way and, as I have described elsewhere, we became bogged down in family administration. With the end of the Cold War, the major withdrawal of units and families from the continent and the reduction in the overall size of the Army, arising from 'Options for Change', we have the opportunity to pause, take stock and re-examine our recruiting policy and welfare needs. I believe that in this context we should first go, in the main, for the young, fit and sparky unmarried. To cater for the inevitable and more senior 'pad' element we should seek to establish permanent UK Stations for both Corps and Regiments as the Parachute Regiment have done in Aldershot. Having set up these firm home bases, then the unaccompanied tour, of up to nine months duration, should become the vogue. In this respect we have a great deal yet to learn from the Royal Navy. Never again should we ever attempt to recreate the BAOR style families administrative monolith, one on which some families became so dependent that hubby's departure to the Gulf War produced unbelievable trauma and the hitherto unknown need for such as counselling; for, hard as it may seem, father was a soldier and he was only being called upon to do his proper duty.

In my Aberdeen University thesis on the 'Rationalisation of the Support Services' I had, in fact, gone a good deal further than to recommend the creation of separate Logistic and Administrative Corps within the Army. For afforded the option, in my final chapter, to extend my study into the even longer term (or the later 1990s) I had advocated an eventual fully integrated and unified tri-Service support organisation. Or, put more simply, the extension of the Logistic and Administrative Corps principle across the support structure of all three Services. My argument had been largely based on the premise that, with the ever increasing costs associated with the major expense items in the Defence Budget, manpower and equipment, something 'had to give' if we were to be able to meet future bills. To my mind this demanded, and still does, fully unified Support Services in such as the supply, transportation, repair and medical fields. It is, for example, both ludicrous and costly that we retain three separate medical and nursing services and single service establishments to both train and administer them. If proof is needed of this fact we only have to look back to the recent Falklands and Gulf conflicts. The surgical teams deployed, both afloat and ashore, in the first instance were a glorious 'mix' of the best we could muster and 'all hands', whatever the colour of their tunic, were deployed to meet the feared Gulf casualty forecast. The three services all fly and maintain a variety of helicopters. I am sure that, in this day and age, it is both illogical and unduly costly, that we maintain three separate repair agencies to service the aircraft and differing systems to train and administer the work force. I am aware of the argument that says that too many single Service interests are at stake and that with the best will in the world this is not an issue the Services are capable of resolving on their own. It does not, however, submerge single combat identities as did the Canadian initial unification moves. Against ever increasing budgetary constraints, and the rising costs of manpower and equipment, it is a proposal deserving of further consideration. For if the Services were to accept such adjustment to their present support organisation, it could avert further erosion in both equipment provision and 'quality of life' standards. I say this since, as the Services are presently constituted, each successive Defence Budget cut leaves the policy makers and planners with little option than to effect further savings by delaying (or even cancelling) equipment projects, reducing the Works Service Vote, or simply cutting manpower (by amalgamating or merging famous teeth-arm units). By integrating the tri-Service support structure I believe we could go a long way to counter these problems.

The scope of the charity market never ceases to amaze me. Year by year it seems to increase in both variety and size and, with it, the demands on the pockets of a kindly and supportive public. There must, however, be a limit one day to the bounds of their generosity. So perhaps it would be wise for those concerned with the charitable needs of the ex-serviceman and woman to combine their efforts more closely; for like those concerned with the aged there are, I believe, too many Service related charities 'fishing in the same depth of water in the great charity lake'. For example, we have currently the Royal British Legion (RBL), the Soldiers', Sailors' and Airmen's Families Association (SSAFA), King George's Fund for Sailors, the Royal Naval Benevolent Society, the Army Benevolent Fund (ABF), the RAF Benevolent Fund, the Ex-Serviceman's Mental Welfare Society, the British Limbless Ex-Serviceman's Association (BLESMA), the Forces Help Society and Lord Roberts Workshops, the Star & Garter Home, to list but a few, all competing with each other from much the same section of the community. In some instances, from my ABF experience, we were making annual grants to certain of the charities listed above, or we were 'taking from Peter and passing to Paul' in sharing out the public's generosity. I, for one, also had some difficulty in explaining to people, and especially potential donors, the difference between the functions of the ABF, SSAFA and the RBL to the Service charity cause. I was, frankly, never quite sure myself and so could not have sounded very convincing on the subject. To my mind it is an even bigger nonsense, especially in these hard times, that we should vie with each other over what the public is prepared to offer up to help the ex-service charitable cause. For example, I can recall an instance out in the shires where the local ABF and SSAFA County Committees were in virtual 'conflict' over who should have annual lien on the President's Tent on the evening prior to the opening of the County Show; the aim being to run a reception and beating retreat charitable event. The invitation lists, I suggest, were virtually identical across the County. Despite the fact that the event was for a Service charity, neither party could agree to a joint occasion nor even an alternate year turn in the tent. Small minded, one might say, but it was never my experience in the time I spent with the ABF that much jointery was in evidence. I can also remember a luncheon at Dover Castle when the Deputy Constable was handing over cheques in sharing out the profits of a recent successful Tattoo. The lady next to me, and from another Service Charity, openly queried why she had got less than the ABF. Whilst a few heads might have to be knocked together, and this could hurt the pride of a few, I am sure we really need to take a long and hard look at this one. For, as I mentioned earlier in these pages, had we all been working in concert we might have saved Osborne House. In short, I am advocating something such as a 'Combined Services Charitable Ex-Servicemen's Fund' which handles all aspects of ex-servicemen's welfare from homes to handouts: a single all-purpose charity which is readily identifiable to the public and which they can recognise as the single entry point for all ex-service charitable donations. It would, additionally, be much cheaper to administer than the existing splinter group arrangements.

At the time I was commissioned, in mid-1948, any Atlas contained large and small chunks of real estate shaded red or pink on its each and every page. This represented the lands and islands across the several continents that then went to make up the British Empire. We had garrisons in many and officered the various Colonial Forces. Though about to leave the Indian sub-continent, we were still to retain sizable forces in both the Middle and Far East. We had recently concluded a terrorist campaign against the Hagana and Irgun Zvai Leumi in Palestine, were currently engaged in active operations against the Communist Terrorists (CTs) in the Malayan jungle and had deployed a battalion in northern Kenya to counter cross-border raids by shifta bandits. Additionally the Cold War had begun in earnest with the Berlin Blockade and we retained a very considerable force in BAOR as part of the NATO Shield. This was then the vista open to the young officer joining his Regiment or Corps from Sandhurst. It was both varied and widespread. It was also 'tinged with the smell of cordite' and the distinct possibility of an early tour of active service. Within a couple of years with, first, the start of the Korean War and then the beginning of the withdrawal from Empire, this possibility became an increasing fact of life. The young officer leaving Sandhurst today is sadly faced with no such exciting nor varied prospects. All is, however, not gloom and the young man on top of his profession will, I believe, still have the opportunity to enjoy his soldiering but in a rather different manner than did I and my generation. It is these openings that I now intend to look at in more detail.

The Cold War has ended but it has seemingly left a highly volatile and dangerously nationalistic cauldron simmering in both the Balkans and Eastern Europe. The UN has entered the arena in the former Yugoslavia in the strictly peacekeeping role. British troops have been deployed to assist in this task. I consider it is one which will increasingly come their way as the world looks more and more to the UN in tackling peacekeeping and, hopefuly, peacemaking problems. It can, though, only tackle the latter as in Korea and the Gulf, if afforded real teeth to do the job. This may, in time, demand the creation of some permanent or standing UN Force in which we British are required to produce a contingent; or alternatively the new NATO Rapid Reaction Corps, in which we are to retain a Division, could be deployed under UN auspices to separate contestants in a nationalistic small war scenario somewhere about Europe. So apart from Ulster, which will sadly continue as a military commitment for some years to come, there will still be the chance of active duty.

We travelled far and wide both at duty and on training. Perhaps the opportunities for the next Sandhurst generation will not be quite so diverse. They will still exist, however, but in probably rather less scope and numbers. In most recent times British Army elements have seen service with UN Observer Teams in Cambodia, Sinai, the Sahara and Namibia. There is no reason to suppose that there will not be similar calls for UN Observer assistance in the years ahead. There will also, I'm sure, continue to be a demand, world-wide, for BATT type assistance especially in the Third World. The British Army remains widely respected and its training methods are regarded as second to none. In the same context one would hope that we could extend the individual 'Exchange au Pair' programme more widely and build on such exchange enterprise as was displayed in the Ex LONG LOOK deal. This was initiated by the then CGS; General Sir Peter Hunt, when it was feared that we were losing close contact with both the Australian and New Zealand armies since our pull out from the Far East. The exercise involved the six-month exchange of a VC10 load of a cross section of all Corps and Services. I can recall having an Australian Subaltern and Sergeant at our Depot at Bassingbourn in 1980. They actually saw one platoon completely through their training period and the scheme was generally adjudged a huge success by all concerned. One also hopes too that we might be able to widen the scope of our overseas training sessions beyond the very attractive outlets that already exist in such places as the US, Canada, Kenya and Brunei.

The Sappers have for long maintained an extensive 'Hearts and Minds' programme near world-wide. Whilst I was at Bassingbourn the neighbouring RE Regiment at Waterbeach invariably had at least one squadron deployed in distant parts sinking wells, building roads and so on to improve the lot of some local community somewhere or other. In most recent times the Royal Marines have 'held the hands' of the Kurdish peoples in northern Iraq. Now that the Cold War is over, perhaps part of the 'peace dividend' will be that, in this context, we will, in future, be able to deploy more military manpower and resources to meet such as famine and flood disasters and especially in the Third World. I am one, for example, who genuinely believes that many of the problems associated with the distribution of relief supplies in Somalia and elsewhere would probably be solved if we were to deploy a proper military logistic staff backed by a recognised military transportation and maintenance system. I have enormous admiration for the various charities involved (though once again perhaps there are too many of them around). They are, however, not professionals when it comes to major logistic play. Finally there is always the unexpected or unforeseen contingency. I don't believe many anticipated the actions in either the Falklands or the Gulf. We cannot, therefore, entirely rule out the unforeseen next month or next year. We should remain alert to this possibility and retain the flexibility of mind to cope with it. I also hope that, as pressures ease and time permits, we will see more young officers following such as Tim Rodber back into the International sporting ranks. For all work and no play still makes for a very dull and unhealthy officer!

As General H Norman Schwarzkopf wrote in his excellent book, '*It doesn't take a Hero*,' a pert concluding comment was, 'I feel that retired Senior Officers should never miss an opportunity to remain silent concerning matters for which they are no longer responsible. Having said that, I believe a few general (no pun intended) comments are in order.' It is precisely the latter advice that I have sought to follow in this final chapter. It is, as I have said earlier, always easy to be wise in hindsight. Experience should have taught us, however, that there are even lessons to be learned in success. For on analysis it sometimes appears that there might have been better ways of achieving the same aim. In outlining a few thoughts on what might have been, where different policies might have changed things and the way ahead for the twenty-first century young Serviceman, I have relied on the benefits of hard experience rather than pure conjecture. I stand to be corrected with the passage of time. I likewise hope that the book overall has been of some general interest and that it will have provoked some thought and the odd smile. I hope it gives my fellow Rear Rank 'scruffs' as much pleasure reading it as it gave me writing it. They say we all have one book in us. This has been mine!

Author's Note

Since STAND EASY went to press further cuts in the TA ORBAT have been mooted. It is said that upto 12 infantry battalions will be disbanded. It appears, however, that no general re-roling of the Reserves is as yet envisaged.

Sizable cuts have since also been announced in the overall Army Band strength. The final demise of the regimental band, as my generation knew and cherished it, will result. Following such a break in hallowed tradition perhaps the time has now come to safeguard the long term future of military music with the creation of a single Band Service or Corps? For as Carlyle once said, 'Change indeed is painful, yet ever needful.'